THE
BASTARD'S SONS

THE
BASTARD'S SONS

ROBERT, WILLIAM AND HENRY OF NORMANDY

JEFFREY JAMES

AMBERLEY

First published 2020

Amberley Publishing
The Hill, Stroud
Gloucestershire, GL5 4EP

www.amberley-books.com

Copyright © Jeffrey James, 2020

The right of Jeffrey James to be identified as
the Author of this work has been asserted in
accordance with the Copyrights, Designs and
Patents Act 1988.

ISBN 978 1 4456 8314 0 (hardback)
ISBN 978 1 4456 8315 7 (ebook)

British Library Cataloguing in Publication Data.
A catalogue record for this book is available
from the British Library.

Typesetting by Aura Technology and Software
Services, India. Printed in the UK.

CONTENTS

The British Isles and key locations.

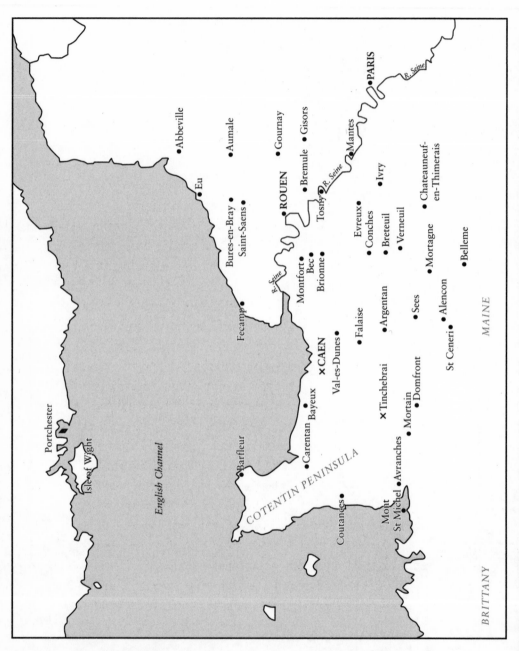

Normandy and key locations.

Robert Curthose's route to Jerusalem during the First Crusade.

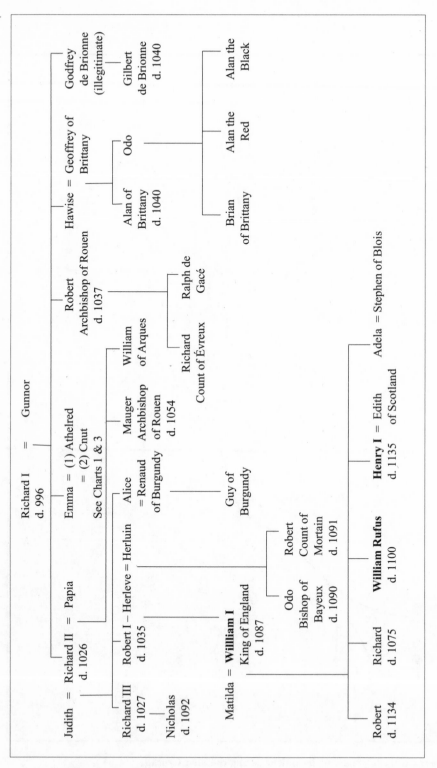

Descent of the sons of William the Conqueror.

TIMELINE

1028	Birth of William the Bastard
1031	Birth of Matilda of Flanders
1035	Death of Robert the Magnificent at Nicaea
1047	Battle of Val-ès-Dunes
1049–50	Marriage of William and Matilda
1051	Birth of Robert Curthose
1054	Battle of Mortemer
1057	Battle of the River Dives/Varaville
1058–60	Birth of William Rufus
1063	Norman occupation of Maine
1066	Battle of Hastings
1068	Birth of Henry
1069	Harrying of Northumbria
1072	Treaty of Abernethy
1073	Re-conquest of Maine
1075	Revolt of the English earls
1076	Battle of Dol-de-Bretagne
1078	Robert Curthose's rebellion against his father
1080	Birth of Edith (Matilda of Scotland)
1082	French reoccupy Vexin
1083	Death of Matilda of Flanders
1085	Domesday Book survey launched 1086

1087	Death of William the Conqueror and coronation of William II (Rufus)
1088	Rebellion in England against Rufus
1090	Insurrection at Rouen
1091	Treaty of Rouen
1093	Battles of Brecon and Alnwick
1094	Battle of Mondynes
1095	First Crusade announced
1097	Battle of Dorylaeum
1098	Fall of Antioch to the Crusaders
1099	Crusaders capture Jerusalem
1100	Death of William Rufus and coronation of Henry I
1101	Treaty of Alton/Winchester
1102	Births of William Adelin and William Clito
1103	Death of Sibylla
1106	Battle of Tinchebrai
1118	Death of Queen Matilda (Edith) of Scotland
1120	The *White Ship* disaster, death of William Adelin
1128	Death of William Clito on campaign
1134	Death of Robert Curthose, Duke of Normandy
1135	Death of Henry I

I

GOD'S GIFT

To him the fierce Normans faithful homage paid,
And lordly Maine his stern commands obeyed.

Thomas of Bayeux

William of Normandy, as everyone knows, won the crown of England in 1066 at the point of the sword. Less well known is that twenty-one years later, when aged sixty or thereabouts, he lay dying of wounds incurred fighting the French. The priory of St Gervase, located on a hillslope to the west of the bustling riverine port city of Rouen, became his hospice. Monks maintained a barrage of prayer; bishops, abbots, trusted barons and numerous servants attended upon him more directly. Only one of William's three surviving sons – the youngest, Henry – stayed with him throughout this last ordeal. The eldest, Robert, known by the childhood nickname Curthose – meaning, colloquially, 'shorty' – was just a few days' ride away, but remained unaware his father was dying. The middle son, the Conqueror's namesake, tagged with the nickname Rufus for his florid looks, had already hotfooted it to the coast to await news of his father's passing. He planned to cross the English Channel and seize the crown of England before anyone else did.

William in later life had become increasingly overweight and prone to fatigue. King Philip of France unkindly likened him to a pregnant woman close to the onset of labour. William in turn threatened Philip with 'a hundred thousand candles', a somewhat obscure reference to the pillage and rapine he would unleash on the French when he was good and ready. His subsequent campaigning against Philip may have been vengeful but it also served to parry French raids launched from across the ill-defined border country, known as the Vexin, which buffered Normandy from the Île-de-France.

The part of the Vexin lying between the Epte and Andelle rivers was claimed by the Normans; the territory between the Epte and Oise to the east remained under the control of the French. Within the region a number of great fortress towns – Mantes, Chaumont, Pontoise, Gisors and Vernon – abutted one another, and it was an aggressive midsummer assault on Mantes, a halfway point between Rouen and Paris, which proved William's undoing. Astride a panicked horse, with his midriff crushed against the heavy pommel of his saddle, intense heat from the flames of burning buildings likely worsened his plight. Two monks we know about were burnt to death in the conflagration. According to the chroniclers, their deaths and the destruction of Mantes' churches caused God to punish William by later bringing about his death. William sought to atone by gifting money to the Mantes authorities to rebuild the destroyed churches, just one of several sweeping gestures designed to curry redemption from on high in his final days.

*

William the Conqueror's father, the thirty-year-old Robert I, Duke of Normandy, had fallen ill and died at Nicaea on his return leg from the Holy Land in the summer of 1035 when William, his only son, was just seven or so. The duke had never married. He had maintained a long-term mistress named Herleva, William's mother, the daughter of an artisan. Partnership arrangements in the first half of the eleventh-century, known as handfast marriages, reflected long-held pagan practice. Vows were exchanged but without the formality of a religious ceremony of any kind. To be born out of wedlock was commonplace at a time when many Europeans were still emerging from a non-Christian past. The succession of an illegitimate minor to the dukedom of Normandy in normal circumstances would nevertheless have done more than simply raise eyebrows: when told a seven- or eight-year-old bastard would succeed to the dukedom, the powerful Roger de Tosny point-blank refused to recognise him. Violence erupted. Medieval commentators wrote of men fortifying their towns, building towers, collecting stores of grain, fearing long-term dislocation. Normandy became torn by internecine broils and its frontiers compromised.

Norman society was intrinsically volatile. The eight-year-old William had inherited a lawless land, said to have been 'debauched by anarchy' – a continuation of civil strife which had polluted his father's ducal tenure, mitigated to an extent after Robert's death by the efforts of William's guardians. Dangerous rivals were abroad. William needed protection at all times to avoid being waylaid and becoming a puppet for some ambitious nobleman. One or other of his maternal uncles slept at his side, sword at the ready to parry any assassination attempt. On occasion the ducal party even hid out in the houses of the peasantry to frustrate their enemies. William spent much of his youth on high alert and several of his protectors lost their lives in violent circumstances. One, named Osbern, had his throat cut while sleeping at William's side. The duke, by then in his early teens, must have witnessed the dying man's death throes. Trauma in childhood and early adolescence, as we now know, re-emerges in later life and expresses itself in anger. William grew up to be a violent man, lacking empathy. He had to grow up fast to survive a murderous political climate. His military training was a focus of necessity, not a routine syllabus item.

In the summer of 1047, when aged around nineteen, William defeated an army of Norman rebels at the Battle of Val-ès-Dunes. The battle has since been portrayed as a proving ground for the young duke, who until then must have been considered little more than an apprentice in arms. Fought on a rolling plain to the south of Caen that was said (as if trumpeting the emergence of a major military talent) to have inclined toward the rising sun, the subtext for the battle was to quash an attempt by a nobleman named Guy de Brionne to enforce his own claim to the dukedom. Brionne had a good pedigree. He was legitimately descended from William's paternal grandfather.

The battle consisted of a series of cavalry skirmishes, followed after the defection of some of the rebels to the duke by the complete rout of Brionne's forces and a frantic dash across the River Orne. The bloated bodies of those who drowned are said to have blocked up a nearby mill-race at a place called Borbeillon before they were swept down the river *en masse* – a harrowing baptism in battle for the young duke. Described by his chaplain, William of Poitiers, as crushing 'the reckless necks of his enemies under his feet', William had on the day proved himself to have all the makings of a formidable warrior and a man to be feared. Once a fighting man himself, Poitiers wrote of him seeming 'at once beautiful and terrible' when in battle.

Fighting at the duke's side had been Henry I, king of the French, who it seems may have almost lost his life when unhorsed by one of the rebel leaders. The king's assistance was payback for a favour sixteen years earlier during Henry's own minority, when he had been offered support from William's father during a French succession dispute. The French king's cooperative policies now in large measure helped William to survive *his* own minority. There were also economic and political reasons for Henry to underwrite William's security, in particular the free flow of trade goods down the Seine and the Loire, which might otherwise have been interrupted. Henry also needed allies against the burgeoning power of Anjou to the south, where Geoffrey Martel, Count of Anjou (a treacherous man known to history as 'the hammer'), posed a growing threat.

Normandy after Val-ès-Dunes became a more ordered place, evidenced by a spike in church building. After a truce-making ceremony at Caen, compliant Norman noblemen sent William hostages and hurried to pay him homage. Those who held back faced draconian measures. Grimout de le Plessis from the Calvados region, for example, suffered incarceration at Rouen and remained chained in fetters until his death thirty years later. William of Poitiers claimed the duke had by the early 1050s 'attained his manly vigour' and become 'an object of dread to his elders'.

It was likely a growing fear of the young duke that led to an otherwise unlikely Franco-Angevin coalition forming to oppose him. Normandy for a time fell under a vice-like blockade. In early February 1054, two allied armies attacked the duchy, launching pincer movements with the aim of capturing Rouen. William waited to see which direction the attacks would take; he then split his forces to separately confront them. His own knights blocked one division to the west of the Seine, while other knights engaged and routed the enemy rear-guard force at a place called Mortemer, located in the modern-day Seine-Maritime region of France. The unengaged enemy contingent, prevented from advancing, withdrew back across the border.

Another Franco-Angevin alliance threatened William three years later. The allies this time attacked Bayeux and Caen. William concentrated his forces at Falaise, a stronghold built upon a rocky crag overlooking the River Ante. He again awaited an advantage and then struck out and defeated one half of the enemy's strung-out and divided army on the tidal banks of the River Dives; the other division bolted, said by Poitiers to have preferred 'headlong flight to battle, spurs to spears'. It seems the Franco-Angevin army struggled to maintain order when crossing the river in the face of an incoming tide, the main cause of the disaster which befell them.

Even though William owed vassalage to the French king and was on occasion at war with him, Normandy at this period operated in all important respects as an independent territorial principality. To save the duke the embarrassment of prostrating himself and having to kow-tow, homage for Normandy was often done by his eldest son, Robert Curthose. This arrangement worked well while

Robert remained underage, but over time, as we shall see, it came to pose problems. Threat of warfare on the duchy's frontiers and an ambivalent relationship with the French must have become an important backdrop to Robert's youth.

Because the subdivisions of what once had been the great Carolingian Empire were relatively recent creations, few of the successor states rested on well-established or continuous frontiers. Normandy has been described in modern times as 'an expression of history rather than geography', so porous were its frontiers. Much the same might be said of Brittany, Anjou and Flanders. Territorial delineations remained fuzzy in western Europe. Hard borders did not exist. Law enforcement, taxation and defence became the remit of men on the make. King Henry of France, and after him his son Philip, controlled just a small region of France, centred on the upper Seine and Loire, with capitals at Paris and Orleans. Elsewhere, dukes and counts (terms often interchangeable at this period) wielded inordinate power as warrior lords and bound others under oaths of vassalage. Where landholdings were extensive, a nobleman might owe fealty to multiple overlords; where kingly or ducal oversight failed, local families filled the vacuum by exercising semi-independent control. Feuding often broke out among these competing families and long-running vendettas inevitably followed.

Hastings, 14 October 1066

By the fateful year 1066, once semi-independent lordships within the duchy of Normandy had been brought under William's control. He could assert the right to garrison his vassal's castles and demand that no new castle be built without a permit. This relative stability allowed him to broaden his horizons to focus on conquest further afield across the narrow seas to England after the death of its king, the childless Edward the Confessor. Despite an earlier alleged promise made by Edward that William should succeed him, the crown of England passed smoothly to Harold Godwinsson of Wessex, a militarily legitimised contender, for whom strength of arms trumped any respect for royal descent. Harold, though, remained at daggers drawn with his exiled brother Tostig, the one-time Earl of Northumbria. He also faced challenges not only from William but also from Harold Hardrada, King of Norway.

After harrying the English east coast, Earl Tostig joined forces with Hardrada. The Norseman's battle fleet struck first, before William's, a consequence of favourable wind rather than logistics. William's fleet remained for a time harbour-bound at Fécamp on the Normandy coast.

Factors in favour of a foreign adventure for William were the recent death of Henry of France and the succession to the French throne of Henry's underage son Philip, who posed no threat. The Duke of Anjou had also now died, and the duchy of Anjou had been wracked by civil war between competing cousins ever since. William also had no close family rivals to fear closer to home. His nearest male relations were his maternal half-brothers, Bishop Odo of Bayeux and Count Robert de Mortain. Both would accompany him on campaign in England. His son Robert Curthose was approaching an age where he could step into his father's shoes should William not return. The young man may already have boasted a talent for soldiering, but the venture in England was deemed too dangerous for a fifteen-year-old, even though the duke had other sons as spares. Robert instead remained in Normandy to assist his mother, the duchess Matilda, who acted as regent during her husband's absence.

William was also able to count on the support of a unified clique of home-grown subordinates. These were men of his own age and mindset from roughly a dozen eminent families in Normandy, some of whom he had grown up with. They had all been bloodied fighting the French, Angevins and Bretons, and had done well materially under William. They now hoped for greater gains. Land hunger was a prime motivation for the Normans, so William had to hold out the prospect of reward and excitement to retain a strong following – a recipe for violence which helps explain why western Europe up until the First Crusade became such a dangerous place. The duke also attracted active allies from outside Normandy, including many Bretons and Flemish. Crucially for what followed, he also had papal backing for the venture. This gave him and his men a moral boost by providing legitimacy, not unlike a UN mandate today.

By the time of William's invasion of England, two battles fought by the English against Earl Tostig and Harold Hardrada in Yorkshire (Fulford Gate, an English defeat, and Stamford Bridge, an English victory) had served to divide and diminish the local defence forces available to meet the threat from Normandy. Harold of England might have done better to play for time and build up his army before committing himself to battle. The Norman army has been estimated at around 7,000 men; Harold would have been lucky to have brought back with him 3,000 fit men, and to have raised perhaps a further 1,000. It is possible Harold hoped to surprise the Normans, but instead he found them well prepared.

Given the disparity in numbers, that the battle lasted as long as it did might best be put down to the difficulties the invaders faced when attacking uphill against an entrenched and stubborn enemy fighting on a narrow frontage that nullified the Normans' numerical superiority. One contemporary Norman source, the *Carmen de Hastingae*, described the battlefield as a 'mons' (a hill) and a 'vallis' (a valley or slope), the bottomlands of which were likely waterlogged; the English frontage may also have been staked to deter horsemen. So crammed was the hilltop that the English dead, wedged in between live compatriots, are said not to have given way to men from the second line: 'each corpse, though lifeless, stood as if unharmed and held its post'.

Operating in combination with the Norman knights, William's foot soldiers are claimed to have 'shot [their] arrows and thrust [their] spears … continuing their attacks in a series of charges and individual assaults'. Harold exhorted his troops not to be lured from the strong position they held by pursuing runaways. For as long as the English shield wall remained intact, volleys of arrows, spears and the threat of cavalry could not break them. Some commentators consider William capitalised on the English tendency to follow up success by engineering feigned retreats to cut off the pursuers and destroy them. Rather than orchestrated retreats, it may have been the case that when the English strayed too far forward down the slope to engage their tormenters, William simply capitalised on their exuberance by launching well-timed mounted counter-strikes, cutting off and slaughtering those who failed to re-join their main body in time.

Not until late in the day, as shadows lengthened, having parried onslaught after onslaught, did English discipline finally collapse. Already thin ranks became stretched. Just before nightfall, the duke ordered the final cavalry charge of the day, to be shot-in by massed archers. It was make or break! On the famous Bayeux Tapestry, which shows the battle in gory detail, a continuous procession of twenty-three embroidered archers (possibly around two-thousand real ones) are shown elevating their bows and shooting off their arrows. The combination of plunging arrows and the shock of lance on shield won the day. The embroidered King Harold is shown to have been a victim of this combined arms attack, hacked down while dismounted, after receiving an arrow to the eye. Two of the king's brothers also died in battle.

English survivors fled the field of slaughter, some to stumble and be crushed under hooves, others to be speared by their pursuers while in flight. In their haste to close with the getaways, and unfamiliar with the ground, some Norman horsemen plunged headlong into a deep ravine, referred to afterwards as the *Malfosse*. The defile became a hideous tangle of mounts and men, broken limbs and thrashing necks at battle's end. Medieval chroniclers viewed the duke's victory and King Harold's defeat and death as the hand of God at work. The duke had three horses shot or impaled from under him during the course of the battle yet emerged unhurt – proof to a medieval mind that the crown of England had been the Almighty's gift to give, and that William had been identified as its rightful owner.

*

The conquest of England required the winning of this single great victory and then four or five years of intermittent, bloody campaigning. Crowned at Westminster on Christmas Day 1066, William at first controlled little other than the accessible parts of East Anglia, London and the southern counties of England. He nevertheless felt comfortable enough to leave the running of his affairs in southern England to his half-brother Bishop Odo, whom he made Earl of Kent, and his childhood friend William Fitz Osbern, Lord of Breteuil, who became the first Earl of Hereford. Both men proved hard taskmasters over the English; Fitz Osbern, in particular, became one of the conquered land's great castle builders.

The Conqueror returned from Normandy in early December 1067 to face the first stirrings of revolt. In the aftermath of Hastings, many Englishmen remained unconvinced they had lost. Several members of the English royal family were abroad in Ireland, threatening a comeback via the West Country. Not until the early spring of 1068, after an eighteen-day siege, was the important city of Exeter secured by the Normans. It otherwise might have been used as a base for an English re-invasion. One of the Saxon defenders at Exeter bared his buttocks and broke wind in the direction of the attackers – a comic but ultimately costly gesture which resulted in the Conqueror blinding a hostage he had taken in recompense. The garrison submitted soon after this. Exeter had been where the late King Harold's mother Gytha had fled after Hastings; she again managed to avoid falling into Norman hands by escaping by sea to Flat Holme Island (the southernmost point of Wales). The *Anglo-Saxon Chronicle* records that in 1067 Gytha Thorkelsdottir hid out on the island before travelling to Saint-Omer in the Pas-de-Calais.

William ordered the building of the Rougemont Castle at Exeter, part of which, the stone gatehouse tower, is still extant. The castle would have been an earth-and-timber fortress to begin with and was positioned on the highest point of land within the surviving Roman defensive walls of the city. The gatehouse came to dwarf all other buildings around it, a metaphor of

Norman power and permanence. The castle's construction, as with others elsewhere in England, required the pressganging of local labour. Forty-eight houses had to be demolished to make way for its construction. Strategic necessity, it seems, trumped scruples (assuming the Normans had any). William placed Baldwin Fitz Gilbert in charge at Exeter. Like Fitz Osbern, he was also the son of one of the Conqueror's trusted guardians. Fitz Gilbert's commission was to suppress further revolt in the West Country and to protect against seaborne attack from Ireland.

Other early castles were built at Warwick, Cambridge, Nottingham, Lincoln and Huntingdon, becoming outposts for William's campaigning into Mercia and jump-off points for campaigning further north toward York, where two castles eventually had to be built, one on either side of the River Ouse – an acknowledgement of the city's dangerous environs. Campaign castles like these served as stores for supplies for the armies of knights and archers soon to occupy these regions.

Another flashpoint zone was the Welsh Marches. Welsh eruptions into the counties of Herefordshire and Gloucestershire before the Conquest had tested the armies of Edward the Confessor. Because of near-constant fighting on the Welsh borders in the years before the Conquest, the famous Golden Valley of Herefordshire had become a depopulated wasteland, which only recovered under more effective Norman oversight. During the early Norman period many castles were raised along the marches to keep the Welsh at bay. Used as boltholes by what have been described as 'the brigand-like Normans', castles allowed a relatively small number of knights and auxiliaries to lord it over very large areas. The Norman adventurers and castle builders were described by the twelfth-century chronicler Orderic Vitalis in his *Historia Ecclesiastica* as 'raw upstarts, almost crazed by their sudden rise to positions of power'. Orderic would have it that manifestations of unfettered supremacy by a land-hungry minority over a dispossessed people became long lasting and corrosive. Men like Bishop Odo and William Fitz Osbern acted largely independent of the Conqueror (often as a matter of necessity, as William had on occasion to be in Normandy), but they are said by Orderic to have plundered the land almost at will:

> The English groaned under the Norman yoke, and suffered oppressions from the proud lords who ignored the king's injunctions. The petty lords who were guarding the castles oppressed all the local inhabitants of high and low degree and heaped shameful burdens on them ... the king's vice-regents were so swollen with pride that they would not deign to hear the reasonable pleas of the English or give them impartial judgement. When their men-at-arms were guilty of plunder and rape they protected them by force, and wreaked their wrath all the more violently upon those who complained of the cruel wrongs they suffered.

William may have wished to keep a hard core of Anglo-Saxon lords onside to police the marches of his newly won domain rather than tying up Norman garrisons, but the problems he came to face gradually divested him of the notion. In the words of his biographer David Bates (*William the Conqueror*), William wished to involve his new subjects in his rule 'to stress continuity and legitimacy'. During the turbulent year 1069, described as one of violent crisis, it for a time seemed touch and go whether William might lose control of the situation in England entirely. Not only were the north, the West Midlands and East Anglia up in arms by then, but there were also renewed attacks in the south-west being mounted by the English: as an example, the Norman castellan at Montacute, in Somerset, came under attack and its relief necessitated the assembly of a sizeable force made up of soldiery from the Norman garrisons at London, Winchester and Salisbury. The fighting men mustered were led into battle by the warlike bishop Geoffrey of Coutances, who stood to lose land to the rebels. It is tempting to imagine the Conqueror's son Robert Curthose, aged around eighteen, riding out at Geoffrey of Coutances' side on campaign in 1069.

Certainly, his mother, Matilda of Flanders, is known to have been in England at this time, having just given birth to her youngest son, Henry (*c*. December 1068); possibly this occurred at Selby in Yorkshire, on the fringes of another dangerous warzone.

The Normans used the surviving network of old Roman roads when striking north. Extensive regions of marshland and riverine channels funnelled movement for land armies along well-worn route-ways in medieval times. Areas like the Humberhead Levels, circumscribing the borders of Yorkshire, Lincolnshire and Nottinghamshire, now dry land, were in those days permanently or seasonally waterlogged and subject to regular inundation from the sea. Several major rivers, all liable to flooding, converged on the Humber estuary. The political term Northumbria attests to the Humber acting as a major barrier between north and south.

Northumbrian nationalists made scant distinction between Saxons or Normans; both were to them the product of alien cultures. In part because of the fierceness of the defence they put up, the destructive instincts of southern-based rulers could not be moderated when operating upriver of the Humber. Like earlier Saxon kings such as Ethelred II (d. 1016), the Normans acted with extreme brutality in the region. Tracts of already marginalised lands were in some areas made totally uninhabitable by Norman harrying, with consequent population loss. Yorkshire was the county where the desolation wrought was most keenly felt, but records from Evesham Abbey indicate the harrying also extended into Cheshire, Shropshire, Staffordshire and Derbyshire.

William afterwards ordered the construction of a fortress at Richmond in Yorkshire to become his sentinel toward Cumbria. The king entrusted the castlery to a loyal kinsman named Alan Rufus of Brittany and the Breton lord went on to carve out for himself an extensive private fiefdom, largely free of oversight. Alan's holdings comprised parts of eight counties, and amounted to one of the most extensive Norman estates in England. Alan had led the Breton contingent at Hastings in 1066 and had also later fought bravely at Exeter. Further north still, on Tyneside, it would take until 1080 for a castle to be built, called the New Castle; its construction would be commissioned by Robert Curthose, not by his father or Alan Rufus.

Northumbrian churchmen from Durham carried off the relics of St Cuthbert, a long-dead but still powerful Northumbrian spiritual figurehead, for safe keeping to the Isle of Lindisfarne. So frightened were the monks of the Normans that the saint's relics did not return to the mainland until the spring of 1070. The English Church had good cause to fear the incomers; denigration and oppression by the Normans saw the destruction of many English churches and the replacement of whole tiers of the English clergy, as well as the plundering of much monastic wealth. William transplanted churchmen from Normandy to England as part of a more extensive programme whereby English bishops and abbots were ejected from office and replaced. Ecclesiastical revival and reform may have been the price for papal support in 1066. An archdeacon named Hildebrand had been the de facto power behind the papacy that year. As Pope Gregory VII, he later wrote to William (dated 24 April 1080) to call for a continuation of Church reform with a reminder that he had diligently laboured for William's advancement to royal rank. He wrote,

> I believe it is known to you, most excellent son, how great was the love I ever bore you, even before I ascended the papal throne, and how active I have shown myself in your affairs; above all how diligently I laboured for your advancement to royal rank. In consequence I suffered dire calumny through certain brethren insinuating that by such partisanship I gave sanction for the perpetration of great slaughter.

Incoming French priests and administrators from the Continent looked down upon their English counterparts as inferior, uncouth and untrustworthy. They occasionally used draconian methods when imposing themselves. Turstin, Bishop of Glastonbury, banned the tradition-honoured Anglo-Saxon Gregorian chant in favour of a mantra imported from the Continent. He resorted to violence when the Glastonbury monks objected. Several were mortally wounded when laymen under the bishop's orders attacked them with spears and clubs.

Other Continental churchmen, just a few, saw the invasion and landgrab for what it really was and voiced criticism of the Conqueror's methods. Guitmond, from the diocese of Evreux in Normandy, refused an offer by the Conqueror of high ecclesiastical office in England and accused William, whom he described as a master and a tyrant, of subjecting the English to an unjust and intolerable slavery. He said he would have no part in robbery, and spoke of his kinsmen acting like Vandals, Goths and Turks, whose sole purpose was to ravage and rob and to tread underfoot every vestige of peace. England, he said, is now a vast heap of booty, its peoples defeated and wretched, laid low by the sword and unlawfully disinherited. That the Conqueror continued to hold Guitmond in high esteem afterwards highlights the deference in which he held the monk in a superstitious age. Guitmond, in turn, is said to have feared the terror invoked by the Conquest might presage God's promise of the world's end, a time when nation would rise upon nation, and kingdom upon kingdom. Despite his candid criticism, Guitmond, it seems, held a distinctly negative view of the English. The monk said he would in any case have been averse to ministering to the conquered race, adding it would be difficult for him to deal effectively with such barbarously spoken foreigners.

*

By the early 1070s the Normans had to all intents and purposes secured their dominion over England south of the Tees. The first phase of conquest was over and what has been described as a more permanent pattern of Norman settlement began to emerge. Historians have likened England after 1066 to a vast building site, where castles, churches and cathedrals were erected across the country. The English were being lorded over by a Norman elite, placed around the English shires in positions of authority, much in the manner of a colonial power. A harsh, well-regulated regime did at least free England from banditry. The good security imposed by William is said to have meant that any honest man might travel over his kingdom without injury, even with 'breast pockets full of gold'.

Tight policing, though, did not prevent the expropriation of much of England's landed wealth through confiscations or tax levies. The early acquisition by William the Conqueror of so many rich southern and marcher shires enabled him to lavishly reward his foremost knights. Commandeered land, some of which was parcelled out at the Conqueror's Christmas Court at Gloucester in 1067, benefited approximately three hundred prominent Normans, of whom forty or so gained very substantial landholdings. William's forfeitures and dispossessions of lands are held to have severely exceeded what might have been expected of an incoming king and were therefore widely resented. William's half-brother Odo became one of the greatest beneficiaries of William's largesse. He gained, as mentioned, the earldom of Kent, plus control of Dover Castle and landholdings in England comprising 456 manors, valued at £3,050 – a colossal sum at this time. All were lands taken from Anglo-Saxon thegns who had fought at Hastings.

Forfeiture of English land occurred in stages, following a series of rebellions, with the last major upheaval occurring in 1075. The army yield for William from accrued obligations after 1066 is estimated at around 5,000 knights, a very sizeable Anglo-Norman levy. Those obligated to serve came from both lay lords and the clergy. Barons as well as bishops were charged to maintain knights within their household to meet the king's demands. In 1072, William called on the Abbot of Evesham to 'bring to my presence all the knights [within your jurisdiction] you owe me, in a state of readiness, at Clarendon a week after Whitsun. You too should come before me on that day and bring with you those five knights you owe me from your abbey.'

The term Anglo-Norman in the context of the military may be a misnomer. Historians writing in the twelfth century typically differentiated Norman and English elements within the armed forces. Knights partaking in the campaigns after 1066 considered themselves French, Breton, Flemish or Norman, not Anglo-Norman. The latter term, used to describe the armies of the Conqueror and his sons, is first come across in the writings of a monk from Lewes Priory during the reign of King Stephen when describing a muster of troops in southern England as *Normanangli*. The army unleashed by William in Maine in the 1070s comprised Norman and English soldiery, but the constituent elements were separately mustered and commanded: the divisions of horse and foot are said by William of Poitiers to have been 'skilfully arrayed under their several commanders'.

As late as the reign of Richard the Lionheart (d. 1199), the kings of England classed themselves first and foremost as Normans, this despite many of the notable personages of the twelfth century being of mixed race. Most of the major chroniclers of the period, including Orderic Vitalis, William of Malmesbury and Henry of Huntingdon, were of mixed marriages. Malmesbury, the author of the *Gesta Regum Anglorum*, regarded as the most astute and reliable of our twelfth-century medieval historians, claimed 'he drew his blood from English and Normans alike'. Orderic, who died in 1142, and who is the main primary source for much of this book, was a Benedictine monk and chronicler of mixed English and Norman parentage. His *Historia Ecclesiastica* has been described as the greatest English social history of the medieval period. Orderic's biographer Marjorie Chibnall (*The World of Orderic Vitalis*) writes in the preface how 'Orderic's outlook was moulded by the interests of the people amongst whom he lived, particularly the monks of Saint-Evroult and their patrons, the Anglo-Norman and French knights and magnates'. Her subject's intellectual horizons were, she says, 'widened by books of theology, history and hagiography he copied and studied in the library of the monastery'.

Tenurial arrangements William established in England placed all land ultimately under the king's control and served to discourage factional fighting, which remained a curse on the Continent. William's mark is that he conquered England and sought to enforce a degree of unified control from the outset. Through impositions he made his power largely unassailable, creating what has been termed by historian Frank Stenton (*Anglo-Saxon England*) 'an institutional despotism'. Strongly sited castles remain the most visible secular manifestation of this.

> The Conqueror had castles built and wretched men oppressed; the King was so very stark, and seized from his subjects many a mark.
>
> *Anglo-Saxon Chronicle,* 1087

Castles had first appeared in Continental Europe during campaigning by Carolingian Franks against the Vikings. Other than crumbling Roman fortifications, such edifices can scarcely have been known in England and Wales until the Norman occupation. A lack of them is held to have speeded the country's collapse in 1016 to Cnut, and again in 1066 to William. Prior to the Confessor's time, private fortifications may even have been outlawed by the crown, with just a few exceptions. Instead of castles, Alfred the Great and his immediate successors in the tenth century had relied on fortified towns, maintained by royal forces or under charter. Known as burhs, they protected Wessex from marauding Viking armies and became marshalling centres when fighting back to recover lost territory further north. Their geographic siting may have been planned by Alfred so that nobody living in Wessex would have been more than half a day's march away from one. Thirty or more burhs are listed in the Burghal Hidage, our earliest surviving administrative document of central government. Among the largest were Winchester in Hampshire, Alfred's capital, and Chichester in West Sussex. To what extent the stone or earthen walls of these burhs had been maintained up until the time of the Norman Conquest is questionable.

In any event, strategically sited castles, not burhs, became the essential Norman campaign accessory in England. It is estimated that by 1088 there were roughly five hundred castles in England.

The front-line county of Shropshire still boasts the remains of eighty-five castle earthworks. Between Llangollen and Betws-y-Coed, along the modern-day A5, several are still visible from the road, interspersed like grim station posts. An additional thirty-six castles were built in neighbouring Montgomeryshire, the northern march into Wales, where it is reckoned that almost every village had one of these structures. The rectangular stone hall-keep at Chepstow, built by William Fitz Osbern, is the oldest dateable secular stone building in Britain, and very similar to others on the Continent built at around the time. Chepstow was a stone castle as early as 1071. From its turrets crossbowmen would likely have been within striking shot of hostile Welshmen massing on the west bank of the River Wye.

The sheer scale of William's conquests meant he came to face an ever more complex and challenging political landscape. He struggled to hold back forces ranged against him. In the thirteen years up until his death he won no battles, nor did he capture through military means any fortress to which he laid siege. His recovery of Le Mans, the capital of the county of Maine, in 1073 marked the high point of his military success.

Two years later, a serious rebellion broke out in England, the harbinger of future setbacks. The plotters were spurred to revolt on learning that William, while in Normandy, had fallen seriously ill, close to death, and that his son Robert, then aged around twenty-four, was away campaigning in Maine and so posed no threat; when the revolt erupted, however, the bulk of the castellans of England and its sheriffs remained unblinkingly loyal to William. What fighting there was saw the destruction of one rebel army at Fawdon in Cambridgeshire and the neutralising of another in Herefordshire. In East Anglia the rebel forces faced the combined armies of the bishops of Bayeux and Coutances, Odo and Geoffrey, and a company of knights led into battle by the veteran commander William de Warenne, one of the Conqueror's foremost and most loyal magnates. In Herefordshire, another powerful lord, Walter de Lacy, rounded up the insurgents waiting to cross the

Severn without a battle having to be fought. He had with him his own knights and those owed the king by Wulfstan, Bishop of Worcester, Ethelwig, Abbot of Evesham, and Urse d'Abetot, sheriff of Worcester. At Christmas 1075, several of the rebels were blinded or otherwise mutilated, while others faced exile and imprisonment. Only one was ordered by the Conqueror to be executed outright.

Deprecated at the time and ever since as a flash in the pan, the 1075 insurrection nonetheless had the potential to become the most dangerous of the several insurgencies after Hastings. It had occurred in the southern half of England, not the more distant north, and had involved at least three high-born earls, plus the fighting retinues of two of them, a force of soldiery from Brittany and the depredations of a loosely allied Danish fleet.

William's subsequent campaigning in Brittany against his rebels proved to be a major failure of Norman arms. In the autumn of 1076, he was defeated in open battle at Dol-de-Bretagne by one such group. The normally resourceful William was badly out-generalled on the day; it was his first ever major military defeat we know of, and one notably costly in men, horses and treasure. William's authority and reputation were severely dented. If Robert Curthose, by then in his mid-twenties, fought at Dol has gone unrecorded, but he may well have done. Much moral capital was raised by the Conqueror's defeat. Chroniclers alleged God to have been displeased a bastard still ruled His realm.

By the following year William had given up on all attempts to bring his remaining rebels and their unruly Breton allies to heel. His own position in Normandy now became his key focus. Not only did he have to deal with an untoward and damaging rebellion initiated by his son Robert, but the French reoccupied the disputed Vexin in breach of earlier agreements. King Philip of France sought to benefit from William's setbacks and militarily impose himself on the area – hopeful of forcing a realignment of power at the Conqueror's expense. It took five years for the Conqueror to strike back, but by then he was attempting to redeem a military career which had long since peaked. His end was near.

2

THE BASTARD'S SONS

Born around 1051, Robert Curthose was in his mid-thirties in 1087, the year of his father's death. Given his later well-proven prowess as a knight, the derogatory sobriquet *Curthose* cannot have been used to his face without blows being exchanged, but the nickname will, albeit reluctantly, be used in the narrative to differentiate him from the many other Roberts who feature. Immediately prior to the conquest of England, when still an adolescent of fifteen or so, he had been knighted by the slightly younger Philip of France (b. 1052). Echoing earlier Germanic rites of passage for young warriors, knighting involved the investing of the recipient with a hauberk and helmet, dubbing him with a sword, and girding him with the belt of knighthood. Robert became referred to afterwards as the Count of the Normans, and was described by the contemporary chronicler William of Jumièges (d. c. 1070) as a young man 'brilliantly shining in the blossoming flower of his handsome body and advantageous age'. His parents made proud reference to him as 'our son, whom we have chosen to govern the regnum after our deaths'. An early announcement that Robert would one day rule Normandy was a useful way for William to gain affirmation of loyalty for his son from the Norman nobility. The best men in Normandy swore the prince oaths and took him as their lord in waiting. Before the invasion of England

and eight years later in 1074, when he fell ill, William restated Robert's rightful claim as heir to Normandy.

As a boy of twelve, Robert had been betrothed to Marguerite of Maine, a young girl described stereotypically by Orderic as 'a noble virgin, more beautiful than any pearl'. Both being too young to wed, formalities had been placed on hold. Marguerite for a time became a ward at the Norman court. She died suddenly soon afterwards, though not suspiciously. Maine was already under Norman military occupation and William had no intention of pulling his troops out of the county after the princess' death, even though war with Anjou might result; the Angevins still claimed lordship over Maine.

Once part of the Carolingian duchy of Cénomannie, the marcher county of Maine in the mid-eleventh century was a heavily forested region, squeezed between Normandy to the north and Anjou to the south. Described as William's first real conquest, it had been occupied by his forces three or four years before the invasion of England; despite stiff opposition, he in large part controlled the county by the beginning of 1064. Securing his southern borders from Angevin attacks while absent abroad was an important enabling factor for the campaign of 1066. The decisive action of a short war had been the capture of Mayenne, a fortress sited on a rocky outcrop commanding the route south to the county capital at Le Mans, which in turn fell to the Normans soon afterwards. William claimed to have freed Maine from Angevin oppression, yet the fragility of his hold on the county soon became clear when, in 1069, the Manceaux nobility rebelled. Many Normans then fell victim to a fierce insurrection. The county was lost more quickly than it had been gained. Only with great difficulty four years later did William manage to reoccupy the capital at Le Mans and re-garrison it, so complex had it become by then to administer a dukedom (Normandy), a rebellious county (Maine) and a great kingdom (England).

In 1073, when William again campaigned in Maine, his son Robert, aged around twenty-two, likely rode at his father's side.

The main fighting consisted of a series of brutal sieges at places like Fresnay, Beaumont and Sillé-le-Guillaume, all of them in the modern-day Pays-de-la-Loire region. Arriving outside the gates of Le Mans, the city garrison submitted to the Normans without putting up a fight, so dire had been the reports of fighting at these other places. They are said by Orderic to have capitulated 'to avoid the horrors of fire and sword'. William's method of reannexing Maine in some respects paralleled his better-known harrying and terrorising of the north of England four years earlier.

Ravaging enemy lands played an essential part in weakening opponents. If carried with the vigour displayed by William, it might lead to artificial famines, widespread destruction and even economic collapse. Harrying was an overtly warlike activity, designed to deny resources to an enemy or to punish transgression. Areas targeted were systematically destroyed, villages razed to the ground, seed corn for the following year's crop burned or carried off, and inhabitants indiscriminately slaughtered. Medieval chroniclers express horror when recounting the atrocities committed during these harrying sprees. Orderic, when writing about the Conqueror's Maine campaign, cites 'the plight of children, young men and women, in the prime of life', of 'hoary greybeards perishing', and of wholesale massacres being enacted. Terror was a decisive weapon when wielded by the Conqueror.

The following year, 1074, Robert confirmed a gift to the Abbey of St Vincent at Le Mans – an act linked to a serious illness William suffered around this time while domiciled at Bonneville-sur-Touques, to the north of Lisieux. The gift represented a tender for God's mercy for his father. While ill and fearing death, William, as earlier mentioned, recommitted the Norman succession to Robert and tasked him with the governance of Normandy – but after making a full recovery he is claimed to have shouldered his son aside and settled down to spend more time in the duchy than he had done hitherto – in effect, relegating Robert to a role as an enforcer, ever at his father's beck, without a court of his own. The relationship soon became strained. A charter dated to 1076 refers to Robert as the son of the king of the English who governed the city of the men of Maine, but it makes no mention of Normandy. An undervalued son of the king might better sum up the prince's straitened status as he, Robert, saw it, something which came to rankle more and more. The prince enjoyed only an almost meaningless comital title. He came to realise his father's promises in the past that he should share in the rule over Normandy had been little more than artifice – possibly done to appease the French king, who, for security reasons, backed a separation of rule over England and Normandy: what we might call today a separation of duties.

Deep-seated anxieties traceable back to childhood may have been the cause of William's reluctance to share or to let go the reins of power and to more closely involve his son in the governance of Normandy. The Conqueror has been applauded for recognising and harnessing the potential of young men keen for adventure – his targeting of England is a prime example of such untapped potential unleashed – so it is surprising he appears not to have better utilised the latent energy of his eldest son. In fairness to William, it may have become apparent that Robert had all the makings of a fine warrior and enforcer but did not have the qualities needed for a successful governor. His son had undoubted charisma – all descriptions style him as ebullient, easygoing and generous to a fault – but perhaps not yet the experience or acumen required to rule a turbulent duchy, let alone a major west European kingdom.

William's own achievements, of course, set a very high bar against which Robert would be measured, and the king may have been a very harsh judge. He is said to have looked down on his son. Was he perhaps challenged by his son's youth and energy? The Conqueror was tall, ambitious and domineering, whereas Robert by all accounts was shorter and more easygoing, a man claimed as loath to rail or disappoint. This latter characteristic is mainly noted by the chroniclers in the context of Robert's dealings with his close associates, the sons of men who had helped conquer England and who now craved the opportunity to emulate their fathers and win glory. Robert valued his friends very highly. He would have wished to reward them in the manner of any other lord: Orderic wrote, 'When the duke had no more money to give ... he made promises ... He promised much, but gave little.'

Generosity in the prince has sometimes been spun as a failing rather than a positive attribute, and it may have been a reaction to his father's notorious meanness. So tightly did the Conqueror hold on to the duchy's purse strings, Robert never had enough money to manage his own court. His early years, when dependent on his father, have been described by William of Malmesbury as 'constricted by meanness, laced with mockery'. A dominant and sometimes frightening parent, William not only kept his son ruinously short of money but also undermined him in public on occasion. Because of these prohibitions and his father's bullying ways, Robert was handicapped when attempting to attract and retain a knightly following. Ostentatiousness was a norm for leaders in medieval times – having the wealth to fund lavish display, patronage and good works an essential, not simply a bonus. Even after William's death, when Duke of Normandy in his own right, Robert would never be able to match the financial reach of his younger brothers William Rufus and Henry. Like their father, they would come to enjoy the vast financial resources of England, whereas Normandy would become much poorer in comparison. In later life they would be able to afford to buy mercenaries, bribe enemies and financially undermine their elder brother... but this is to get ahead of ourselves.

In the late 1070s, after a violent and protracted rebellion by Robert against his father, interaction between the two men remained problematic up until the eve of William's passing. Unaware of his father's worsening condition after the fighting at Mantes, Robert, likely two or three days' ride away at Abbeville on the coast, did not attend the deathbed or funeral. He may have been deliberately kept in the dark by his brothers so that they could better progress their own agendas (this, though, smacks of retrospective conspiracy theorising). Other than the coffin being too small for William's great girth, convincing evidence is lacking for what actually transpired upon William's death. A despatch at some point must have been sent to inform Robert and to confirm he was now Duke of Normandy. It is said to have been delivered by a knight named Aubrey (a former Earl of Northumbria), but arrived too late for Robert to make arrangements to attend the funeral.

*

Robert's accession to the dukedom of Normandy was very much a given. His rights to the duchy had been underwritten by the great and good, through sworn oaths of allegiance made on Bibles and holy relics. The Normans were politically and morally invested in Robert as their duke-in-waiting. The honour of the dukedom of Normandy, the emotional heart of the Anglo-Norman realm, could not be taken from him without undermining earlier promises, breaking accepted laws of inheritance and attracting intervention of a military nature from the French, whose king, Philip, backed the prince to succeed to the dukedom. William Bona Anima (Good Soul), the powerful Archbishop of Rouen and a key advisor to the Conqueror, also supported the prince's accession.

Robert being the rightful heir to Normandy did not mean he would necessarily gain the English crown. The way inheritance worked in Norman society was for elder sons to gain their father's acquired patrimony (in this case Normandy), and for second sons to gain lands acquired through conquest. William Rufus, the king's second surviving son, would on this basis have hoped to gain all or some part the kingdom of England. Henry, the youngest surviving son, would have been lucky to get any land at all (albeit his mother's lands in England may have been promised to him).

This whole subject of how the realm was to be apportioned after the Conqueror's death remains something of a grey area for historians, blurred to a very great extent by the moralising scribbling of later chroniclers, like Orderic, who claimed William felt a deep unwillingness to bequeath land acquired through the shedding of blood. The intimation from this would be that if the Conqueror's sons wanted England badly enough they would have to fight over it. Such religious and moral opaqueness may in fact have masked a degree of uncertainty in the king's mind as to the long-term viability of a conjoined realm. William would have questioned whether any of his sons (with the possible exception of the youngest, Henry, already obviously clever, ruthless and determined, though too young to be considered) had the necessary credentials to single-handedly rule the troublesome amalgam of England, Normandy and Maine. Recent military reverses might have persuaded him that defending Normandy and Maine from the attentions of aggressive neighbours would be a full-time job for his eldest son, without the added complexity of overseeing an overseas kingdom.

This is how twelfth-century poet and historian Robert Wace imagined William's last words on the subject:

Normandy, I give to Robert, my eldest son ... if the Normans have a good chieftain, their company is greatly to be feared ... but if they have no fear of a lord they will begin to give bad service ... Robert, who has to watch over such men, has much to do and to think about.

The sheer extent of the Anglo-Norman realm had increased problems inherent in the passing on of land after death; not least would have been the impact on cross-Channel landowners, who, should the realm be split up, would naturally have been averse to serving two competing masters. There were no clear rules regarding the English succession as part of an Anglo-Norman enterprise.

Had William's affairs on the Continent been more settled and had he trusted his three sons to work together, he might have looked to unite his lands under the eldest and made provision for the younger two to gain sizeable fiefdoms, known in France as appanages. Consolidation should have been preferable to fragmentation. Under the earlier Frankish Capetian kings, younger brothers sometimes gained land concessions as fiefs instead of kingdoms. The basis for this had been that siblings would more likely be trustworthy than distant relatives and would selflessly share the weight of governance and take risks on the battlefield. Henry I of France, for example, gave the substantial fiefdom of Burgundy to his younger brother. The Conqueror's second son, Richard, who died accidentally in the New Forest when a teenager, may have had the Cotentin Peninsula in Normandy earmarked for him.

Little is really known of this short-lived second son, so close in age to Robert. He is known to have been alive at Easter 1069 and a date for his death has been suggested as late as 1075. The Conqueror is claimed to have held out high hopes for him. Richard may have been better favoured by William than Robert, though this is just surmise. The latter would have been around twenty-four in 1075, the year of the earls' rebellion in England, and therefore well aware of the extent and impact of the loss felt by his parents at such a difficult time. Tellingly, just three years after Richard's death – assuming it to have been in 1075 – Robert would launch his own destructive rebellion against his father.

William Rufus

The Conqueror may have enjoyed a much easier relationship with his second surviving son and namesake, William, born at the end of the 1050s, possibly as late as 1060 – therefore aged around twenty-seven in 1087. A ruddy face may have been the origin of the younger William's post-mortem nickname Rufus and is the name by which he will be known in this narrative. French-speaking contemporaries may have known him as Guillaume le Ros (or le Rou). There is also evidence to suggest he may have been referred to on occasion as William Longsword, after an ancestor, Vilhjálmr Langaspjót, who died in the year 962; none of the near-contemporary chroniclers refer to him this way, however.

Rufus' alleged ruddy complexion and blond hair reveal something of his genetic heritage. The Icelandic sagas speak of the founding brothers Grimr and Helgi, both Scandinavians, as each going their own way in appearance: Helgi was tawny-haired and ruddy-faced, while Grimr was blond and tousle-haired. In the only near-contemporary portrait we have of Rufus he is claimed to have been of square build, red-faced, with blond hair swept back (noted sometimes with a central parting, the fashion at the time). Rufus' beard, like his hair, may also have been blond. The only description of the Scottish King Macbeth, courtesy of the Irish chronicler St Berchan, describes him as yellow-haired and red-faced, much like Rufus. Macbeth was known as the Red King (though perhaps for his bloody reputation, not his looks). An eleventh-century poem, the *Duan Albannach*, begins by addressing learned Scots in this way: 'O all ye learned ones of Alba, stately yellow-haired company.' The famous Norman warlord Robert Guiscard, Duke of Apulia and Calabria, is said to have been ruddy-faced, with flaxen hair and broad shoulders. His son Bohemond was blue-eyed and had yellow hair and a red beard. Bohemond, of whom more later, was an exceptionally tall man, narrow in the waist and loins, with broad shoulders, a deep chest and powerful arms. His hair was said to have been cut short to the ears, and 'a certain charm' hung about him, though marred by 'a general air of the horrible'. He is described this way by Anna Comnena (*The Alexiad*).

Rufus is characterised by his loyalty to his father. He is depicted at William's side in battle, sharing the Conqueror's uncompromising fighting spirit. William of Malmesbury wrote that Rufus was the first to issue a challenge or to hit back when opposed. He is claimed to have 'feared God but little and men not at all'. Blunt and sharp-spoken, his father had been similarly forthright. Both men are alleged to have had bad tempers. Rufus is sometimes held to have become almost incoherent with rage when aroused, leaving him lost for words or struggling to pronounce them. He is said to have stuttered (menacingly so) and to have sometimes outstared men at formal gatherings. Multi-coloured flecks in the king's eyes are claimed to have flared alarmingly when aroused. Sometimes the two orbs appeared to be of different colours. These negative characteristics may have been conjured using earlier exemplars; in a sense, they were made to fit a paradigm of what a cloistered monk might imagine a reputably fierce king to have been like. There is in fact good evidence to suggest Rufus was markedly chivalrous and courteous and always scrupulously correct in his dealings with social equals. His sense of courtliness and gallantry may well have been better developed than that of many of his contemporaries. His fair treatment of captives became something of a hallmark. He was also an innovative, naturally gifted and practical man, full of good ideas, with a down-to-earth, get-things-done persona; it is the latter trait that may have made him appear brusque.

On his deathbed King William is said to have kissed Rufus and urged him to make the sea crossing to Kent and gain the Archbishop of Canterbury's blessing to be crowned King of England... or so the story goes. Orderic takes great pains to stress the dying king's lucidity and intent, so this version of events has become the dominant narrative. Frank Barlow, Rufus' academic biographer, describes, in his Oxford DNB entry, his subject's move on the crown as a legitimised coup, made possible only by the Archbishop of Canterbury's deference to what he thought to be the late king's wishes. Another of Rufus' biographers, John Gillingham (*William II, The Red King*) says royal successions were normally disputed, the outcome decided by 'politics and war', even if the previous king's wishes were regarded as creating acceptable title: in other words, Rufus would have to fight for his rights as his father had done. Katherine Lack (*Conqueror's Son*) suggests William may have died more quickly than is allowed for by the chroniclers and therefore was unable to make his last wishes known; her intimation is that Rufus took it upon himself to seize the crown of England.

Already at the coast when news of his father's passing reached him, Rufus hurried across the Channel to England and secured the treasury at Winchester and a number of key southern coastal sites, the most important ones being Pevensey in Sussex and Dover in Kent. He likely travelled with a knightly retinue and is said to have carried with him a sealed letter of recommendation from his father as well as the Conqueror's sword, sceptre and crown, plus a number of hostages from the time of the Conquest. The cross-Channel dash must have seemed to Rufus a great adventure. He had to avoid being waylaid by enemies and would have been dependant on favourable wind and tide for a timely crossing. Getting to England as quickly as possible was vital. News of the king's death would create a vacuum at Westminster, which might attract pretenders to the throne. Pauline Stafford (*Unification and Conquest*) says the Conqueror's accession in 1066 had come at the end of 'an exceptionally complicated succession dispute'. As late as 1087 the Norman hold on England remained a developing process, one which William's three sons cannot have banked on remaining irreversible.

Rufus' crossing proved expeditious and free of incident, and Lanfranc, Archbishop of Canterbury, crowned him William II of England at the Church of St Peter the Apostle, Westminster, on 26 September 1087, three days before the feast of St Michael, patron saint of high places and heavenly protector against dark forces. A late harvest that year had proved to be poor, so the news of Rufus' bloodless takeover would have come at a premium in a year described in the *Anglo-Saxon Chronicle* as 'heavy and pestiferous'. A virulent fever is said to have affected one man, woman and child in every two, and to have often proved fatal; this had then been followed by further bad weather and a great famine. The last thing the country would have wanted would have been a period of protracted in-fighting.

Archbishop Lanfranc's acceptance of Rufus' claim marked the most crucial hurdle for the aspirant king. Had the archbishop objected or procrastinated for any reason, Rufus might not have been in a position to force the issue. Even contemporary commentators were in no doubt that without the archbishop's consent Rufus could never have gained the kingdom. Lanfranc would in any event have wanted to play the kingmaker. There had been a great rivalry between Canterbury and York for religious primacy in Britain, and the nature of the relationship between the two archbishoprics remained undefined in 1087.

When in 1072 the Conqueror had selected Thomas of Bayeux for the see of York, Lanfranc had refused to consecrate him unless the nominee made a written undertaking of submission. Thomas did so but with the reservation his pledge was made subject to papal decree. This remained outstanding, so his profession remained qualified. Had Rufus looked to York to be crowned, this might have served to undermine Canterbury's claim to primacy.

Rufus took time out to ensure the security of the royal treasure and the mounds of fiscal documents housed at Winchester Castle. The great trove of booty comprised plundered precious metals and the proceeds of taxation in the form of masses of silver coin. By ensuring its safekeeping Rufus acted no differently from other kings of England in the past. Edward the Confessor's first act as king had been to take over control of the royal treasury from his mother, Emma, with whom he was at odds. Rufus should not be viewed as overtly self-enriching. He made financial restitution in accordance with his father's last wishes, splitting benevolences among the principal churches of England. Some minsters got ten marks of gold, others six. Each country church got sixty pence. The newly made king commanded that crosses, alters, shrines, copies of the Gospels, candlesticks, sacred vessels, pipes for the communion wine and various ornaments, received in exchange for jewels, gold, silver and precious stones, should be divided among the more important churches and monasteries. Additionally, each English shire had money allocated to be portioned out to the poor and needy. Even the lowliest of his subjects mattered. The poor would be expected to offer up prayers for the king in consideration.

Another beneficiary of the new king's largesse was Battle Abbey, built by his father to house monks to pray for the souls of the dead at Hastings. The abbey and its adjacent manor gained a £40 annual grant. The monks in residence also received gifts of golden and silver reliquaries, plus the Conqueror's gem-studded mantle. Rufus would later have a bejewelled monument erected above his father's tomb at Caen. If later known as one of England's most irreligious kings, Rufus gave no advance notice of the fact.

Seen in a thirteenth-century coloured miniature, Rufus' likeness is of a fierce, bearded man of firm resolve, holding an impressive sword at the ready. His coins show him this way too. In one issue, he is depicted actually wielding his sword. He of course would have wanted his image to portray someone intimidating, a man his people could trust to protect them. A distant figure to all except the men of his household and those who toiled at his hunting lodges, the likeness of Rufus on coins was the main way to make himself known to his common subjects. His image had to be impressive. The consensus is, anyway, that Rufus was moulded from the same energetic martial cast as his father. He ticked all the boxes required of an outward-going, magnanimous, medieval prince. The English monk who penned the *Anglo-Saxon Chronicle* entry for the year 1100 called him 'strong and violent ... and very terrible': all three attributes were good press for an eleventh-century monarch, who had to be seen as both terrifying and just.

On a less wholesome note, the king has been accused of maintaining a riotous court. Unmarried and without his late mother to intervene and censure conduct, there were almost inevitably bound to have been behavioural issues raised at court by churchmen. Gillingham points out that apart from domestics (laundresses, dairymaids and probably prostitutes) the royal household would have been overwhelmingly masculine. That Rufus never married, had no known mistresses and suffered from the scribblings of the chroniclers has been taken to indicate he was gay. However, we should be wary of antique narratives written by men largely cloistered and denied outlets for their sexuality, ready to believe any tittle-tattle they heard. The king's character has been described as 'finely balanced between vice and virtue', so we should probably leave it at that.

Rufus' not marrying and siring heirs must nonetheless be seen as the great failure of his reign. Waiting until middle age to marry and have legitimate children cannot have been unusual in medieval times, but it might have been expected that Rufus, as a crowned king, would seek out a bride sooner rather than later and that if he did not his advisors would have pressed hard the case for him to do so. There are indications in the 1090s that he may have considered marriage into the Scottish royal family, but any hopes along these lines were scuppered when relations between the English and Scottish kings suddenly worsened.

Much better attested than the intimate details of Rufus' personal life is that his court embraced the new fashions of the age, including long hair, pointed shoes shaped like scorpion's tails, and elegant shirts with hanging sleeves. He had extravagant tastes. Emma Mason (*William II*) calls him 'a power-dresser'. A long-haired look harked back to a Viking past, but it seems the Normans of the Conqueror's generation more typically wore their hair short at the back and sides. The Church disapproved of the new fashions. They may in a sense have been hitting back. Disparaging the clergy became fashionable in Rufus' circle, though not necessarily because Rufus gave a lead in this respect. We should in fact not really make too much of any of this; conservative elders and Church apostates locking horns verbally with an upstart generation is hardly novel. At some point, Rufus may have relented to pressure and opted for a more sober look. Traces of stonework on a capital at Westminster have been taken to suggest a man with quite short, curly hair and a trim beard. Impartial stonework may more accurately depict an otherwise shadowy historical personality.

Henry

William's third surviving son, Henry, was still a teenager at the time of his father's death. By all accounts, he was more circumspect than his elder brothers, and less headstrong. Henry's reserve has been taken to mask a considerable shrewdness. His sobriquet *Beauclerc* indicates him to have been a well-educated and bright scholar. He could perhaps both read and write at a time when the secular nobility could at best sometimes read. His tutor may have been Osmund, Bishop of Salisbury. Henry is known to have visited Abingdon Abbey with him at Easter 1084, when the prince would have been aged around sixteen. Henry's signature is found beside Osmund's on several royal charters from this period. Henry has been claimed to be the first intellectual King of England since Alfred the Great (even at the time he was referred to somewhat sycophantically as 'a portent and a wonder'). He is claimed to have looked down on men less well educated than himself, once declaring, 'An uneducated king is no better than a crowned ass.' The precise context is not known for sure; it might well have been said in a jokey way. Modern scholars, however, doubt the veracity of Henry's scholarship and consider such attributes applied to him as overblown. As the last child of a long marriage, Henry, more certainly felt he had something to prove. Other than a good brain he developed sharp elbows and a measured wait-and-see approach to getting his own way.

Dubbed a knight by his father at Whitsuntide, 24 May 1086, at Westminster, Henry was by then a dark-haired, dark-eyed youth of medium height. His dubbing had been followed by a bout of crown-wearing on the part of his father – a highly symbolic and formalised ceremonial which at the time attracted widespread interest. At Salisbury on 1 August 1086, at a great gathering of all the important nobles of the land (called in the *Anglo-Saxon Chronicle* 'a great convocation'), William seems to have placed Henry centre stage when seeking to enforce the allegiance of all his important Anglo-Norman subjects – a repeat of the submission William had once called on for Robert to receive when at much the same age. Henry was the only one of the Conqueror's sons to be born in the purple – in other words, born after William became anointed King of England. He was also likely the only son of the Conqueror to have been reared in England. He may have remained in the country apart from occasional trips to Normandy right up until his knighthood in 1086, and, on this basis, he may have considered himself to have enjoy greater legitimacy to the throne of England than either of his brothers.

As mentioned earlier, there is a strong tradition linking Henry's birthplace (*c.* Christmas 1068) to Selby in Yorkshire. His mother, Matilda of Flanders, had already given birth to seven or more children by the time Henry was born. She may have eschewed the risks of travelling north while pregnant, hopeful of joining up with her husband at York before her confinement, but may have had to make an emergency stop at this otherwise obscure northern outpost when her waters broke. However, travelling north at a time when a major rebellion was in full sway is now considered unlikely. The queen, some argue, remained in southern England throughout her confinement, within easy reach of Southampton or Portsmouth and a passage back to Normandy. Should anything untoward have happened to her husband, or should the troubles in the north have sparked unrest south of the Thames, she would then have been better able to embark for Normandy at a moment's notice. The queen is known to have lodged at Winchester during Easter 1069, when Henry would have been less than six months old; soon afterwards she did in fact travel back to Normandy. The Conqueror is said to have sent his beloved wife back across the narrow sea, 'away from the English tumults, to keep the duchy secure'.

As an alternative scenario, it may have been while William was at Selby, or encamped nearby, that the news of the birth of his son reached him from the south of England. This would help explain the royal charter for an abbey to be built there. The only other abbey founded in England during William's reign was at Battle in Sussex, raised to make restitution for the deaths of the many men killed in 1066. The establishment of a religious house at Selby, to offer thanks to God for the gift of a son born in the newly conquered land, may also have addressed the need for the establishment of a northern foundation at a time when Northumbria remained a much-disputed and fought-over theatre of war. Wherever in England Henry was born, he could boast that he was an Englishman, upstaging his brothers.

3

NOBLE WIFE AND
WORTHY DAUGHTERS

Aged around thirty-seven when Henry was born, Queen Matilda lived an exhaustingly peripatetic life, always on the move. It is a mark of her great stamina that she made the arduous crossing of the English Channel on several occasions during her married life. The passage of water was considered so dangerous that many noblemen and women with lands on both sides of the English Channel never had the nerve to brave the journey. Matilda's near continuous pregnancies and travails are all the more incredible if the bones unearthed in 1961 from her tomb in the choir of L'Abbaye-aux-Dames in Caen are really hers. They would establish her to have been a diminutive woman, hardly five foot tall. There is, though, a question mark now over the provenance of these remains. Like the bones of our early kings and queens, housed at Winchester Cathedral and once plundered by Parliamentarian troops during the English Civil War, dead French royals also had their relics kicked around and muddled up during the Wars of Religion. In any event, at five foot, Matilda might not have been considered unusually small in an age when the average height of a man was just around five inches taller. One interesting observation, assuming the bones unearthed to have been hers, is that the pelvic bone was found to be wide compared with her supposed height, an anatomical advantage for a woman who would endure at least eight or more pregnancies.

Historians extoll Matilda as a model of active queenship. Her progresses have been tracked through her charters, the number and frequency of which are claimed as evidence of her own personal power. Her crowning at Westminster was a well-orchestrated State occasion, played out to enormous fanfare, the first great State occasion of the Norman era in England. William's own coronation in 1066 had by contrast been a hurried affair. The queen became a powerful ruler in her own right, with vast resources at her command. She is known to have witnessed one hundred charters, signing them carefully with a distinctive Jerusalem-style cross. Her signature mark appears more frequently than any other save William's. She occupied an unusually elevated position in government, and she maintained her prominence at court up until her death in 1083. She was described later, with misogynistic directness, as 'a woman of masculine wisdom'. As had become typical of the more active medieval queens, she played a central role in governance and family matters. If, in her husband's absence, the government of Normandy became a collaborative arrangement with her eldest son, Robert, charter evidence indicates she most often took the lead role. This may have been insisted upon by her husband, who, as we have seen, after 1074, blocked Robert from acting on his own initiative. Matilda may have wanted Robert to have the freedom to take the reins of power more often than he did. She would have been aware that having his authority constrained fuelled a growing sense of anger and frustration in him, and for her to witness this at first hand must have been the cause of considerable distress.

Matilda also suffered obstacles to overcome when young. Her marriage to William was at the time viewed as both politically provocative and proscribed within parameters allowed to cousins by the Church. William and Matilda were fifth cousins, descended from Normandy's founder, Rollo the Viking. The Church closely regulated marriages where pairings were thought to be within certain degrees of kinship. Even engagements between common ancestors where no formal marriage had occurred, just the promise, might be proscribed. William and Matilda, as well as being fifth cousins, had relatives who fell into this category. Matilda's mother, Adela, had once been betrothed (though not married) to William's uncle Richard III, Duke of Normandy. For this reason alone, some in the Church may have viewed William and Matilda as too closely related in the sight of God.

Because of the risk of papal censure, the couple's wedding had been a closeted affair, of which we have few details. Marriage negotiations had probably started in 1048 and were well under way by October 1049. At the Council of Rheims, Pope Leo IX (having been lobbied by naysayers) first questioned the union between the two cousins. Putting aside the possibility of some genetic link, which can hardly have been provable, the conjoining of a Norman prince and a Flemish princess was also deemed dangerous for political reasons. The German Emperor Henry III (an enemy of Matilda's father, Baldwin of Flanders) was one of several Europeans, albeit the most powerful, who considered the marriage to be provocative. Henry III was the Pope's mainstay. Papal proscription followed hot on the heels of imperial anger. William had great need of a Flemish alliance to bolster his position, so was not to be deterred. His prospective father-in-law, Count Baldwin, also wanted the union to go ahead. He needed a strongman like William as a son-in-law to back him against his own unruly neighbours. William's illegitimacy and papal blocks came far behind the duke's martial prowess as considerations.

The newly married couple had also faced censure closer to home, where the Archbishop of Rouen, Mauger, William's uncle, opposed the union. Mauger is said to have found it intolerable that two blood relations should share the marriage bed. For such a tirade to be taken seriously seems remarkable, but, later, taking their cue from him, die-hard English patriots would disparage Matilda as William's *gebedde* or concubine. Mauger may have upped the ante on the already threatened papal proscription by threatening, himself, to excommunicate his nephew and place an interdict on the duchy – a dire prospect for any medieval ruler. William did not, however, back down; he would later depose and exile his uncle for backing a rebellion against him, so in a sense got his own back. On his deathbed, William is said by Orderic to have ruminated over the damage that had been done to him by both archbishop Mauger and by another of his uncles, William, Count of Talou. He said they had treated him with contempt because he was a bastard. After defeating the pair in fighting near Arques in 1053, William had banished them from Normandy and had revoked their titles. After his uncle's stronghold at Arques fell, following the news of a ducal victory at Aubin-sur-Scie (located five miles south of Dieppe), the garrison are said to have marched out from the castle 'with heads bowed, carrying only their saddles'. Mauger went on to settle in the Channel Islands, where he is said to have gone mad and consorted with demons; Talou found sanctuary at Boulogne. Even so, the marriage issue was not formally closed until 1059, when, at a Lateran Council convened at Easter that year under the authority of a new pope, Archbishop Lanfranc succeeded in overturning the injunctions.

Matilda may have been no more than eighteen or nineteen years of age when she wed. Described formulaically as 'a beautiful, gentle bred woman of pure mind', she travelled from Flanders to the fortress at Eu on Normandy's eastern border to be married, accompanied by her father. The royal party were met by William, his mother Herleva and his stepfather Herluin de Conteville, the father of William's half-brothers, Odo and Robert. It may have been at Eu that the wedding took place. A further round of formalities then followed at Rouen in the late autumn of 1049. The earliest direct reference to Matilda as the duke's consort is not in fact to be found until a charter for 1053, but their son Robert's name appears on a charter dated to 1051, when he was a new-born baby. Since there have never been aspersions made as to his legitimacy, his parents must presumably have been married by then.

Matilda may have considered herself William's superior in the medieval pecking order. A direct descendent of Charlemagne and Alfred the Great, she counted the King of France and the Duke of Burgundy among her uncles. Her mother, Adela, proudly styled herself 'the sister of the King of France'. She nurtured a fierce pride in her ancestry. She may at first have baulked at the idea of marrying the twenty-something William. Independent minded and resourceful, she is claimed to have initially resisted William's courtship advances, saying to one of the duke's emissaries she would never marry a bastard. In truth, more of an issue than bastardy may have been the low status of her suitor's mother, Herleva, a commoner. By the time Orderic Vitalis, William of Malmesbury and Henry of Huntingdon were writing of these events in the following century, bastardy had become a bigger issue than before. Social values had by then changed significantly.

William nevertheless may have had to press his suit in dramatic fashion to gain his prize, and a failed attempt to abduct Matilda against her will cannot be dismissed as mere storytelling. A bastard daughter of the late King Harold II, named Gunnilda, would in 1092–3 be abducted from Wilton Abbey by Alan Rufus, the powerful Lord of Richmond. In 1015, Edmund Ironside, the rebellious son of King Ethelred II of England, kidnapped and married the princess Ealdgyth, who at the time was housed at Malmesbury Abbey by the king for her own protection. Kidnap and rape were extreme ways to gain a bride's dower lands and titles. In the case of William and Matilda, lurid tales of a rough wooing were soon circulating. One tells of William dragging Matilda from her horse by her plaited hair while on her way to church, in Bruges or Lille. Another imagines William confronting her in her bedroom, dragging her out and violently throwing her onto the muddy ground outside. The sources for this are late. If they are to be believed, we might as well accept Matilda to have been upended and thrown over William's saddle and carried off in the manner of his Viking forebears.

Other than the lingering issue around consanguinity, relations between William, Matilda and the papacy appear to have been good throughout the 1050s. The commentators at the time, all of them religious men, may in fact have made more of the threat of papal censure than was really warranted. In an attempt to draw a line under the affair, the duke and duchess endowed two new monasteries at Caen: one for monks and one for nuns (known today as 'his' and 'hers'). When, in 1059, Pope Nicholas II retrospectively approved the marriage, he may have done so on the proviso the couple founded one monastery each. Monks and nuns at Caen from then on prayed for the souls of their sponsors.

It must have come as a great relief to Matilda and William to have their marriage recognised by the Church, especially in the context of their children's legitimacy: by then, one or more daughters and perhaps another two sons (Richard and William Rufus) had been born. At Matilda's foundation in Caen, which she dedicated to the Holy Trinity, the Abbaye des Dames, the duchess is said to have endowed it with studied care, with lands and goodly objects: splinters of the True Cross, crumbs from the bread broken at the Last Supper, strands from the Virgin's hair, one of St Cecilia's fingers and numerous embalmed corpses of saints. William, meanwhile, had a hundred benefices established throughout Normandy, built to feed and clothe the poor and the maimed. These places still existed at Cherbourg, Rouen, Bayeux and Caen well into the mid-twelfth century, and are said by the twelfth-century historian Robert Wace to have remained just as they had been established. Their funding may have represented penance for any residual sin accruing from the marriage. Uppermost in the thoughts of the duke and duchess would have been the desire to shore-up their legitimacy as a couple. Robert's birth early in the marriage would have helped buttress their union. A male heir would have been viewed as God's blessing, helping to silence any lingering criticism. Further children would follow in short order.

In later life, Matilda spent many hours at another of her foundation churches, the small Benedictine priory at Notre-Dame du Pré. Here, on the banks of the Seine near Rouen, she prayed for her husband's safety when he first campaigned in England. When news of William's triumph at Hastings reached her, she ordered the priory's name to be changed to Notre-Dame de Bonnes Nouvelles (Our Lady of Good News). She also initiated a torrent of alms-giving, targeting the poor, done to 'bring succour ... to her husband, struggling on the field of battle'. It may have been Matilda who encouraged her chaplain, Guy of Amiens, to compose the epic poem known as the *Carmen de Hastingae*, a work praising William and condemning King Harold of England. It is the earliest Norman source for the Battle of Hastings. Guy accompanied Matilda to England for her coronation at Whitsuntide 1068, having by then likely completed the work (if, indeed, he was the author). The *Carmen* was commissioned as a gift from Matilda to her husband upon her coronation. It is the *Carmen* which tells us the battle was fought on a 'mons' and in a 'vallis', and also that the English on the day of battle 'scorned the solace of horses ... trusting in their strength, standing fast on foot'.

Papal authorities came to greatly value Matilda's benign influence over William. The Holy Father, Pope Gregory VII, once wrote to encourage her to act as a guide for her husband, quoting a passage from the Bible that explained how an unfaithful man might only become faithful through his wife. This was to inspire a faith in God and was not a reference to faithlessness in a sexual sense. There is in fact no compelling evidence to support any claim William was a womaniser, which was very unusual. A keen focus on legitimacy overrode any urge to indulge in extramarital affairs. He is the first Norman duke for whom no evidence of consorting with concubines or the fathering of illegitimate children survives. He remained true to Matilda. On one notable occasion, he stated how he loved his wife 'as my own soul'. The feelings were reciprocated. When William took ill at Cherbourg in the years leading up to the Conquest, Matilda, unkempt and visibly distraught, paced the floor and demanded the attention of courtiers and churchmen to attend upon him.

Matilda continued throughout her life to make bequests to the Norman church of religious artefacts, draperies and other regalia. One gift we know about of 100 Rouen livres was made to the Abbey of Saint Evroult, located on Normandy's turbulent and semi-barren southern borders, later to become the home of the historian Orderic Vitalis. The abbot there built a refectory with the money for the monks to take their meals together. The money might better have been spent on defence, for the abbey is said to have been surrounded by the most villainous of neighbours. In addition to the money, the foundation received gold, a chasuble decorated with gold and pearls, and a cope for the chanter. Gifts were also made by Matilda to monasteries and abbeys in England, notably Malmesbury Abbey and Wells Cathedral. The only sour note in an otherwise unanimous barrage of accolade as to her charitable nature is that a number of disgruntled English churchmen remained hostile to Matilda up until after her death. They referred to her as a virago, a foreign despoiler who carted off many of their treasures.

The queen died on 2 November 1083, aged around fifty-one. The nature of her final illness is unknown, although an outbreak of plague is sometimes held to have been responsible. William went into deep mourning. The marriage had navigated heavy turbulence, yet had remained a happy one. Robert, too, must have deeply mourned the death of his mother, as would, no doubt, his younger siblings. Matilda had been Robert's only source of parental comfort. Her burial took place at her foundation abbey of St Trinité at Caen. The original tombstone, with an inscription carved around the edge, still survives intact. She bequeathed her crown and sceptre to the care of the nuns at St Trinité. Her unimpeachable bloodline had helped strengthen William's position as a prince on the European stage. She had brought no dowry or land or titles to the marriage. Her strong pedigree was seen as enough of a settlement in itself. All her epitaphs stress her royal pedigree, passed on to her sons and daughters.

*

William and Matilda were also blessed with at least four daughters we know about: Adelida, Cecilia, Constance and Adela. There may have been more; an Agatha and a Matilda are also mentioned. A girl with the same name as her mother might be expected, but, if there ever existed a daughter of this name, nothing at all is known of her life. Matilda of Flanders' fertility was remarkable, especially if, as alleged, she was short of stature. It is not known if any of the daughters were at William's bedside during his final days, but one or more of them might well have been. Princess Adelida is usually considered to have been the eldest of the four girls (b. *c.* 1053), named perhaps after the Conqueror's sister Adelaide. She heads most lists of William and Matilda's daughters. Sometime after 1066 she entered into vows at the Benedictine abbey of St Léger at Préaux. She may have been brought up under the guardianship of the powerful Norman magnate Roger de Beaumont, her second cousin and the abbey's patron. A belief she was at one time destined for a royal marriage stems from a story of an unnamed daughter of William's linked in marriage at different times with an Englishman, a Manceaux and a Spaniard: almost the opening line of a bad joke. One story tells of her terror at the thought of having to submit sexually to an older Spaniard, whom she had never met. Another claims her to have been betrothed in 1064 (when aged just eleven) to the ill-fated Harold Godwinsson, killed at Hastings. The fact she entered cloisters after 1066 may be pertinent in this regard.

Who and when to marry cannot ever have been a personal choice for sons and daughters of the nobility in medieval times. A sense of wretchedness and desperation is sometimes evoked by historians when describing the string of collapsed marriage betrothals Adelida may have suffered. There is of course no way of knowing how the princess felt, or of the precise truth of these multiple engagements. She might have been relieved they fell through, preferring a cloistered life. An early piety in her is noted by contemporaries, who make reference to calluses on the princess' knees from incessantly praying, and not necessarily for a husband. Whether or not Adelida came to take the veil as an oblate or as a lay princess is not known. Her academic biographer Elizabeth van Houts writes that meditations were dedicated to her by the Archbishop of Canterbury, who referred to her as 'our venerable lady of royal nobility'. In 1072 she received from him a number of prayer books, meditations and extracts from the Psalms, along with an accompanying letter describing her as a young woman starting out 'on the frontiers of religious life'.

A monastic career was a life choice for eleventh-century noblewomen, not a sacrifice or a fallback in the event of the collapse of marriage plans. The Church in the second half of the eleventh century provided women with the possibilities of stimulating roles otherwise closed to them, a re-continuation of females acting as Church leaders in Italy from as early as the fifth century. An abbess would have executed responsibilities of both a religious and secular nature, including the spiritual and temporal supervision of nuns and novices, and the collection of tithes – in effect, estate management. Religious foundations of the day were extremely labour intensive. The early Church taught an equality among all believers in the eyes of God. It did not differentiate markedly between men and women in the exercise of administrative and ecclesiastical power. The spread of the monastic movement in western Europe between the sixth and tenth centuries was often fronted by women from royal and noble backgrounds. Anglo-Saxon monasteries were sometimes called double-houses, accommodating both men and women. Typically, they rested under the command of an abbess, not an abbot. Change was in the wind: the so-called centralising tendencies of the eleventh century onwards, which saw the role of women in the Church downgraded. We would now consider these changes misogynistic. One prominent ecclesiastic who is known to have foisted such views is St Thomas Aquinas (d. 1274). He considered only the male essence could beget priestly authority. As early as the 1070s male leaders within the Church may have started to exercise supervisory powers more directly over old and new monastic foundations, with abbesses relegated into a subordinate role.

The second daughter, Cecilia (b. *c.* 1056), became an oblate (a holy handmaid of Christ) at her mother's Benedictine foundation of St Trinité at Caen, just months before the invasion of England in 1066, when just ten years old. Offering Cecilia to the Church when so young may have been done for a variety of reasons, but the most likely motivation would have been to gain God's blessing for William and Matilda's cause in England. The document confirming the offer of Cecilia to the Church is witnessed by the duke's three sons then living: Robert, aged around fifteen; Richard, aged around thirteen; and William Rufus, aged around six or seven. Professed a nun in 1075, when aged nineteen, Cecilia went on to become St Trinité's abbess when aged around fifty-seven. Earlier than this, she had taken a lead role in the running of the abbey, acting as a deputy to its long-lived abbess.

Both her parents are known to have attended her ordination ceremony in 1075. The lateness of her ordination (considering the gap between 1066, when first offered, and 1075, when professed) has been taken to indicate William may have been hedging his bets as to whether or not his daughter would in fact remain cloistered. In unpredictable times this must have seemed the sensible thing to do. Her parents may have waited before having her consecrated until her sisters designated for political marriages survived into childhood. Her ordination may also have been timed to thank God for William's unlooked-for recovery from his illness the year before in 1074, mentioned earlier in the context of Robert's gift to St Vincent's at Le Mans. Confusingly, Cecilia is once said to have declared she was 'the only daughter of my father and my wholly wretched mother'. Two other sisters were alive at that time. Cecilia must have meant she was the only unmarried daughter left alive, therefore the only one able and available to console her mother while in mourning for Adelida. Robert and Cecilia remained on close terms, as too did Rufus and Cecilia. Her monastery would later have lands in Norfolk bestowed on it by Rufus. She died in the summer of 1126 and was buried within St Trinité's walls. Her tomb is now (and may have then been) inaccessible.

The third daughter, Princess Constance, married the twenty-something Alan IV, Duke of Brittany, at Bayeux in 1086. Queen Matilda was by this time dead and William had just a year or so to live. Anecdotally, Constance, whose age is unknown, had been her late mother's favourite daughter. She is considered to have been the most gifted of the sisters. William may have hoped to end long-running hostilities between Normandy and Brittany by closing this marriage deal. If so, he achieved his wish.

It was good politics. There are, though, contradictory accounts of Constance's popularity in Brittany. She is said to have been disliked by courtiers for her haughty demeanour. The countess may possibly have been a severe and conservative woman, who looked down on the Breton nobility. She took her responsibilities to the common people seriously, championing their welfare. She was said to have been loved by the commoners, though kept at arms' length by the nobles. She died childless, not yet thirty, in 1090, and was interred at Rennes in the Church of Église Saint-Melaine.

The daughter about whom we know the most is Adela, born just after her father's victory in 1066, therefore the youngest of the four daughters. Henry and Adela were the only two children born after their father and mother became King and Queen of England. Named after her maternal grandmother, Adela's literacy and her patronage of the arts indicate her to have been carefully educated, like her younger brother, either in a monastic setting or by private tutors. She is said throughout her life to have made time for learning, becoming the patroness of the noted poet and historian Baudri, Bishop of Dol, who once eulogised her in verse, writing how 'no-one returns empty-handed from the princess' uprightness'.

When just a child, Adela had been promised as a bride to the later sanctified Simon de Crépy, the son of the powerful Ralph IV of Valois, who held comital title to a large number of French counties. A papal injunction scuppered the union, however. Much of the French Vexin lay under Simon's control. He had been brought up as a ward at the Norman court. William is said to have considered him akin to a son and Robert Curthose to have loved him as a brother. The two, Simon and Robert, may have been close in age, with Simon a few years the elder. With William and Robert's assistance, Simon, a man never really cut out for soldiering, fought a three-year-long war with Philip of France for control over his inherited lands in the Vexin. Sickened by the violence he witnessed, he entered religious orders, possibly as an escape from worldly care. He would later play a role in helping reunite the royal family after Robert's rebellion in 1078–9. That William was weakened by Simon's decision to seek a career in the Church was underlined when the parts of the Vexin which had been under Simon's remit fell back under the authority of the French king. These were territories which had in the past buffered Normandy's borders with the French. It now became a jumping-off point for further warring, the cause of the Conqueror's demise in 1087.

Sometime after the turn of the year 1079–80, Adela became betrothed to Stephen, heir to the rich county of Blois, a man said to possess as many castles as there were days in the year. Celebrated at Chartres, the principal town of Blois, the wedding must have been a lavish affair. The alliance it secured proved of immense importance to both parties. The bride can have been little more than fourteen years of age, yet the bards sang of her beauty, valour, learnedness and generosity, and prophesised she would make Stephen a worthy wife. They were proved right. The marriage yielded a large brood of children. One of them, Stephen, named after his father, would one day become King of England.

Adela inherited her mother's fecundity, plus the strong, decisive character traits of both mother and father. When her husband left Blois on crusade in the mid-1090s, she took on the full comital court role and managed the county's finances and the royal household. Like her mother, she took immense pride in her lineage. Her palace at Blois was adorned with wall hangings, woven from gold and silver silk thread. These may have been tapestries to match in ambition and scale the famous Bayeux Tapestry. On her bedhead there were depicted the carved symbols of planets and the signs of the zodiac. As this might suggest, Adela aspired to and maintained a lofty moral stance. When her husband Stephen unexpectedly and somewhat shamefully returned home early from the First Crusade, she became so angry with him she immediately ordered him back. We might consider her an overly authoritative spouse and Stephen weak-willed, but this would be to overlook the existence of letters between husband and wife which suggest a close, loving marital relationship and a husband severely homesick for his wife all the while on crusade. (See Appendix 1.) Stephen starts one letter with the words, 'My Countess, my sweetest friend, my wife.'

4

REBEL PRINCE

Fair prince, rouse yourself manfully, and demand from your
father a share of the kingdom of England, or at least claim
the duchy of Normandy, which he long ago granted you …
assume the lion's part.

Orderic Vitalis

On 13 November 1077, Robert Curthose was among those
who attended the dedication of his father's new abbey church of
St Etienne at Caen. It is possible that Rufus might at one time have
been destined to serve there, but Richard's death in the New Forest
had likely upset his father's plans. Cecilia had been committed to
her mother's twin foundation at St Trinité two years before. If not
on campaign at the time, Robert may have witnessed the event.
It must have been sometime after this that he famously accused his
father of treating him little better than a soldier for hire. We have
no firm details precisely when or why this argument occurred and
can only assume that William's relationship with his eldest son had
now come under increasing strain, almost certainly because of the
king's reluctance to allow Robert a fuller rein over the governance
of Normandy.

A growing rebelliousness had asserted itself in the Conqueror's
son, further stoked, according to Orderic, by Robert's confederate

knights, who cajoled him to act assertively and demand more than simply to serve as a frontier ranger. As earlier posited, William have come to fear his son as a rival. Robert is claimed to have challenged his father to make good on his earlier promises, only to be rebuffed. His squaring up to his father in this way would not simply have been youthful muscle-flexing or done when angered by the antics of his younger male siblings as is sometimes imagined. The prince was closer to thirty years of age than twenty. His actions more credibly marked the start of a dangerous power play. As we have seen, William had been damaged politically after the fallout of the rebellion in England in 1075 and his defeat in Brittany the following year. Orderic says William cautioned the prince against incitement into 'some absurd attempt to commit evil with impunity'. The chronicler writes as if William were aware of what was about to happen, but Robert would not have gifted his father with advance notice of his intent to rebel. The historical setting for the breakaway was a military encampment at L'Aigle, on the duchy's south-eastern border, abutting the feudal manors of Perche, Mortagne and Bellême; the timing, the autumn or early winter of 1078/9, on the eve of a campaign to be launched on the frontiers.[1]

The prince picked his time to exert maximum damage on his father. His plan was to capture Rouen, some sixty miles away, and set himself up in opposition to his father. The coup de main failed. He and his knights were beaten off by ducal forces under the command of Rouen's castellan, Roger d'Ivry, a man who doubled in an honorific sense as William's butler. The abortive strike did, however, herald an outbreak of civil war. The king's son and his knights were soon ravaging the borders of the duchy from Rémalard Castle in the modern-day Orne department of Normandy. William abandoned his planned move against his marcher rebels and instead bought the services of a number of them: one was the renowned warrior Rotrou of Mortagne. Internecine warring was vicious; in part this was because of the number of mercenaries like Rotrou fighting on either side.

A knight named Aymer de Villerai became an early casualty of the fighting. He is said to have been captured, slain, and then slung across the saddle of a horse like 'a slaughtered cow'. Aymer's corpse toured Normandy to act as a deterrent to others, a spectacle justified by writers nearer the time as a measured response to 'the great and frequent ravages' of ducal lands by Robert's knights. Aymer's son is said to have become so traumatised when witnessing his father's gruesome fate that he immediately submitted to William; afterwards he became one of the Conqueror's most loyal subordinates. On Robert's eventual expulsion from Rémalard Castle, William is claimed by Orderic, somewhat fantastically, to have driven his son into exile with laughs and jeers and afterwards to have roared out for all to hear, 'By God's resurrection, he will be a hero, will our Bobby Curthose.'

The rebel prince is conjured by the chroniclers as riding out with a swarm of obsequious sycophants in the manner of a robber baron, restlessly eager for some new disturbance. It is in keeping with 'the Norman myth' that he and his companions should be singled out in this way; and yet the Normans were not in any way racially distinct – they were neither wholly Scandinavian nor French. William's sons had a Flemish mother and a father who was part Scandinavian and part French. They also had great-grandparents who hailed from Brittany. Important families on Normandy's southern borders were not Norman at all but Frankish. To say 'scratch the surface of a Norman and you would have a Viking' would be no more or less accurate than to say the same of Edward the Confessor or Harold II, both of whom had Scandinavian ancestry.

Robert took with him into exile many knights, all cavalrymen, trained and equipped at the Conqueror's expense. These were his *fideles* or faithful men, companions-in-arms and landless bachelor knights, seeking their way in the world. Their loss added to William's anger against his son. Rather than a cause for mocking jeers, the drain of young knights from the duchy would have been of serious concern. Knight errantry was closely monitored by men like William and was heavily proscribed. The status of a knight-bachelor typically lasted until a man came into his inheritance, married and began to raise a legitimate family – benefits for too long denied to Robert. Among the coterie of young men who rallied to the prince's banner were Robert de Bellême and Robert de Mowbray, both of whom we will hear much more of. They too may have sought independence from their families and an opportunity to win fame and glory.

As a group these men fit the voracious stereotype of the Normans as penned by the chronicler Geoffrey of Malaterra when describing the Normans operating in southern Italy as 'a cunning race, vengeful of injuries, despising their own patrimony in the hope of gaining more elsewhere'. Although championed as the optimal warriors of the age, with the mounted knight and the castle their iconic trademarks, the Normans were in reality no better or worse in a fight than any other Frenchmen. The early Northmen (Normans) had quickly jettisoned their more unruly Viking attributes to adopt the ways of their more sophisticated Frankish neighbours. At Hastings, the English fought in the manner of the Vikings of old, whereas the Norman knights fought on horseback like the Franks on whom they now modelled themselves. Taking to the sea in longships had by 1066 become something of a novelty for the Normans. They may no longer have retained the seagoing acumen or daring of their Scandinavian forebears. The Conqueror was undoubtedly a first-rate commander, but a more general reputation for military prowess among the Normans is now considered to have been largely their own later invention. William at the time was just one of several eleventh-century Frankish rulers to set out on a path of conquest, albeit, arguably, the most successful of them.

Robert Curthose must have been in his element on campaign. He was the antithesis of the effete courtier, a soldier through and through. Avoiding the nuanced subtleties of the ducal court, riding out with men of his own age and outlook would have suited his open and accommodating martial nature. Swapping the ducal straitjacket imposed by his father for the camaraderie of camp life and the cut and thrust of battle must have served as a palliative for the fractious and undermining paternal relationship he had endured. If a shorter man than his father, his martial skills argue against him being in any way unfit for the life of a warrior knight. An instinct for marauding and rapine, dormant until assuaged on chevauchee, might almost be seen as a violent and long-overdue coming of age.

Though not implicated in inciting her son to rebel, Queen Matilda put herself out on a limb by backing and providing her son with financial and material resources. She may even have made soldiers available to him from her estates in Flanders. All this must have been done covertly, but she was eventually found out. William flew into a rage, threatening the arrest and blinding of one of the queen's confidants for acting as a go-between. The terrified messenger, a man named Samson, had to be smuggled from under the Conqueror's nose and was sent into hiding at the monastery of Saint Evroult, where, years later, Orderic would have heard all about it. Matilda became so upset by her husband's antagonistic responses that she had to choke back tears.

Such first-hand drama helps highlight the flesh-and-blood immediacy of medieval courtly life, of generational animosity, and of passions raised in close confines, with sometimes violent outcomes. In desperation, the queen is claimed by Orderic Vitalis to have consulted a German hermit and soothsayer to help her gauge her son's future. The hermit allegedly foresaw the Conqueror's death and Robert's coming into his dukedom. He then foretold Normandy's ruin under her son's rule, describing the prodigal as akin to 'a wanton cow', trampling Normandy underfoot, plundering the wealth of the Church to distribute it to 'panders and lechers' – it is a striking example of hindsight mixed with malice, the product of the monk's vivid imagination.

After the loss of Rémalard Castle, Robert continued raiding into Normandy. He was now riding out in the company of Hugh de Chateauneuf-en-Thymerais, a man who took his name from a commune in the modern-day Eure-et-Loire department of northern

France; he was the same man who had earlier made Rémalard Castle and two other castles at Chateauneuf and Sorel available to the rebels. Hugh's father-in-law was a powerful cross-Channel magnate and close associate of the Conqueror, Roger de Montgomery, the father of one of Robert's main confederates in arms, Robert de Bellême (sometimes also referred to in the sources as Robert Talvas). Bellême was close in age to Robert, probably a little younger, and the wilder of the two. He had been knighted at Fresnay by the Conqueror in 1073, when aged sixteen, at the height of the campaigning in Maine that year.

With Bellême in mind, Orderic claimed the duchy of Normandy had 'given birth to a generation of wicked sons who cruelly devoured their mother's bowels'. Hailing as he did from a rapacious clan, typical of the more driven families in Normandy and on the duchy's frontiers (men who had in the past sought to carve out for themselves semi-independent fiefdoms), Bellême may have personified this charge, and may even have helped inspire the legend of Robert the Devil: a mythical figure alleged to have been a Norman knight fathered by Satan. It is a story that originated in France in the thirteenth century, featuring a wicked knight who could not be surpassed for strength or courage and who eventually becomes a bandit, robbing, burning, murdering and ravishing. On one occasion we know about, Bellême press-ganged monastic labour from the monastery at St Evroult to demolish a rivals' castle at Montaigu. He also purloined the revenues of the bishopric of Sées, which constituted Church income belonging to St Evroult.

These were hardly wickedly dark power plays worthy of a devil incarnate, unless of course seen through the eyes of the victims: the monks, the only people around at the time with the time or ability to write. Orderic Vitalis, for example, wrote on this subject,

> They only rejoice ... who can rob and thieve without restraint ... the respect for the priesthood, to which once all did reverence, is nearly extinct in the flood of calamities which so violently rages ... those who are plunged in the gloom

of the world's troubles can neither enjoy the light of true wisdom nor extricate themselves from the snares of vice ... The infernal furies made human beings, villages and houses, the victims of fire and slaughter ... at the sight of so many evils the impoverished Norman clergy weeps, the convents of monks lament, and the helpless people are everywhere desolate and sorrowful.

Anti-clericalism was a trait Bellême may have shared with many other Norman noblemen. The Church had amassed much land and was seen by the knightly classes as a territorial competitor, helping explain the sometimes strained relations between lords and bishops. Modern commentary regarding the lord is more nuanced. Bellême is now considered to have been little worse than others at the time: a knight who like his peers sought a degree of autonomy from the centralising inclinations of the dukes of Normandy and the fetters placed by them on when enacting vendettas.

Aggressive interplay within kinship groups was very much a feature of the '88 revolt, but so too was foreign intervention. Robert Curthose called on the support of his feudal overlord King Philip of France, who at the time may have been campaigning to push back Norman encroachment in the Vexin – the same heavily contested royal demesne to the north of the Seine that would later prove a fatal step too far for the Conqueror. Though likely something of an exaggeration, Norman and French interests are said to have become irreconcilable by this time, so a disunited Anglo-Norman realm would have been very much in the French king's best interests. Philip remained Robert's feudal overlord, and therefore held a duty of care. He became the prince's ally and enabler. Robert also sought out and gained the help of his maternal uncle and namesake, Robert I of Flanders, known as the Frisian, a determined opponent of the Normans. His usurpation of Flanders after the Battle of Cassel (22 February 1071), where the rightful Flemish heir Arnulf and Queen Matilda's champion William Fitz Osbern were both killed, had angered his sister, the queen, and had sullied relations between the county of her birth and the dukedom of Normandy ever since.

Under the rule of the Frisian, Flanders became a refuge for enemies of the Norman duke. Robert Curthose's travelling there and feting a sworn enemy of the duchy (even if the Frisian was his maternal uncle) was a major lapse of judgement on the prince's part. An uncompromising war resulted. Even Philip of France in the end became alarmed at the instability engendered. He had already ceded to Robert Curthose the strongly sited and walled castle at Gerberoy, located midway between the Somme and the Seine, on the northern marches of the Vexin. Increasingly concerned by the growing levels of violence, he likely broke his pact with the prince; but withdrawing support was one thing, and ousting the incumbent from Gerberoy Castle another.

The Battle of Gerberoy, Winter 1078/9

At a midwinter battle fought outside the castle, probably the culmination of several engagements fought outside the castle walls, Robert's military acumen came to the fore when launching a sortie from the castle gates with his knights and routing the opposing force outside led by his father and the French king. The two monarchs fought alongside one another that day in an otherwise unlikely alliance. High-bred participants in those times did battle as mounted knights. Backing them up were archers and crossbowmen. Warhorses, known as destriers, were bred for strength and stamina, and trained not to panic in battle. Only men rich enough would have ridden such horses. Others may have had to make do with infeior mounts. Fully helmeted and mailed, with their well-protected legs held straight in the box-like saddles of the time – which provided the rider with a secure seat and helped him withstand the shock of impact when couched lance splintered against raised shield – such men defied death when launching their charge against an enemy similarly accoutred. The Bayeux Tapestry shows cavalrymen with lances both couched and held overarm. Expensive mailed leggings are shown only on representations of the Conqueror and Count Eustace of Boulogne on the Bayeux Tapestry, indicating only the wealthiest wore such apparel. The same would have been true of mail armour worn on the body. A full mail coat would have been twice as expensive as a less effective padded shirt. Knights also donned the trademark spangenhelm with nasal guard.

William may have relied on Norman and English contingents to back him up at Gerberoy, whereas his son Robert had his own knights as well as Flemish and French mercenaries on his payroll. Both men led from the front and may have clashed head-on in the first jarring crash of battle. A later twelfth-century account of a similar conflict, contained in Robert Wace's *Roman de Rou*, provides us with a vivid indication of what such a contest might have been like:

> The knights attacked each other in tight formation, striking each other with lances lowered. On both sides they received blows on their shields from the lances. When the lances shattered and broke, they attacked each other with their swords, not seeking jousts but striking each other in the battle itself, just as champions do when they, alone on the battlefield, fight one against one. They strike and hit each other and turn aside when they are afraid. Each man is ashamed to flee and each wants to win the day; each advances as best he can.

The Conqueror was immediately wounded and unhorsed when the battle lines met (and not for the first time in his life: at Hastings, as we have seen, he is claimed to have had three horses brought down from under him). Once again, he was vulnerable to being trampled or battered to death. Did Robert's lance in fact unhorse his father as has sometimes been claimed? The combat occurred before the days when men wore armorial bearings or displayed heraldic devices, and yet it is unlikely Robert would have failed to recognise his father's bulky frame at the outset. If he did knowingly strike out at his father it would underline just how fractious the father/son relationship had become. Re-horsing the king cost his groom (an Anglo-Danish nobleman named Toki Wigodsson) his life when struck by an incoming crossbow bolt – an event overlooked when discounting a less general and unforgiving encounter than a semi-regulated joust. That crossbowmen were actively employed at Gerberoy implies a close siege with all the viciousness this entailed.

William Rufus, then a knight aged around twenty, also suffered wounding at Gerberoy. Sharing the risk of battle was expected of any member of the royal family who had reached an age to do so. Death or wounding of kings and princes was by no means an uncommon outcome of inter-generational feuding. Rufus would most probably have fought in the front line alongside his father. His bravery would in later life become legendary. He might already have been a well-accomplished warrior and Gerberoy may not have been the first occasion Rufus gave full reign to his martial nature, even though he would probably have been too young to have fought at the Battle of Dol in 1076. The main wound to the Conqueror at Gerberoy was not to be measured in cuts and bruises but to his pride. Successfully defending a castle under siege and routing a besieging army stood at the pinnacle of the medieval art of war. Robert Curthose had bested his father fair and square. Embarrassed that the son and father had so openly clashed, an English scribe that year struggled when attempting to assess the damage done to the Conqueror both physically and morally. Part of the page he worked on for the *Anglo-Saxon Chronicle* is torn away as if in disgust. The words on the page end saying, 'we do not want, though, to write more here of the harm which he [Robert] did his father'.

*

In the summer of 1079, the Scots launched a major foray into northern England. King Malcolm III of Scotland, known as Malcolm Canmore (from the Gaelic *Ceann Mor*, meaning great chief or more prosaically big-head), judged it an opportune time to strike at his ancient enemies – a predictable response down the centuries to English vulnerability. His raiding occurred just six months or so after the fighting at Gerberoy. It is tempting to speculate his raids were designed to test the resolve of the now divided Normans. The attacks were made between 15 August and 8 September 1079, between the two feasts of St Mary. Out of reverence or fear of the long-dead local saints of the region, only the church and environs of Hexham were spared the horrors of fire and sword. Malcolm would not have wanted to get on the wrong side of the powerful bishops Eata and Acca, dead or not.

The following summer (*c.* May 1080), Bishop Walcher of Durham – 'a saintly man, but an unworldly one' – was murdered at Gateshead. This was followed by a more general massacre of Norman and Flemish settlers by Northumbrian militants. The Northumbrians had been heavily politically and emotionally invested in their late earl, Waltheof, executed by William in 1076 after the failed rebellion the year before. They had never taken to Bishop Walcher. The Frenchman's presence at Durham was begrudged, especially as he proved unequal to the task of governance. Day-to-day administration of the region was delegated to others, some of whom proved equally clueless. King Malcolm's raiding parties faced little or no resistance in the summer of 1079: this, credibly, may have acted as a catalyst for the insurrection that followed. However, there is also anecdotal evidence of a vicious blood feud being waged in Northumbria, which the bishop somehow got entangled in. Whatever the spark for the protest, locals with a grudge cornered him and his entourage at Gateshead. Walcher is said to have covered his head with the border of his robe and stepped forward from the porch of the church to meet his fate and then to have been cruelly cut down by the swords of his enemies. Afterwards, for a time, all order in the region was lost. A large number of Normans and Flemings were slain and the late bishop's castle placed under siege.

With the Anglo-Norman realm rocked on both sides of the Channel, power brokers in Normandy sought to reconcile William and his wayward son. The great Norman magnates, some of whose sons had followed Robert into rebellion, pressed the king to retract threatened censure and restore Robert into his confidence. Even the French king and the Pope pressed the case for a rapprochement, the Holy Father writing to Robert to remind him of his duties as the son of a king. For Philip and the Pope to intervene diplomatically indicates the havoc caused by Robert's rebellion had plunged the Continental order into crisis.

The first moves toward reconciliation may in fact have been initiated by Philip of France earlier than the news of Walcher's killing first reaching Normandy, perhaps as early as Easter 1080, when Robert and Rufus are known to have been together witnessing a charter of their father's. The former was back with his family again when attending the betrothal of his sister Adela to Stephen of Blois. This event took place at Breteuil Castle, where the castellan had supported Robert's rebellion. Breteuil in this sense was a safe place for father and son to meet. William and Robert would not have wanted to spoil the smooth running of proceedings; their meeting, the first since the Gerberoy battle, must have been a muted affair, overshadowed by the glamour and excitement of Adela's engagement festivities. Normandy and Blois united through marriage headlined the proceedings, not the hope of a father-and-son reconciliation which at this stage may still have been very much a work in progress. William at first refused to give ground, saying his son had stirred up much dissent against him and had lured away his young knights and supported his enemies. He may only have yielded to petitioners when the ill tidings from Northumbria reached the court.

Prominent among those who then acted to reconcile father and son was the monk Simon de Crépy, previously mentioned in the context of his one-time engagement to Adela. Simon may have been invited to court by Matilda to attend the princess' betrothal celebrations. He had once been, and likely still was, a part of William's wider *familia* – a grouping of close relations, boon companions and court allies who provided the core support for any medieval prince. When domiciled at court, Simon may have taken the place of William and Matilda's late son Richard in both the parents' affections and in a brotherly sense Robert's too. Still loved and respected by king, queen and prince, Simon's timely intervention may have proved decisive by facilitating closure on the issue without the protagonists losing face. Yet even Simon's best efforts are claimed to have failed at first. Matilda is said to have at one point become so upset she was reduced to tears, and not for the first time. After the king and prince in the end shook hands in reconciliation, Simon returned to his home at the Abbey of Saint-Claude in the modern-day Jura region of France. Sometime later he set off on pilgrimage to the Holy Land, where he died around 1081.

The Conqueror must have been deeply frustrated by the turn of events in northern England; because of this, as much as the prompting of others, he embraced the stark imperative for the Normans to close ranks. Robert's bad behaviour was agreed to have been incited at the urging of wayward friends – always a useful diplomatic excuse in a crisis. Father and son accepted they had to enter into a cooperative understanding so as to put plans in place to travel together to Northumbria. It may have been a strained arrangement nonetheless. We will never know if they ever became close. Their subsequent presence in Britain in the months to come is in fact the only reliably documented occasion when the king and heir were at each other's side outside of Normandy and Maine; so little is really known of Robert's youth that it may have been the first time Robert had ever been abroad in England.

Even before William and Robert arrived in Northumbria, the king's half-brother Odo of Bayeux, Earl of Kent, had subjected the lands of Walcher's killers to a bout of punitive harrying. He ransacked Northumbria's churches and monasteries, carrying off booty in time-honoured Viking fashion. Many Northumbrians caught up in the furore sought exile in Scotland to avoid death or mutilation. So robust was Odo's action against the Northumbrians that it achieved what has since been termed 'a

Carthaginian peace' in the region; but it was not Odo or the king who spearheaded the riposte against the Scots. Robert Curthose, in sole command, rode north through a thoroughly ravaged no-man's-land at the head of a large force of knights and mounted archers, leaving his father and uncle south of the Tyne. For William to choose his recently reconciled son to head up the taskforce might be seen as belated recognition he needed to be kept gainfully employed. William may also have wished to test his son's loyalty and diplomatic skills as well as to keep him away from Normandy and his mother. The support Matilda had given to her son during his rebellion may have undermined trust to a greater extent than is evidenced in the sources.

The last time the Conqueror had been on the Scottish borders had been eight years earlier, in 1072. On that occasion, William had led an army and a fleet as far north as the River Tay and confronted Malcolm at a bridging point eight miles to the south-east of Perth. The advance into Scotland that year had been carried out in the wake of a Scottish scorched earth policy, denying the Anglo-Normans supplies. Malcolm had afterwards recognised William's claim to the English throne and the two men also likely agreed the bounds of their geographic remits. By treaty (known as the Treaty of Abernethy) the King of the Scots formally acknowledged William as his overlord, albeit this would have been in respect of lands he had held in fief from Edward the Confessor, including the Lothian region north of the Tweed and Cumbria south of the Solway Firth, not lands further north and west into Scotland.

For Robert to travel into East Lothian, a recent war zone, so late in the year would have been a hazardous undertaking. Few expeditions made into the north in winter can ever have been made without a land army accompanied by a fleet to carry essential supplies. Not to have done so risked starvation for the land army in an uncharted, unpredictable and inhospitable landscape. We do not have details of the size and composition of the forces under Robert's command. Conjecturally, his land army occupied key centres in Lothian and in doing so may have threatened a further northward advance into Fife. Malcolm up until then may have avoided battle by retreating in the face of the Anglo-Norman advance in much the same way as he had done in 1072. There may have been a stand-off of some sort and some desultory skirmishing, but in the end the Scottish king agreed to meet with Robert at Falkirk, south of the Forth in modern-day Stirlingshire. Precise details are lacking as to what then transpired but the sense of what occurred from the scant sources is that the two men embraced in guarded fellowship. This may have been because Robert Curthose had in the past befriended Malcolm's brother-in-law, Edgar, a prince and the great-nephew of Edward the Confessor and brother of the Scottish queen; Edgar now likely welcomed his old friend, the Conqueror's son, with open arms and introduced him to the Scottish royal family.

Prince Edgar (Atheling)

Tagged with the cognomen *atheling*, meaning throne-worthy or princeling, Edgar might with some accuracy be portrayed as the last remaining male representative of the ancient royal line of Wessex. When putting in a good word for Robert with King Malcolm, he would have stressed the enduring tensions between father and son and lauded Robert as trustworthy and by nature generous and therefore a good man to deal with. Born *circa* 1052, probably in Hungary, where his family had earlier sought exile from Cnut after the Dane's conquest of England in 1016, Edgar had returned to England in 1057, aged around five, with his father, Edward, mother, Agatha, and his two sisters, Margaret and Christina. Edward was the Confessor's heir, but died shortly after arrival back in England (as far as we know of natural causes). Upon the Confessor's death nine years later, the teenaged Edgar might have hoped to gain the crown of England, but if so he was quickly disabused. Without powerful backers, he could not compete with a man as powerfully placed and militarily empowered as Harold Godwinsson had by then become.

His position had, however, improved for a time after Harold's death, when he briefly became a rallying point for English patriots and loyalist churchmen at London in the winter of 1066. Some Englishmen even wanted to elevate him then and there to king. Archbishop Ealdred of York considered Edgar to have been 'right-worthy as was proper due to his birth' and saw that he was elected rightful King of England by the Witenagemot, the formal Anglo-Saxon council. However, he was never crowned. Without an army to back him, the nascent bid was tamped out by the speed and ferocity of the Conqueror's campaigning. He submitted to William at Berkhamsted in December 1066 and was taken to Normandy in the spring of 1067 with other captive Englishmen, including the earls Morcar and Edwin, who had separately submitted to William at Barking in Essex shortly after the Conqueror's coronation. Edgar may have been paraded before the Norman gentry in the manner of a trophy of war, but was nonetheless treated well and came to strike up a lifelong friendship with the similarly aged Robert Curthose. William's tolerance and fair treatment of Edgar and his family has been favourably contrasted by historians with King Cnut's starker behaviour towards the English nobility in 1017, when five notables were murdered on the Dane's orders, including Eadwig, Edgar's great-uncle.

Edgar and his mother and sisters returned to England with the Conqueror in December 1067. William distrusted leaving them at large in Normandy, from where Morcar and Edwin had already flown the coop to raise rebellion in the north of England. One source claimed they planned on returning to Hungary (via the North Sea and the Baltic), where Agatha, Edgar's mother, was a princess in her own right. The presumption must be that William gave them leave to do so, but it is also possible they got caught up in the fighting in the north of England. We have no firm dates for any of this. The traditional story has them suffering shipwreck off the Scottish coast and being rescued and landing on the north bank of the Forth Estuary at North Queensferry, where the riverside frontage is still called St Margaret's Hope. They came to settle at the Scottish court, where Malcolm Canmore, a widower, and a man already with grown-up children from his first marriage to a now dead Orcadian princess, set out to woo the elder sister Margaret, the eldest of Agatha's children. The other sister, Christina, an altogether more austere woman, would later become an abbess at Romsey in Hampshire.

Edgar is said to have first resisted Malcolm's move for his sister's hand, but continuing to do so proved difficult once the English royals were beholden to the Scottish king for their safety. Margaret too at first forbore the Scottish king's demands, allegedly saying she would not have him because she might better please the Almighty 'with pure continence in maidenhood in this short life'. In the end she had to yield. We should, though, be cautious accepting this dramatic version of events. Chroniclers were writing of Margaret's courtship after the queen's death, when her sanctification was being proposed by the papacy. For all we know the king and the princess may have immediately hit it off together. Margaret would bear Malcolm six sons and two daughters. She proved to be as fecund as Matilda of Flanders. Three of her sons would become future kings of Scotland. Of the two daughters, one would become an English queen and the other a Continental countess.

Margaret would later lead a thorough Anglicisation of the Scottish court. Less uncouth than Malcolm Canmore and an allegedly pious and literate woman, she established the first European-style cathedral at Dunfermline in Fife, dedicated to the Holy Trinity, where Benedictine monks in Scotland toiled and prayed. The foundations of great religious centres were a feature of this period. The queen's ferry on the Forth, which, as mentioned, is held to have been her first docking point in Scotland, is said to have been improved by her to enable pilgrims to move freely between Dunfermline and St Andrews. In *The Life of St Margaret, Queen of Scotland*, it is said to have been at her instigation that the natives of Scotland first purchased Continental wares and fashionable costumes. She is credited with having 'polished away the accumulated rust of Scottish barbarism'. The Scots who wore these new clothes are said to have appeared like a new race of beings. Through marriage into the old English royal family Malcolm had in a very real sense been promoted from a minor to a major player on the European political scene and one who could boast the potential prize of England's crown for one of his many sons. No wonder the Conqueror had at the time considered the marriage to be a provocation.

With powerful allies, Edgar had now been freed to reclaim his birthright. His grandfather Edmund Ironside, when combating Cnut in 1015–6, had attracted a powerfully loyal response from the English; he is said to have raised the whole nation against the Danes. His emblematic nickname still today conjures the image of a man somewhat larger than life: strong, charismatic and capable of taking hard knocks. Much the same might have been expected of his grandson, and Edgar rose to the occasion. He and his supporters for a time came close to succeeding in prising Northumbria from the Normans. At the head of a combined Northumbrian and Danish army, his forces captured the Norman castle in York and wiped out its garrison before being driven off by William's advancing army. In the winter of 1069/70, Edgar was at sea with the Danes and on one occasion we know about he evaded capture by the Normans when raiding into Lincolnshire. The Danish king, Swein, may have backed Edgar's dynastic claims (albeit there is no firm evidence for this: what is more, Swein just as likely had his own dynastic agenda). Norman military acumen and greater decisiveness in the end crushed this polyglot threat, placing Edgar very much on the back foot and again reliant on Malcolm Canmore for refuge. He played no part in the fighting in East Anglia in 1071. Even so, he remained a threat to the Conqueror, who, in 1072 outside Perth, pressed Malcolm to order Edgar's expulsion.

The *atheling*'s movements immediately after this become hazy. He perhaps sought allies in France, and is said to have spent some time in Flanders. He may have been offered military support by the French, and a base of operations in the Vexin, but was again somehow shipwrecked off the British coast. Back in Scotland, he got a less welcoming reception from Malcolm, who must have feared another Norman punitive incursion into Scotland to root out his brother-in-law. In the end, a reconciliation between William and Edgar was arranged: the latter swore his allegiance, and was likely urged on to do so by Queen Margaret.

Edgar never went back on his word and avoided getting entangled in the rebellion of 1075; this, though, attracted the reproof of the nationalistic twelfth-century chroniclers.[2]

*

Robert had arrived in Scotland at a happy time for Malcolm and Margaret. After a succession of sons, the Scotsman had just been presented by the queen with a baby daughter named Edith, born probably in the autumn of 1080. Robert stood as her godfather at a christening held at Dunfermline, where Edith had likely been born. To be asked to stand as the child's sponsor was a singular honour for Robert which linked him spiritually to Malcolm and Margaret's family – he became what in medieval times was termed a God's sibling (or gossip) of the Scottish royal family. King and queen would almost certainly have anticipated Robert becoming the next King of England. A tight bond between their daughter and the likely English heir would have been favourable for future Anglo-Scottish relations. The new-born girl had immediately become an important addition to the British royal estate. Through a later marriage to one of the Bastard's sons or grandsons she had the potential to bring the Scottish and Anglo-Norman polities into dynastic accord. William and Matilda would have been fully cognisant of this.[3]

The relative success of Robert's mission speaks well for his interpersonal skills and likeability. The role he played has been considered by historian R. W. Southern as 'the right sort of work for the king's eldest son'. An awareness of the need to secure better arrangements with the Scots is evident and argues that Robert had the future kingship of England in mind while operating north of the border. As stated above, Malcolm would have looked upon Robert as the Conqueror's rightful heir, but he was measuring inheritance and the succession through the prism of Scottish practice, where a strong son, though not necessarily the eldest, would enjoy the most compelling case for enthronement.

Robert did not take the friendship afforded by the Scots at face value: a serial plunderer, Malcolm remained a threat to Northumbria. Even so, there was only a limited amount Robert could do to bolster Norman power north of the River Tweed without attracting a warlike response from the Scots. Moreover, critics of the prince fail to take account of the difficulties involved for armies and fleets navigating rugged, unyielding landscapes and stormy seas to confront better-placed and well-supplied neighbours within their own domain.

One major task initiated by Robert while at Monkchester on the Tyne was the ordering of the construction of a 'new castle' on the north bank of the river. Jim Bradbury (*Medieval Warfare*) considers Robert Curthose in this sense to have played an important role in completing the conquest of England. In 1068, Edgar and Malcolm Canmore's forces had based themselves at Monkchester before confronting the Conqueror's army on Gateshead Fell. The fortress town had afterwards been levelled by the victorious Normans. The old castle at Monkchester may have been a pre-existing Roman bastion, known as Pons Ælii. Newcastle, as the new castlery was soon known, became the principal bastion for the Normans in the far north and became Robert's main legacy in Britain.

Robert was again with his father in February the following year at Salisbury to celebrate the feast of the Purification, and afterwards he rode at his father's side through south Wales to St David's, in the far south-west of the future principality. The progress through south Wales was the headline event; in fact, it was the only event recorded in the *Anglo-Saxon Chronicle* that year: 'In this year the king led an army into Wales, and there freed many hundreds of men.'

First and foremost the travail must have been a military mission. A flotilla of Anglo-Norman longships might be imagined progressing westward in tandem with a larger land army, the former hugging the coastline and keeping in touch, through signals, with scouts and scurriers, maintaining observation at all times. As mentioned earlier, the famous single-masted longships of the period made good use of favourable winds and could when becalmed make a fair headway when rowed with the mast lowered. Though renowned as seafarers, with a good knowledge of rudimentary astronomy, early medieval mariners did not take unnecessary risks. They stayed well in sight of land whenever possible, making use of estuarine islands and inlets as safe havens. There must also have been the need to regularly take on fresh water and re-victual, in itself necessitating frequent landfall and stopovers. Eight knots might have been a likely maximum speed for a medium-sized longship under oars, though this would not have been a pace likely to be kept up for long, and would have been impossible to achieve against a swift tide. For long passages, the Vikings must have changed crews at regular intervals to ensure the oars remained continuously manned. The crewmen, two or more men to each row-lock, remained rooted to benches until handover took place. In Viking times, they had been sailors as well as fighting men, but whether this was true of the Norman craft in 1081 is questionable; the ships were carrying supplies not soldiery as their primary cargo. Viking fleets did still plague the British Isles on occasion, and faced little opposition while at sea.

Welsh chroniclers claimed a religious motive for the Conqueror and his son to have made the long and dangerous trek westward in 1081, saying the royal party wished to pray at the shrine of Saint David. William and Robert would have recognised the site as enormously prestigious. Praying there can be seen as an act of respect, helping to underpin wider diplomatic objectives. While at St David's, William is held to have recognised the Welshman Rhys ap Tewdwr as the legitimate ruler of South Wales – albeit under Norman overlordship and for an annual fee of £40. Many Englishmen and women enslaved by the Welsh were freed as part of this recognition event; the *Anglo-Saxon Chronicle* mentions hundreds of men freed, but does not state their ethnicity; most likely, prisoners were freed by both sides as an equitable exchange. That same year Tewdwr had defeated and killed his great rival Caradog ap Gruffydd, the King of Gwent and Morgannwg. Known as the Battle of Mynydd Carn, the fighting took place somewhere in southern Cardiganshire. The victory secured Gwynedd and Deheubarth – comprising the whole of the west of Wales – for Tewdwr and his allies, so it seems likely William and Robert had made the journey into Wales as a consequence of the fighting. Norman mercenaries may have fought on either side at Mynydd Carn, as had by then become common practice, so perhaps it was to free captives who had been taken at the battle that the exchanges were made.

Wales was not at this time unified. The depredations of the Vikings from the ninth century onwards had severely disrupted the future principality, which still retained its ancient subdivisions: Gwynedd in the north-west, Powys in the east, Morgannwg and Gwent in the south-east and Deheubarth in the west, with further divisions within these kingdoms also of political relevance, as in Ceredigion in the far west and Dyfed in the far south-west. Coexistence between the Anglo-Normans and the Welsh must always have been a decidedly edgy affair. English stereotyping of their Welsh neighbours as treacherous may stem from this time, based on a fear of the other. The Welsh were an increasingly encroached-upon people, always prepared to strike back. When operating west of the Wye, the Normans were pushing against a relic British society fractured by geography as well as by internecine warfare.

Welsh eruptions into Herefordshire and Gloucestershire before the Conquest had on occasion tested the armies of Edward the Confessor. The famous Golden Valley of Herefordshire (the valley of the River Dore) had for a time had become a depopulated wasteland because of near-continuous harrying. Only later, under more settled Norman stewardship, did the region start to recover. The famous Domesday Book noted, 'On these wastelands woods have grown up and here [the lord] Osbern [Fitz Richard] hunts and takes what he can get.'

The aggressiveness of the Normans in the Welsh Marches engendered otherwise unlikely defensive coalitions between Welsh warlords and Mercian rebels. In 1067, for instance, Welsh and Mercian insurgents under the command of a rebel warlord named Edric the Wild had attacked Hereford and devastated Norman estates on the Welsh borders. Two years later his Mercians and Welsh allies had assaulted the Norman marcher castle at Shrewsbury. They would have gone on to lay waste to Staffordshire had not the Conqueror marched at the head of a strong army against them in the winter of 1067/8 and defeated them at Stafford. In February 1070, William had again attacked and wreaked havoc across the West Midlands – a harrying spree frightful enough to be noted by the monks at Evesham. Caradog ap Gruffydd, killed by Tewdwr at Mynydd Carn, had in 1075 sided with the Conqueror's rebels – his Welshmen had supported the second Earl of Hereford's rising, which attracted harsh payback from William when launching punitive strikes into modern-day Glamorganshire the following year.

Aged thirty, Robert had now fulfilled major ambassadorial roles in Scotland, Wales and Northumbria. His expectations in the longer term (the duchy of Normandy and county of Maine to one side) must have remained unclear to him. No less so for Rufus and Henry. King and prince returned to the duchy after their excursions to confront an aggressive Angevin move into Maine. There was no let-up. Robert forced the interlopers to negotiate and attracted the intervention of Angevins. The last time Robert had performed homage for Maine to an Angevin duke had been in 1078, the same year that he had rebelled against his father, said to have been done that day as was proper 'for a vassal to a superior lord'. This time his embracing his liege lord at the so-called Peace of Blanchland reconfirmed Robert's rights to Maine.

The prince may been have acting independently of his father in the county; the years spent waiting to don the ducal mantle had by this time served to blunt his sharper edges, making him less ambitiously inclined, though no less of a warrior for that. William can by now have had little reason to fear his eldest son as a rival; he likely encouraged Robert's campaigning in Maine in the same way he had done in Scotland, as a way for his son to stamp his mark as the future ruler. William oftentimes had to be away from the duchy. He would not have taken his knights and younger sons with him had Robert posed any great danger to him. Father and son may nevertheless have continued to clash at a personal level over inconsequential domestic issues, and William may have been unable to restrain himself from on occasion pouring abuse and reproach on Robert for unspecified failings. He may of course have never really forgiven his son for rebelling five years earlier. William was likely a man who nurtured grudges.

The relationship between father and son may have worsened after Queen Matilda's death in 1083, fracturing when harsh words were spoken in the context of their loss. There is a sense of inevitability about this. Matilda had been the glue holding the royal family together, especially with regard to her husband and Robert. Still denied lordship over Normandy and now without a maternal anchor, Robert is held to have announced he would no longer act at William's beck and call, taking orders in the manner of a hired mercenary. This was how he had now come to see himself. The breach between the two men became irreparable, and at some unspecified point Robert broke away from court completely.

There is no reliable information about Robert's career for the four years or so up until his father's death in 1087. He has been imagined to have been in league with the king of the French, but there is really no firm case to answer that Robert ever aligned himself with any of his father's enemies. Flanders, Aquitaine, Gascony, Italy, Germany and Ponthieu are all linked to his wanderings. There is even a tradition that he became prominent on the tournament circuit in northern France. In Italy he is claimed to have proposed marriage to the Countess of Tuscany, who turned him down. Princes did not as a rule act as matchmakers on their own behalf. Without his father's agency, Robert's gaining the hand of a rich noblewoman would always have been an unlikely outcome. His spats with his father may in large part have been to do with his continued unmarried status; for too long he had been denied an independent household and therefore unable to sire legitimate heirs. For an undoubtedly heterosexual man, now approaching his mid-thirties, this must have intensified as a point of contention as the years rolled on. His lifestyle while away from court was not all tourneys, raids and rallies, however; at some point he must have made time for other types of 'r and r'. He is known to have fathered two illegitimate sons and a daughter, possibly by different women. One of the sons would become famous as William Fitz Robert, a noted crusading knight; the other, like his late uncle Richard, for whom he was likely named, would one day lose his life in the New Forest.

Robert was at Abbeville when the news of his father's death reached him. He straightaway rode to Caen and later honoured his father's memory by making donations to Normandy's monasteries, churches and the poor – done in the same manner as Rufus in England, for the repose of his father's soul. The new duke had less money for donatives than Rufus. He nevertheless acted with generosity, freeing his father's political prisoners. They included Ulf, one of Harold II's many sons, and Duncan, the son of Malcolm Canmore by the Scotsman's first marriage, made hostage by the Conqueror in 1072, the year Edgar *atheling* had been expelled from Scotland. Because Robert had no land border with Scotland to concern him, and was now in a sense related to Malcolm through Edith's christening, by freeing Duncan he may have hoped to gain the Scottish king's support in any coming struggle with his brother Rufus. Rufus, though, embraced Duncan and knighted him, precluding such an outcome. Duncan remained intermittently at Rufus' court up until the death of Malcolm III in 1093. He must have felt comfortable in his adoptive culture. He had spent fifteen years of his life at the Norman court. Moreover, his father by this time had recognised Duncan's half-brother Edward as his heir, so there was nothing for him north of the border.

Rufus held on to his own hostages. They were Wulfnoth, another of the remaining sons of Harold II, and Morcar, the former Earl of Northumbria, whose elder brother Edwin of Mercia had been was killed in 1071 during the rebellion that year. Both men must have accompanied Rufus when he sailed from Wissant to claim the throne. Wulfnoth had been a prisoner since boyhood. It may have been a kindness to keep him at court in the company of men and women he had known since childhood. Morcar's case is more complex. As a young man he had fought the Norman invaders in the company of the legendary Hereward the Wake, in the fenlands of Cambridgeshire. He had been tricked by William into surrendering on a false premise and then made a political prisoner. In 1087, when dying, the Conqueror is said to have wished to atone for his trickery by having Morcar released. Rufus denied his father his wish, fearing a nationalistic backlash in England should the old earl be freed. Like Hereward, Morcar defied the usual Norman negative stereotyping of the English. Even when abandoned by his Danish and Northumbrian allies in 1070, he had continued to resist the Norman occupation and had avoided capture for over a year. Other die-hards and their successors, known as the *silvatici* (the outlaws of the woodlands), were still claimed to haunt England's great forests well into the 1090s. Around such men patriotic legends took shape. With tankards in hand, having drunk deep into the early hours, Rufus' companions may have laughed at the notion of the *silvatici* posing a threat to them, but fretted when the firelight faded.

5

A GREAT CHANGE AND A COLD FEAR

Rufus' coronation took place at Westminster on 26 September 1087, shortly after his reception with Lanfranc, Archbishop of Canterbury: the *Anglo-Saxon Chronicle* states, 'William was blessed as king in Westminster by Archbishop Lanfranc, three days before the feast of St Michaelmas, and all the men in England submitted to him and swore him oaths'. We can imagine Lanfranc lobbying on the future king's behalf, striking deals if necessary to get the great and good of the country to accept his charge's claim. The time between Rufus' arrival in England and his coronation was just enough for all this to take place in an orderly manner while allowing too little time for his elder brother to intervene. Rufus can have had few ready-made allies in England. He needed to quickly attract a following. Generous donations were made (or promised) to the Church to ease acceptance of Rufus' title to the crown. Archbishop Lanfranc clasped hands with him and made him swear on the Gospels to be a good and true lord to the English people provided that they would be loyal to him, and to preserve the English Church. Clasping hands in church was a sign of an absolute commitment in the eyes of God through the conjoining of Church and State.

As to whether or not the archbishop was a willing agent in the king-making, the sources are contradictory. It is not even known for sure if Lanfranc had already been appraised of the Conqueror's demise when first confronted by Rufus. Some sources suggest this to have been the case, others not. That Lanfranc embraced the king's son's claim so quickly is the best evidence we have for a sealed letter stating William's dying wishes in categorical fashion. Rufus and Lanfranc were in fact already well known to each other. The churchman was once Rufus' tutor. Stories that Lanfranc may have been a harsh master with respect to Rufus are anecdotal. If Rufus and Lanfranc later sparred sometimes, they did so good-naturedly. We know that the churchman once gently reproved the young king for not making good on promises made at the time of his coronation, to which Rufus shrugged and replied in jovial manner, 'What man alive can fulfil everything that he promises?'

Archbishop Lanfranc

A Lombard by birth, Lanfranc had quickly risen under the patronage of the Conqueror to become William's main ecclesiastical advisor and chief justiciar. He can be reliably placed in Normandy in the 1030s, teaching at Avranches, a Norman city still said to have been recovering from earlier Viking raids. From around the mid-1040s, he held the position of prior at the Abbey of Bec. In 1063 he became the first abbot of the Conqueror's newly built abbey at St Étienne in Caen, where Rufus may for a time have become his pupil. Lanfranc energetically oversaw the construction of St Étienne's church and the buildings there. Five years later he gained an exemption from Pope Alexander II, which freed the abbey from the authority of the bishopric of Bayeux, the remit of William's half-brother Bishop Odo. The separation may have worsened already bad relations between the two men and set Lanfranc and Odo on a collision course for the future, of which we will hear more. Among Lanfranc's other pupils was Anselm of Aosta, who would one day succeed him at Bec and later at Canterbury. Anselm acknowledged Lanfranc's overriding influence over him as a mentor, even though the morbidly self-abnegating priest was cast in an altogether different mould from his more energetic and outgoing guide. Anselm has been described by his academic biographer R. W. Southern as 'a man ablaze within', compared with the outwardly cold Lanfranc.

It may have been Lanfranc's worldliness that had first most impressed the Conqueror. Even so, the two men had their spats. An example is when Lanfranc opposed William's marriage to Matilda and had as a consequence faced exile. An anecdote tells of Lanfranc setting off to leave the duchy on a lame horse; because of its slow pace, he requested the duke provide him with a faster one. The jokey way this was done served to reconcile the two men. Although the tale sits at odds with portrayals of Lanfranc as 'lifelessly urbane' and comfortable only when fully in control of a situation, it may contain a grain of truth. By 1059, the year sanctions on the Conqueror's marriage to Matilda were formally lifted in Rome, Pope Nicholas II observed how William habitually followed Lanfranc's advice. Other royals in Britain also valued the archbishop's counsel. Margaret of Scotland once appealed to Lanfranc for one or two religious men to be sent to her to support her in challenging tenets of the Celtic Church and eliminating outdated practices. Lanfranc sent her three, under the authority of a clergyman named Goldwinus.

After August 1070, Lanfranc had often acted as the Conqueror's deputy in England. In William's absence, he is said to have become 'chief and keeper' of the realm. A stern test came in 1075, when quelling the king's rebels that year. We know of this from his letters to the king. One urged William to remain calm and not to hurry back to England from Normandy, telling him that such perjurers and brigands could be sufficiently dealt with by the king's subjects, adding that he had everything in hand. The archbishop made sure all loyal castellans looked to the security of their castles and alerted the coastguard to prepare the defences of the realm against the possibility of an invasion from Denmark, whose king had allied himself to William's opponents in England: a distant echo from the dangerous days when the likes of Eric Bloodaxe and Swein Forkbeard had been abroad. In the end, the threat of a Danish landing in strength failed to materialise and the insurgencies in Herefordshire and East Anglia were quickly stifled. Lanfranc wrote to William to confirm the realm had been purged and the noise of warfare silenced.

Lanfranc's influence over William had its limits. He had not been able to moderate the Conqueror's ire with regard to the fate of the captured leaders. Roger, the second Earl of Hereford, and the son of William's great friend and ally William Fitz Osbern, was sentenced to life imprisonment. Even when the Conqueror lay dying, pleas from Lanfranc for the earl to be released went unheeded. Another plotter, the Anglo-Danish earl Waltheof, faced execution. As he had done for Roger of Hereford, Lanfranc tried his best to have the earl reprieved. The prisoner, just a young man, had redeeming qualities more apparent to a prelate than to a king. Described as tall, handsome and a patriot, and likely the vector for the conspiracy against the Conqueror, Waltheof had afterwards spent long months in prison, praying and fasting. He is credited with continuously chanting the one-hundred-and-fifty psalms of David he had learnt by rote as a boy. He confessed to conspiring against the king but argued in mitigation that he had not played an active role in the rebellion.

All niceties were set aside on the morning of Waltheof's execution. The distressed prisoner was dragged from his dungeon to St Giles Hill outside Winchester's walls before first light so as not to stir the sleeping citizens, who might otherwise have risen up in arms on his behalf. After the executioner struck, the lips of Waltheof's severed head were seen to move, as if continuing the closing lines of the Lord's Prayer. It was later claimed the condemned man had fought back tears when attempting to finish the prayer, but had promptly been beheaded by an impatient executioner. The earl's decapitated corpse was discarded in a ditch skirting the killing site, and only later recovered to be brought to the chapterhouse at Crowland Abbey in Lincolnshire, where formal interment took place. The late earl became a cult figure at Crowland after a series of miracles were reported at the grave site. This drew flocks of pilgrims. Another cult to Waltheof is said to have grown up at Romsey Abbey in Hampshire. A school of thought today still considers Waltheof (like King Harold on the field of battle) to have died on the scaffold for 'the good old cause' of English nationhood.

That it had taken almost a year for William to order the earl's execution indicates a grudging hesitancy on the king's part to invoke the normal Anglo-Danish method of despatch for traitors, rather than maintain longstanding Norman punitive methods of imprisonment, blinding and emasculation. William's judicial preference was spelled out in a surviving edict, where he wrote, 'I forbid that any man be executed or hanged for any offence, but let his eyes be gouged out and his testicles cut off.'

*

At Rufus' first Christmas court, held in London, the top churchmen of England assembled. They included Archbishop Lanfranc, Thomas of York, Maurice of London, Walkelin of Winchester, Osbern of Exeter, Wulfstan of Worcester, William of Thetford, Robert of Chester, Remigius of Lincoln, William St Calais of Durham and Bishop Odo of Bayeux. Rufus' first seal was designed in much the same way as his father's had been. Continuity was the byword. Only the nomenclature of the inscriptions was changed: the Conqueror had been recognised as duke and patron of the Normans, as well as the King of England; Rufus, on the other hand, made sure to be known unambiguously from the outset as William II, by the grace of God King of the English. Fears that long-term English opposition might see the conquest of England prove only temporary had finally been laid to rest. Even so, loyalties in England were soon being tested as men sought to come to terms with the reality of a divided Anglo-Norman realm. Orderic says that 'a great change and a cold fear' gripped men on both sides of the English Channel.

In the spring of 1088, a group of conspirators moved to unite England and Normandy under Duke Robert. Given that it occurred just a matter of months after Rufus' coronation the conspiracy against him might at first be seen simply as routine Norman muscle-flexing, but the stakes were enormously high. Rather than a mere test of Rufus' mettle and a bellicose response to change, the conspirators sought to place the elder of the two brothers in unfettered dominion over all the lands previously ruled by the Conqueror. In this way they might avoid the complications inherent in division. For many, the notion of serving two powerful masters was intolerable. Whichever brother they backed, the likelihood of becoming disinherited by the other appeared a great risk. Even if lands on one or other side of the Channel were passed on to other family members, the possibility they would be rendered apart for all time must have been difficult for noble families to accept.

Cast in a strongly authoritarian mould, Rufus appeared the man most likely to dictate the agenda and be the more heavy-handed and oppressive; in short, he was feared to be as prohibitive as his father had been with regard to noblemen's privileges, in particular the prohibition on the waging of private wars, plus rights to succession over land in England and control over marriage arrangements. When feuding barons clashed, the victims in the main were commoners: crops were destroyed and homes razed to the ground. Such warring was expensive and wasteful. William the Conqueror had sought to rule with an iron fist, and by and large he had kept his knights in check. He had banned private vendettas and had insisted he be allowed to garrison the castles of his noblemen with ducal troops when danger threatened – sometimes even when it did not. There had been pushback on this point: it is thought a so-called baronial liberation movement had existed well before the Conqueror's death, surfacing in 1075 and again in 1078 with Robert Curthose's rebellion. Now, after the Conqueror's death, noblemen looked to liberate themselves from ducal and kingly fetters. They considered Robert, who had himself once rebelled, to be the Bastard's son most amenable to lifting limitations imposed by his father.

Importantly, the majority of barons had sworn oaths of fealty in Normandy to Robert and not to Rufus. Allegiance was given specifically to a person in the late eleventh century, not to a geographic entity or title. A pledge between lord and vassal remained sacrosanct; breaking one was treasonable and, in an afterlife, damning.

Breast-beating by a number of noblemen on Robert Curthose's behalf garnered substantial support. Underlining the broad level of threat brought to bear against Rufus, three of the main conspirators in England – Ralph de Mortemer, Osbern Fitz Richard and Bernard de Neufmarché – boasted strong Welsh followings. Bernard de Neufmarché had married into one of the Welsh royal families, while Mortemer held large estates on the Welsh borders, centred on Wigmore Castle in Herefordshire, probably built by William Fitz Osbern. He had made the parish at Wigmore his family's main ecclesiastical centre of worship and his power base. Very soon after the conquest his family had come to govern extensive tracts of the Welsh borders from there. The extent of Mortemer's lands in England encompassed holdings in twelve counties. The most extensive outside Herefordshire were concentrated in Hampshire, Berkshire, Wiltshire, Yorkshire and Lincolnshire.

An early indication of trouble afoot may have been the absence from court of a number of these men. Their aim was to incite rebellion at different locales in England, with the main centre of the revolt in the south-east, where others who declared for the duke would act as enablers. The conspirators fortified their castles and set out to ravage the king's lands. Auxiliaries from Normandy bolstered insurgent numbers. Later accounts speak of Robert Curthose exultant so many noblemen in England had risen in his favour, but this may be a retrospective embellishment; Robert may not have been minded to lock horns with his brother quite so soon after their father's death because, as his father had foreseen, there was much to be seen to in the duchy itself, and on Normandy's frontiers with France, Brittany and Maine.

Among Rufus' most prominent non-English supporters in England were William de Warenne, Robert of Rhuddlan, Alan Rufus of Richmond, Hugh d'Avranches, Earl of Chester, and the king's right-hand man and some say favourite Robert Fitz Haimon. All were from what has been termed a newly created English aristocratic elite, a select military clique. Rufus could also draw on widespread support from his English subjects. Away from the inhospitable marches toward Scotland and Wales, Norman control over England's legal institutions and martial potential was virtually absolute by 1088.

Warenne was the most influential of Rufus' secular loyalists. His name originates from a village in Normandy called Varenne, just inland from Dieppe. A veteran of Hastings, Warenne became one of the Conqueror's great tenants-in-chief, gaining estates which spanned thirteen counties. By 1087, the year of the Conqueror's death, he was the fourth-richest tenant-in-chief in England. Famously, he crossed swords with the king's rebels in East Anglia in 1071, and is said to have been unhorsed by an arrow shot by the Saxon hero Hereward the Wake – a dubious honour at the time but notable post-mortem. It had been as a young man in the mid-1050s that Warenne first gained a military command. He may have been much the same age as the William. He fought in all of William's early wars, garnering confiscated lands in Normandy at the expense of men who threw in their lot with the duchy's enemies. Included in this list was the important castle at Bellencombre. Less than a day's ride from Varenne, it became Warenne's main seat of power in Normandy. The name Bellencombre has been translated to mean 'the fair mound', probably a reference to the still extant castle motte.

In 1075, the year of rebellion in England, Warenne and his neighbour Richard Fitz Gilbert had commanded the army which put down the king's rebels operating in East Anglia. In the 1080s he had fought in Maine alongside Robert Curthose. By 1088, he held land in the eastern shires of England and manors in Yorkshire, Lincolnshire, Hampshire, Sussex and the Midland counties of

Bedfordshire and Buckinghamshire. Warenne may in fact have been rewarded for his services at Hastings with swathes of the late King Harold's lands. Outside of Wessex, these were somewhat patchy in distribution and shared out with others. Warenne became a noted castle builder. The still impressive castles at Lewes in Sussex, and Conisbrough and Sandal in Yorkshire were founded by him, as were others at Reigate in Surrey and Castle Acre in Norfolk. At Lewes, Warenne also built a priory and church. Close beside the priory stood a great motte, pre-dating Warenne's later, better-known castle, which now dominates the town.

William Rufus would have to fight for the right to rule England. He may always have expected this, but perhaps underestimated the immediacy, depth and breadth of opposition marshalled against him. The proactive hiring of seamen to disrupt English commerce and shipping was an early indication of intent on the part of Robert's supporters to deprive Rufus of the kingship. Records from the Abbey of Fécamp, located in the valley of the Valmont River, roughly twenty miles north-east of Le Havre, describe ducal agents seeking out the assistance of merchant captains to obtain boats and crews. It must have become clear to Rufus through spies that some sort of hostile move was afoot. He too requisitioned commercial craft. Patrolling the narrow seas and coastal estuaries became an urgent priority for him, even though the existence of a number of pro-ducal south coast castellans must have complicated the enactment of these royal countermeasures. An invasion from Normandy on a scale to match 1066 would have been out of the question. Robert's supporters did not have the wide-ranging support William the Conqueror had enjoyed, and even a smaller undertaking would have been logistically complex. It had taken the Conqueror almost six months to secure sufficient transports for his great venture, and then he had to await favourable wind and tide before setting off. Robert's supporters would need make do with fewer ships and troops from the Continent and had less time to prepare; they relied in the main on the localised risings in England to undermine Rufus' authority.

Once Rufus realised the full scale of what he was up against, he commanded every man in England not a scoundrel (a *nithing*) to rise up in arms to support him. A great company from the towns and countryside rallied to his banner. Rufus is held to have gained this support by promising restored hunting rights and more equitable laws, but, in any case, his English subjects would probably have been more likely to heed the call of their own legitimised king than that of a foreign duke, even without handouts and inducements. None of the sheriffs of England left their posts in 1088. All of them, as far as is known, remained loyal to the new king. Reporting to them were numerous deputies, reeves and foresters. These men did not report directly to any of England's Norman magnates, so could be depended upon to maintain the king's writ, enact justice and hold out as castellans against any enemy until help came. Prominent churchmen in England supported the king too. Ely Abbey, for instance, provided its full quota of eighty knights to meet the crisis. It has been estimated the Church might have put as many as 700 knights into the field. Through these ecclesiastical and shrieval networks, plus the support of a select number of loyalist barons, Rufus was able to exert a level of centralised control denied to the duke's supporters.

Chroniclers go to pains to implicate Frenchmen rather than Englishmen in the rebellion against Rufus of 1088. The first stirrings of post-conquest nationalism are perhaps discernible. Bitterness of defeat among the conquered may have begun to abate by 1088: if a tenuous claim, it is supported by the fact the succession of another Norman king had gone down as smoothly as it had, without attracting an Anglo-Saxon counter-claim. Passions inflamed by the Conquest had likely waned. Nobody in England would have favoured an almost unknown Norman duke over an already anointed king. The English had come to accept the gains of the Norman royal house as a fait accompli. Importantly, the Conqueror had encouraged his barons to include Englishmen as well as Norman fighting men in their knightly retinues. Because of this, Rufus could call on large reserves of manpower denied to the rebels.

Another factor at play during the ducal insurgency in 1088 was that lordship over strategic tracts of land in England was something of a mishmash. On the Continent, the consolidation of landholdings into principalities, dukedoms, viscounties and marquisates continued to remain a problem for the King of France. The same practice had once been an issue for the Anglo-Saxon kings. The existence of sizeable power blocs in England in 1088 might have weighed against Rufus. Instead, land grants made by the Conqueror were haphazard and nowhere contiguous. It has been claimed that avoiding the granting consolidated estates was a policy objective, but this is now disputed by academics, who maintain the allotments were more likely arbitrary. Separation and division was particularly evident in Sussex. The county boasted six discrete divisions called *rapes*, from west to east: Chichester, Arundel, Bramber, Lewes, Pevensey and Hastings. Each *rape* had a separate baronial identity and a strong castle protecting ingress from the south coast down tidal river systems. The Sussex castellans became front-line commanders against an invasion from the Continent or against insurrection by any one or more of their neighbours. Although those who rebelled ranged far and wide across the country, making it a nationwide affair, it was in the south-east – Kent, Surrey and Sussex – that the contest teetered on a knife-edge and where the fighting became most intense.

The origin of the word *rape* in the context of the territorial subdivision of Sussex is unknown, but likely pre-dates the Norman period. The great cross-Channel magnate and landowner Roger de Montgomery controlled the two most westerly of the Sussex *rapes* at Chichester, beside the River Lavant, plus Arundel, beside the Arun. The Chichester motte is still in part extant, close by the city walls, in modern-day Priory Park. Better preserved is the motte at Arundel, within the perimeter of the impressive extant castle, one of England's great jewels. Eastward of Arundel lay the *rape* of Bramber, entrusted to William de Briouze, a distant relative of the Conqueror's. Briouze additionally held lands in Dorset, Berkshire and Wiltshire. Built on a natural earthen mound, the castle at Bramber, of which a sandstone gatehouse still stands, was erected around 1070 to overlook the River Adur. It protected the important Norman harbour at Steyning. Briouze was a pious man but this did not stop him getting embroiled in fractious legal disputes with the monastery at Fécamp in Normandy, which owned lands in Sussex nearby. Next along the coast lay the *rape* of Lewes, controlled by William de Warenne. Known at the time as Bray Castle, Lewes Castle was constructed at East Sussex's highest point, dominating the surrounding landscape and the estuary of the River Ouse. Further to the east lay the *rape* of Pevensey, the remit of the Conqueror's half-brother Robert de Mortain. The last of the Sussex *rapes*, at Hastings, lay under the oversight of Robert d'Eu, a nobleman claimed to have commanded sixty longships in 1066, half as many as Mortain. The original castle at Hastings was erected in 1066 just before the battle. As at Pevensey, it comprised a simple prefabricated timber palisade, later rebuilt in stone in 1071. Eu's fighting credentials (he was a veteran of the Battle of Mortemer and probably Hastings) are attested by the fact William trusted him to ride with Mortain to face off a combined Mercian and Danish threat to Norman rule in 1069, at the height of the insurrection that year.

The way loyalties played out among the Sussex barons in 1088 is not well understood. All that is known for sure is that the Lewes castellan, William de Warenne, declared for Rufus, while the late king's half-brother Robert de Mortain, at Pevensey, declared for the duke. According to Mortain's academic biographer Brian Golding, depictions of the Bastard's brother portraying him as uncharismatic, stupid and easily led (he has been described as 'a man of heavy, sluggish disposition') sit ill with the Conqueror's trust placed in him. He was said to have been depended upon by the dying king 'in everything as befitted their close kinship'. By locating Mortain at a key site like Pevensey – the natural anchorage there faced directly south toward the Normandy coast – the Conqueror recognised his brother's martial abilities and implacable loyalty. Mortain is claimed to have provided 120 ships for the invasion fleet in 1066. This was more than any other of

William's supporters, and places him top of the Norman 'who's who' list, on the basis that the ship levy accounting might merely be a method of weighing a man's worth, not necessarily a strictly accurate assessment of ship numbers. Mortain had mercilessly ravaged East Sussex before fighting in the front line at Hastings. Many of his estates were in fact located in the south-west, where he became referred to grandly as the Count of Cornwall.

Roger de Montgomery at Arundel, William de Briouze at Bramber and Robert d'Eu at Hastings are all trickier to call. Nothing much is known of the latter two's activities in 1088. The powerful Roger de Montgomery may at first have declared for the duke and launched a series of piecemeal raids on royal demesne lands in Shropshire, but he later backtracked after a face to face confrontation with Rufus. By this time, one or more of Montgomery's sons had become compromised when besieged by the king's forces and were at Rufus' mercy. Fear of retribution against them may have persuaded Montgomery to switch sides to back the king. Had he come out more strongly for the ducal party, and held his nerve, Rufus' hold on kingship might have been fatally undermined. Montgomery was not only a powerful Sussex castellan, he also maintained control over the Isle of Wight and the Solent, and lands in the Welsh Marches, based at Shrewsbury in Shropshire. His main base in England was Shrewsbury Castle, a stronghold built by him on a hill protected by a great looping meander in the River Severn. From Shrewsbury he and his retainers administered much of the marcher lands along the Severn Valley into Shropshire and Montgomeryshire. He was among the richest men in England, third in prominence at court immediately after the Conquest. Made an earl in 1071, his other title, vicomte of the Hiémois (an area encompassing the upper Orne Valley in Normandy), saw him responsible for maintaining the peace along part of the duchy's porous frontier with Maine. Jobs in medieval times did not come any tougher than this.

Rufus on one occasion is claimed to have pleaded with Montgomery to side with him, telling him that without the earl's support he might have to abdicate. Montgomery had been among those who had tried to persuade the dying Conqueror against dividing the kingdom and dukedom. He had anticipated the certain backlash this would trigger. Now he was very much caught in the middle.

Bishop Odo of Bayeux

East of the Sussex *rapes* lay the great county of Kent, encompassing England's ecclesiastical heart at Canterbury, the important ports of Romney and Sandwich and the crucially sited castle at Dover, protecting the narrowest point of the English Channel. Little wonder, soon after the Conquest, Kent's overseeing had been entrusted to the Conqueror's powerful and supposedly loyal half-brother Bishop Odo, whom he made Earl of Kent. Odo became at once a powerful secular lord as well as a prince of the Church. His ecclesiastical career had been kick-started when appointed to the bishopric of Bayeux by William after the Battle of Val-ès-Dunes in 1047. This had been done as part of a series of appointments designed to strengthen William's hold on the duchy at this difficult time. After 1066, Odo's duties across the Anglo-Norman realm became far-reaching and complex. He is said to have operated more flamboyantly than other magnates, administering his lands in the manner of a regent. The Latin annotation embroidered onto the Bayeux Tapestry above Odo's image in battle reads, 'Here [is] Odo the Bishop holding a club rallying the troops.' Odo likely commissioned the work. The tapestry later proudly hung in his palace at Bayeux. He is shown on it to have always been in the thick of the action. When depicted with William, it is Odo who appears the more active: pointing, cajoling, counselling. His energy and leadership contributed hugely to the success of the Norman Conquest, so he would have been expected to play a pivotal role in the affairs of both Church and State in the newly conquered territories. In the end, though, he had overreached himself and attracted his brother's ire.

The essential contradictions in Odo's character and behaviour are highlighted in the following passage of narrative, courtesy of Orderic Vitalis:

> [Odo] was a person of distinguished eloquence, bravery and high spirit in secular circles and a man of liberality and respectfulness when it came to the Church [but also] a bishop deeply entangled in secular affairs [so that] ... much that was laudable mixed itself with his evil deeds, and [yet] what he iniquitously amassed was freely bestowed on the churches and the poor ... he was a compound of vices and virtues ... dreaded by the English because he issued orders to them as if he were a second king ... more occupied with worldly affairs than in the exercise of spiritual graces. The monasteries of the saints make great complaints of the injuries they received at the hands of Odo, who, with violence and injustice, robbed them of the funds with which the English had piously endowed them in ancient times.

The reasons for Odo's fall from grace in the early 1080s are imperfectly understood. On the basis of what we know of him, hubris, unrestrained ambition and political manoeuvring might be taken for granted. The Conqueror was falling short of men's expectations by the early 1080s. This may have spurred the ambitious to look to others to lead them and reward them. There is no indication the bishop provided his rebellious nephew Robert Curthose with support in the late 1070s; had he done so, the Conqueror would not have promoted Odo to almost vice-regal status when dealing with the Northumbrian crisis in 1079. Rather than this, a growing concern regarding levels of oppression meted out by Odo in William's absences from England must have led to the bishop's demise. William would have expected better of his half-brother than to oppress his subjects and feather his own nest at their expense. William himself could be heavy-handed, and he remained by far and away the greatest landowner in England, but what was good for the goose may not have been deemed good for the gander. Odo may also have headed up a powerful faction in England, considered to be dangerous by William. The bishop is claimed to have enlisted his brother's knights for a foreign adventure to push his candidature for high position at Rome, a project which has since been described by eighteenth-century historian David Hume (*A History of England*) as 'chimerical and simonisitic'.

William would not have approved such a requisition. As we have seen in the context of Robert's rebellion, William placed tight controls on knight errantry. The king would have considered his brother inciting men to leave the king's service to have been wayward and self-serving. Odo may even have nurtured designs on the throne of England after the Conqueror's death. Contemporary chronicler Eadmer of Canterbury thought this to have been the case. When mulling over whether to arrest Odo, at the time holed up at Carisbrooke Castle on the Isle of Wight, Lanfranc advised William to go ahead: 'What, arrest a clergyman?' asked the incredulous king. 'No,' replied the archbishop, 'imprison the Earl of Kent.'

With the benefit of hindsight, it is surprising Rufus allowed his uncle back into England in 1087. The bishop had likely been released as part of a more general amnesty after the Conqueror's death, after several years in prison in Normandy on ill-defined charges of treason. He may have been freed just in time to attend William's funeral, and only after pleas made on his behalf by his brother Robert de Mortain. According to Orderic, William cautioned Mortain that his vehemence in pressing his brother's case was misplaced, saying the imprisoned bishop was 'ever a subtle promoter of divisions'. That Mortain was influential enough to have risked bargaining for his brother's release without censure is indicative of the trust in which he was held by the Conqueror. Robert Curthose, when he became duke, readily confirmed his uncle's parole and Rufus later reinstated the bishop to his lands and earldom in England, perhaps as a conciliatory move aimed at Robert, who may have been closer to their uncle. It was a near-fatal error. Odo immediately stirred up trouble and backed Robert over Rufus. Odo's status in England he found to have greatly changed. Jealousy was stoked when he discovered that high-flying prelates like Bishop William St Calais of Durham now provided the king with counsel behind closed doors. Odo felt excluded and marginalised.

It may have been Odo who first proposed the idea of a conjoined kingdom and dukedom. He sought to turn men away from Rufus. He set out his stall in no uncertain manner when ravaging Archbishop Lanfranc's lands in Kent. He may have been getting his own back on the archbishop for earlier affronts, but an immediate recourse to violence served destabilise the county and may have been the trigger for risings elsewhere across England. Odo, when rebelling, knew he could rely on the full support of his brother Robert of Mortain. He also had other allies nearby, like the Clare family, whose castle at Tonbridge lay midway between Mortain's base at Pevensey on the south coast and the bishop's at Rochester on the Medway. Both places were potential ingress points for ducal reinforcements. Every day, it was said, 'the multitude of accomplices in the conspiracy increased'. The stage was set for an outbreak of vicious internecine strife, when 'fathers would fight sons, brothers fight brothers, friends fight kinsmen, and aliens fight aliens'.

6

STORM OF WAR

Just a few hundred knights and Flemish mercenaries managed to penetrate down the Thames and the Medway to Bishop Odo's castle at Rochester, which became one of three main bases for the insurgents in the south-east; the others were at Pevensey on the south coast and Tonbridge in mid-Kent. Among the knights holed up at Rochester was Robert de Bellême, who had ridden out with Robert Curthose to fight at Gerberoy ten years earlier. The fortifications at Rochester were constructed at the centre of an already formidable defensive site, located beside an important fording point on the main road to London. Excavations in modern times have established that Rochester's medieval defences included a rampart almost seven metres deep, incorporating a section of Roman wall and a ditch. The perimeter defences encompassed stone or wooden tower-like fortifications of a diameter large enough to house sizeable numbers of soldiers. The compound in 1088 accommodated around five hundred fighting men, likely a mix of local and foreign fighters. The knights, with their attendant mounted spearmen and archers – the former likened by Orderic to 'terrible worms in iron cocoons' – burst forth from the castle gates to attack the inhabitants of Canterbury and London. Rochester enjoyed a strategically central position against both these key target cities, an indication of some pre-planning on the part of Robert's supporters.

In a desperate attempt to sever Rochester's communications with the south coast, where reinforcements from Normandy might have been expected, Rufus first attacked and captured Tonbridge Castle. The castle there was manned in strength by the de Clare family and their retainers. It stood, and still stands, though now ruined, on a spur of high land, close to a place where the marshy Medway River could in medieval times be forded, and where a number of ancient trackways converged. Tonbridge Castle's inexperienced castellan, Gilbert Fitz Richard de Clare, the honorific Clare relating to another family castle in Suffolk, was injured during the fighting. The garrison surrendered on the second day of siege, as a consequence of the castellan's wound. Rufus pardoned him and his brother Roger. Both were viewed as acting honourably and in accord with the precepts of medieval warfare. Rufus was nothing if not an honourable man. He accepted the Clares were Duke Robert's sworn vassals and left it at that. The Brionne family, from which they sprang, had enjoyed a long and laudable association with the dukes of Normandy. Richard and Roger's grandfather Gilbert had been killed during the civil war which raged in Normandy when acting as William's guardian. Gilbert's sons had then been placed under the protection of the Count of Flanders. Richard de Clare may even have fought at Hastings in 1066. As a major landowner in England, with 176 lordships awarded to him, he went on to play a major role in confronting the king's rebels in 1075. All this was known to Rufus, influencing his response towards generosity after they surrendered the castle and submitted to him.

The loss of Tonbridge proved a major blow to the duke's supporters, who now found themselves threatened by an enemy operating on interior lines, able to attack northward toward the Medway, or south toward the coast. The counter-strokes made by Rufus at this early stage of the campaigning indicate the young king to have been a considerable tactician. He refused to be drawn into fighting on too many fronts, allowing insurrections flaring elsewhere to be confronted by subordinates or left to run their course.

Bishop Odo fled from Rochester and somehow avoided Rufus' enveloping patrols. He sought refuge with his brother Robert de Mortain at Pevensey Castle. Pevensey's location offered the hope of a relieving fleet arriving from Normandy, and the possibility of taking ship back to Normandy should it become necessary. It must now have been clear to Odo the rebellion had stalled. He hurriedly rode south with just a small bodyguard and a few other followers. These unlooked-for reinforcements at Pevensey represented additional mouths to feed. Their horses may have become prized more for their nutritional value than strength or speed. Robert de Mortain may already have been considering his position even before the arrival of his brother. He knew that after the fall of Tonbridge the king would inevitably turn his attentions to the south coast. Unless a ducal ship-army arrived from Normandy soon, his garrison would remain bottled up without hope of relief. The more optimistic Odo cajoled his brother to remain steady in his resolve and brave it out until help arrived.

Some troops despatched from Normandy did in fact reach the coast near Pevensey, but were prevented from landing by English coastal patrols. English longships blockading the castle's seaward approaches would have been well placed to confront ducal reinforcing squadrons. As has recently been pointed out by John Gillingham, Rufus greatly valued sea power and looked to make good use of it in his campaigning throughout his reign. Bad weather may also have played a part in the ducal fleet's downfall by hindering the Norman captains when attempting to manoeuvre. Flight for the sailors when coming under attack was then fatally hampered when the wind suddenly dropped. Becalmed and struggling under sagging sails, many dived overboard and drowned in an attempt to save themselves from capture and the likelihood of a more painful death.

A number of localised risings in support of the duke at Dover and Hastings had probably been stifled by this time, but there were rebels still holding out at the Tower of London. They posed no real danger as they had been bottled up there by the king's men, but they were safely ensconced nonetheless – the Tower was even then an imposing stone edifice, virtually impossible to take by storm. Built by the Conqueror in the late 1070s and early 1080s to overawe the 25,000 or so Londoners, many of whom may have remained implacably hostile to the Normans, its strong walls are alleged to have been mortared with blood.

Insurgencies that flared further afield, described as scattered diversions, erupted in East Anglia, the Welsh Marches, the East Midlands and Yorkshire. Roger Bigod, a prominent lord in East Anglia, targeted royal lands from his castle at Norwich. His neighbour Hugh de Grandmesnil plundered Leicestershire and Nottinghamshire. More serious were insurgencies in the Avon and Severn valleys. The rebellion against Rufus may in fact have first erupted at Bristol, pre-dating the better-documented fighting in Sussex, Kent and Surrey. From Bristol Castle, rebels under the command of Bishop Geoffrey of Coutances and his nephew Robert de Mowbray, Earl of Northumbria, attacked the walled city of Bath and the district around Berkeley. Named for the honour of Montbrai in Normandy, Mowbray had ridden out in rebellion with Robert in 1078. He was said to have been a man greatly skilled in the art of war, and likely acted as his uncle Geoffrey's military commander ten years later. Like Odo, Bishop Geoffrey had fought at Hastings. For his good service he had gained 280 English manors from a grateful William. As a lay cleric, he continued to don a warlike mantle after the Conquest, demonstrably so in 1075, when, with others, he helped besiege the king's rebels and their Breton allies in Norwich Castle. Orderic claimed Geoffrey to have been a much better drillmaster than a psalmist.

When fighting among themselves, the Normans, including their club-wielding bishops, were likened by Orderic to the Babylonians, as 'men drinking from the same cup of tribulations inflicted by them in the past on others'. Bishop Geoffrey and his nephew fitted this venomous typecasting. They burned and plundered their way into Wiltshire, laying waste a number of towns in the county.

Not until they reached Ilchester, in Somerset, were they repulsed by hurriedly mustered forces loyal to Rufus. The storm of war is said to have raged in every direction, with the rebels carrying fire and slaughter wherever they went.

Another party of ducal loyalists, the previously mentioned Ralph de Mortemer, Bernard de Neufmarché and Osbern Fitz Richard, with others including Roger de Lacy and William d'Eu, savaged Gloucestershire and Worcestershire. Houses and churches were razed to the ground. The rebels might have obliterated the city of Worcester altogether had it not been for the intervention of Wulfstan, Worcester's English bishop – a proper churchman, described as a prelate of 'great piety and dove-like simplicity, beloved by all – even the rebels'. Wulfstan was the archetypal man in crisis. Throughout his life he battled personal demons, while ever teetering on the edge of nervous collapse. His prolonged austerities and lengthy prayer sessions are held to exemplify earlier self-denigrating Celtic saints, some of whose feast-days were observed by him at Worcester. He had played a pivotal role in 1075 when organising the king's defences east of the Severn. Thirteen years later, he again set out to secure the environs of Worcester from the ravages of the forces arraigned against it. It was an age famous for miraculous intercessions. A heavy anathema placed on the insurgents by the bishop is claimed by the chroniclers to have tested rebel resolve and helped bring about their defeat – an early example of psychological warfare paying off.

Late eleventh-century man knew the damning effect of holy censure and the power of prayer. Men who prayed for victory, like Wulfstan at Worcester, were an important ingredient in any medieval warlord's arsenal. Before the invasion in 1066, bishops had led groups of clergymen to the fringes of the battlefield, prepared to fight the enemy with prayers alone. Similar companies of priests and monks had accompanied Edmund Ironside's army when it clashed with Cnut in Essex in 1016, and parties of monks had likely done the same at Maldon in Essex in 991 when ealdorman Byrhtnoth lost his life and much of his army to a large Viking raiding army.

Warrior bishops like Odo and Coutances eschewed the use of the sword or lance when in the thick of the action, relying instead on a club-headed mace with sharpened ridged edges. Canon law forbade churchmen from smiting with the edge of the sword. In St Matthew's Gospel it says, 'All they that take the sword shall perish with the sword.' Clubbing someone to death with a mace was an accepted loophole. The fighting spirit of secular-minded churchmen could not easily be assuaged when their blood was up. On the Bayeux Tapestry, Bishop Odo is prominently arrayed in a haubergeon and carries a mace when rallying his troops.

In 1088, Wulfstan did not rely entirely on prayer and the power of interdict. Nor did he ride out in person, as Odo or Geoffrey of Coutances might have done in similar circumstances. Instead he ordered a blistering counter-attack with fifty knights under his command, counselling them to 'be firm in your allegiance to the king and manfully fight for the safety of the people and the city'. With these words of encouragement ringing in their ears, his knights rode out from the castle gates to give battle. The enemy were some distance away across the Severn but advancing rapidly. Wulfstan's earlier sanction and the ferocity of his knights when charging home are claimed to have unshielded the rebels both figuratively and literally. Only the leaders and their mounted bodyguards managed to escape when set upon. The foot soldiers were likely slaughtered out of hand. Death for commoners remained an inconsequential outcome of any battle in this period, rarely elaborated upon. We have no specific details of the fighting but men led into the battle by the sheriff of Worcester must also have played a part in seeing off the rebels. The main lesson to be taken from the affair is that it took the backing of a brave and avowedly English churchman, once a close confidant and spiritual advisor to King Harold II, to see off a powerful Norman host.

*

With the revolt around the country having stalled, all that the remaining rebels could do was to hunker down and hope for relief from Normandy. Odo's bolthole at Pevensey proved to be a strong, unyielding bastion, withstanding six weeks of attack by land and sea before its half-starved garrison were finally forced to submit. Although Rufus stood ready and prepared to use substantial force to press the siege – engines of war are said to have been shipped to the south coast – Pevensey did not in the end face any direct assault. There was, though, a great deal of skirmishing.

William de Warenne became an early victim of the exchanges. He fell mortally wounded when struck by a crossbow bolt shot from the castle walls. His body was afterwards taken back to his home at Lewes, where he died on 24 June. Cluniac monks interred him in their chapter at St Pancras and lauded his merits on a funerary tablet. The inscription on the earl's tomb reads: 'Who seeks earl Warenne's tomb, may look around, and mark the buildings on this holy ground; for here, with pious zeal, his wealth he spent, in rearing this, his noblest monument.' Not all men favoured Warenne. He retained an evil reputation at Ely Abbey, a place where his war hammer had fallen heavily in the past. The monks there had been punished for the support they offered up to Hereward's rebels in 1071. The Conqueror's forces that year had been forced to blockade Ely using longships on the River Ouse and to have approached the marsh-encompassed island fortress by building a causeway using logs and stones. Warenne's widow's offer of restitution to the abbey for any damage done – a donation of 100 shillings – received a point-blank refusal by the monks. Warenne's academic biographer C. P. Lewis says the monks of Ely spent their long evenings conjuring images of their oppressor's departing soul tormented by demons.

Fright invoked by the sudden and ruthless efficiency of Rufus' response to the crisis of 1088 grew with the dawning realisation the rebels could not expect a decisive intervention from Robert Curthose. There is in fact no real evidence Robert was ever a prime mover. He may have belatedly raised arms and soldiers when informed of the plight of his two uncles at Pevensey; otherwise he had likely been far too preoccupied in Normandy and its frontiers to set aside the time for a concerted move against England. Had Robert ever been minded to intervene personally, coordinated timing on both sides of the Channel would have been critical to success and a much longer period of preparation expended. As it was, synchronisation was quickly lost when the rebels, geographically dispersed and overeager, jumped a gun fired off by Odo's ravaging of Kent. Highly judgemental of all secular rulers and of Robert Curthose more than most, Orderic Vitalis considered the duke to have been 'detained [in Normandy] by sloth and indulgence'. A simplistic and almost certainly imagined scene where the duke stands bereft on a Norman beach wringing his hands and castigating himself for not acting with greater urgency strikes a moral note, not a factual one.

After Pevensey's eventual fall at the end of six weeks of close siege, Odo, either through mischance or design, became holed up again at Rochester. Rufus' troops invested the castle and erected two forts designed to overawe and prevent harassing sorties launched by the knights within. The king's artillery destroyed much of the wooden structure of the fortress and damaged the nearby cathedral. However, when the garrison yielded it was a result of disease, not combat. The plague they endured is said to have been brought on by a glut of flies attracted to the castle ward by the mounds of dung from men and horses. Medieval writers likened the outbreak to a biblical curse. Surrender soon became the only option. Odo requested Rufus desist from any martial victory display when the survivors marched out. The king sensibly ignored his uncle's plea and commanded royal trumpeters sound a triumphant flourish. The bishop then faced immediate exile and the confiscation of his estates and titles. Orderic wrote,

Thus the unholy bishop was banished from England, and his vast domains were forfeited so that the prodigious wealth he had iniquitously amassed, was, by the just judgement of God, lost with signal disgrace. He retired in confusion to Bayeux, and never again set foot in England.

Most others gained their reprieve. This was virtually guaranteed for men who had in the past shown unwavering loyalty to the Conqueror, like Robert de Mortain, the Clares and the Montgomerys. Bishop Geoffrey of Coutances is said to have been winked at by Rufus rather than chastised. Even so, he may have had some of his lands temporally confiscated as a token penalty. The same may have been true of other men too. Rufus did not dispossess them in perpetuity; instead, he left the lands vacant to be repossessed once his subjects' loyalty had been re-established – an incentive for his noblemen to toe the line. Orderic, with Rufus in mind, considered it to be 'lion-like to spare a fallen foe; and lion-hearted kings should thus their greatness show'. Robert de Mowbray, a man with much closer links to Robert Curthose, and therefore more likely to have been mauled than spared, faced a period of indeterminate exile.

At a distance of almost ten centuries we cannot hope to fully understand all the ins and outs of why one man might be pardoned and allowed to resume office while another faced opprobrium. Odo had now shown disloyalty to both the Conqueror and to Rufus; his continued presence in England could not be tolerated. Rufus' ire against his uncle may have run so deep that only with great difficulty was he persuaded not to shed the blood of a priest of the Lord. English thegns in fact cried out for the death sentence, but Rufus could not countenance a Norman nobleman and close relative facing an unseemly death on the scaffold. Remembering Waltheof's ignominious fate, Englishmen muttered at the injustice of this. Nonetheless, Rufus never forgave his uncle. Like his father, he had a long memory and he held grudges.

Bishop William St Calais

The other prominent clerical victim of Rufus' anger in 1088 was the fifty-eight-year-old William of St Calais, Bishop of Durham, who had succeeded the murdered Walcher. St Calais' academic biographer Frank Barlow says the Conqueror's moving of the bishop 'from the marches of Anjou to hold a city and castle in the

Scottish marches shows how much trust [he] had in him'. St Calais had once overseen the ecclesiastical and secular politics of empire from the bishopric of Le Mans. He must have played some part in the plotting against Rufus, since he is named in the *Anglo-Saxon Chronicle* to have done to Rufus what Judas Iscariot did to Jesus. It names him as one of the instigators of 'that foolish plan'.

Described by the contemporary chronicler Simeon of Durham, who knew him personally, as 'subtle and possessed of an excellent memory, an eloquent speaker and a wise counsellor', his experience of diplomacy and innate shrewdness may have inclined him to intrigue. Like Bishops Odo and Geoffrey of Coutances, St Calais was an undoubtedly religious man, though by no means a fanatic. As mentioned, he had gained his wealth of experience managing the sometimes anarchic southern outposts of the Anglo-Norman realm on the Maine frontier and was numbered as one of a small set of valued members of the Conqueror's inner circle at court. Under Rufus, St Calais is held to have operated with the equivalence of a justiciar. He was at Rufus' side at York early in the New Year for the founding ceremony at St Mary's Abbey, and it must have been then or shortly afterwards that the king got wind (possibly from the bishop) of the threat of an insurrection brewing. Had St Calais betrayed the rebels? He later swore under oath that he had not violated his fealty to the king at any time and that he had never directly engaged with the conspirators.

After leaving York, with seven knights to accompany him, St Calais had ridden south with Rufus' main force to reconnoitre into Sussex and Kent. In his later testimony he said he had helped to secure Dover and Hastings for the king and had then spent time in London, spying out the level of support for the insurgency; but, when despatched north by Rufus to raise more troops, instead of re-joining the king, he launched a series of independent raids against local rivals. The details of these harassing attacks are now lost to us. All we have to go on is that year's *Anglo-Saxon Chronicle* entry, which states, 'The Bishop of Durham did what harm he could everywhere in the north.' What he had learned in London may have persuaded him to look to his own interests rather than Rufus'. He may have held out little hope for the king's survival. True or not, his failure to re-join the king was later spun to his dishonour. Symeon of Durham, a man in a good position to know, believed the bishop had been destroyed by the intrigues of his enemies. David Bates on the other hand says there would have been scant sympathy at court 'for a man who had first betrayed the conspirators and then deserted the king'.

The sequencing of events for the 1088 rebellion is problematic. Odo is thought to have been up in arms against the king by April at the latest, and the confiscation of St Calais' northern estates likely occurred a month later in May. St Calais' trial, though, did not take place until 2 November 1088. By then he had twice faced the king's wrath at first hand. At Old Sarum, outside Salisbury, on the second occasion, the bishop insisted he be allowed to take his stand upon canon law. It was as a bishop, not as a baron, that he wished to be judged. Had the trial been heard in an ecclesiastical court, he might have benefited from papal intervention. The English had not yet accepted the authority of the new Pope, Gregory VII, so the bishop's stubbornness in this respect may have been seen as just a ploy, even as a political insult. In the end an appeal made by St Calais to the papal curia failed to prevent the trial from going ahead.

Archbishop Lanfranc, acting as prosecutor for the crown, made a point of confirming St Calais was to be held accountable in respect of dues owed to the king, in much the same way Bishop Odo had been tried six years earlier. Had St Calais thrown himself on Rufus' mercy there might even then have been a reconciliation, but instead he acted defiantly. He raged at having his lands ravaged and demanded the king stop treating him basely and dishonourably. He blamed enemies at court for his unjust treatment and showed little remorse for any part he might have played in the early plotting. Frustratingly for the bishop's enemies (and despite an impressive show by Lanfranc when prosecuting the case), St Calais' keen brain was at its most incisive. He outwitted his appellants time and time again. None of the charges against the bishop could be made to stick. So angry was Rufus that he is alleged to have cried out, 'By the face of Lucca, you'll never escape from my hands before I have your castle. Believe me, bishop, you're not going back to Durham, and your men are not going to stay at Durham, and you're not going free until you release the castle.' The castle at Durham must still have remained under close siege as late as November.

Ultimately, only the bishop's guilt for contumacy was proved (this is defined as an unwillingness to face trial or plead) and made to stick. Rufus forfeited all the bishop's lands, secured Durham Castle and exiled St Calais to the Continent. The king may have been at his most vengeful during these dark midwinter days. St Calais was only allowed to cross to Normandy after promising on oath to return the ships made available to him so that they could not be used by the king's brother Robert in any future invasion bid.

*

Rufus' military and political success in 1088 is remarkable. Few at the time could have foreseen how effective the young king would be as a commander in the field. It may not have been until mid-April, when a number of his noblemen failed to attend his Easter court at Winchester, that he had come to realise the full scale of the problem he faced. He had then been left with little time to react to a fast-moving insurgency, and with only a handful of noblemen he could rely on absolutely. These who backed him unstintingly gained great rewards. Robert Fitz Haimon, for instance, was given the honour of Gloucester, once held by the queen and promised in her will to her youngest son, Henry. Henry de Beaumont was made Earl of Warwick. Simon de Senlis gained the earldoms of Huntingdon and Northampton, and Walter Giffard the earldom of Buckingham.

Much of what Rufus achieved was down to the backing of the English, who preferred to support their own consecrated king rather than suffer a further bout of Norman intriguing and a possible foreign invasion. Although individually less powerful than their Norman counterparts, the thegns of England when united were a force to be reckoned with. The sheriffs of England also backed Rufus. They supported him almost to a man. When proclamations were issued, the English are said to have flocked to Rufus' royal standard. The vast majority of English churchmen also backed the king. All but one of the bishops of English dioceses had supported Rufus' accession to the kingship and they maintained their allegiance throughout the rising. Rufus was said to have been humbled by the resolve of his English subjects; so strong had been the turnout, he might afterwards have worried at the prospect of them ever rising up against him.

Rufus had even managed to attract foreign support. His brother-in-law Alan IV of Brittany, who had not long before married the Conqueror's third daughter, Constance, sent him soldiers. This may have been at the special pleading of the king's sister, and if so would indicate a closer sibling relationship between Constance and Rufus (the two were likely close in age) than with Robert.

If 1088 in England had been a momentous year, when 'the madness of war' had prevailed, 1089 would be more peaceful. The headline events were the sudden death of Archbishop Lanfranc in the early summer and an earthquake on the morning of 11 August, felt the length and breadth of the country. Grinding tectonic plates and funerary slabs were now settling into place in England, but not so the familial schism to play out in Normandy between the Bastard's sons.

7

NORMANDY UNDER THREAT

In the late summer of 1088, with the dust still to settle in England, Robert Curthose shifted his attention away from any belated thoughts of intervention and focused on issues that had arisen on the Norman borders. He concentrated his knights at Mantes in the Vexin, the fortress location where his father had suffered his mortal wounding the year before. Ducal overreach on the frontiers of Normandy had deteriorated even before the Conqueror's death. Robert may have planned to finish off what his father had started. He made little headway. Other, more pressing priorities surfaced further to the south, on the Normandy/Maine borders and at Le Mans, Maine's capital. Robert had inherited many unresolved problems – a fact glossed over by his critics – not least the constant feuding between rival families on the southern borders of the duchy. Private wars and threats to the social order were the curse of western Europe. The death of the Conqueror had seen ducal garrisons evicted by resurgent castellans, who now sought to assert authority free from oversight. Need for prompt action closer to home may help explain why Robert hesitated to commit himself to campaigning in person in England in the spring of 1088, assuming he ever really had any intention of doing so.

The duke rode south and invested the castle at Ballon, on the road from Alencon to Le Mans – a fortress known as 'the gateway to Maine', about twelve miles from Le Mans. A belligerent garrison under the command of Paganus de Montdoubleau, a man named for a town in the Vendome in central France, held out against him there. Pevensey and Rochester had fallen by this time. Bishop Odo had returned to Normandy and now accompanied his nephew on the road south. He headed a reinforcement of twenty knights, the feudal fee he owed the duke. Odo is likened by Orderic at this time to 'a dragon struck to the earth and vomiting flames'. Humiliation in England had exacerbated an already combustible disposition. The fire-breathing bishop is said to have encouraged Robert to act with firmness against all known ducal enemies and to move quickly to stamp out any hint of rebellion or intrigue. He is even alleged by Orderic to have presented the examples of past giants of history as role models for the duke to emulate: Alexander the Great, Pompey the Great and Julius Caesar.

Odo's influence over Robert is portrayed as baleful and the duke is miscast as passively adhering to the bishop's agenda; yet it is unsurprising Robert deferred to his uncle's judgement: no Norman was likely better travelled and versed in the ways of the world than Odo, whose life had spanned the years of greatest Norman achievement in western and southern Europe. He had attended all the important events of the Conqueror's reign and is considered by his academic biographer David Bates to have been the most colourful and flamboyant of the Norman conquerors. An early recognition that the dukedom would be placed under threat from within and without by men now backing Rufus can be credited to the bishop's foresight and experience.

Bishop Odo had the powerful Montgomery family foremost in his mind when counselling Robert to act with haste and not spare the sword: the lands and castles of the eldest of the Montgomery sons, Robert de Bellême, were sighted in his cross-hairs. He knew Roger de Montgomery to have switched his allegiance away from Robert Curthose to Rufus at the latter's prompting, and that Montgomery's sons, including his eldest, had since then been 'turned' by the king. Orderic says that Odo urged Robert to 'cut their horns off'. The target family controlled twelve strong castles in the south.

All of them had likely seen their ducal garrisons ejected by Bellême and his commanders after the Conqueror's death; the lord's forebears had rarely in the past conceded the right for a Norman duke to garrison them. For generations the family had maintained a largely independent regime along the marches with Maine, keeping a tight hold on their domains, regardless of whose vassal they were. As the description 'marcher' implies, their lands and strongholds demarcated frontier zones and advanced bastions toward Maine. Their fortress at Domfront actually lay within the bounds of the county, and their castle at Alencon had once controlled a semi-independent buffer state located between Normandy and Maine, which had not been subjugated to William's authority until 1050 or thereabouts.

When attacked that year, a year before Curthose's birth, the castle garrison, described as 'quarrelsome and scandalous', had paid a fearful price after draping wet animal skins over the castle walls as fire retardants. Robert Wace claimed the defenders to have shouted out, 'The hide – the tanner's hide; that is what belongs to his trade' – an insult aimed at William, the bastard son of a tanner's daughter. William's birthplace at Falaise was renowned for its tanners and tailors. After the eventual surrender of the castle's outer precincts, William had got his own back on prisoners he took: 'By God's splendour,' he is said to have cried out; 'Prune them of their limbs and deny them their sight.' It was a brutal act matching King Cnut's infamous mutilations in 1013, when the Dane ordered the noses and ears of his young hostages to be cut off, a typically Viking response to an insult.

To successfully attack a well-sited castle required a major investment in time and materials. Fire was an important weapon in any besieger's arsenal and was the reason why stone keeps so often replaced wooden forts. At Alencon in 1050, the Normans filled in the defensive ditch around the castle, using planks and pieces of wood stripped from nearby buildings; according to Wace they pulled down the roofs of houses and 'the laths, the beams and whatever else they found nearby', before setting fire to the whole conglomeration.

Roger de Montgomery and His Family

The Montgomery family figure large in the lives and fortunes of the Bastard's sons. Roger de Montgomery had been one of just a handful of confederates the Conqueror trusted implicitly in 1066, a man William had grown up with and who had shared many of the dangers facing the duchy in the early years. So well trusted was he that William had left him behind in Normandy to oversee the duchy as a co-regent that year – the safety of the queen and children were in his liegemen's hands. Non-participation at Hastings for a man like Montgomery must nevertheless have rankled. Born in a region of Normandy between Caen and Rouen, once subjected to intensive Scandinavian settlement, he proudly described himself as a pure-blood Norseman. In a charter (*c.* 1080) he signed with the appellation Northmannis Northmannus (meaning Norseman of Norsemen). He made available sixty longships for the invasion fleet in 1066, placing him in a tier just behind Robert de Mortain, Bishop Odo and William of Evreux in the Norman pecking order. Non-participation had not weighed against him when it came to sharing out the spoils. As we have seen, he gained the Sussex rapes of Arundel and Chichester, plus vast landholdings elsewhere too, notably in Shropshire. He became a pillar guarding the south coast toward the Solent as well as the Marches toward Wales. These were territories later added to, mainly through crown dispossessions in East Anglia.

Landed wealth meant great power. Over and above any booty gained in war, the income from such landholdings and the granting of tenancies enabled lords like Montgomery to handsomely reward their knights and to maintain strong military retinues. Alone of the Conqueror's henchmen, Montgomery gave his name to a county in Britain: Montgomeryshire, named after the Norman lord's ancestral home Montgommeri. The first castle built at Welsh Montgomery, named in Welsh Hen Domen (or Dolmen) meaning Old Mound, was of the motte-and-bailey type, raised to command an ancient road network at the point where two roads crossed, and to control the traffic across the River Severn at a nearby ford. Montgomery Castle had been built with forced labour in the teeth of opposition from hostile neighbours and it survives today in open countryside, albeit now overgrown and neglected. Multiple outer ramparts, ditches and raised fighting platforms attest to the danger from the hinterland it protected. Within this ring of defences lay a bailey with timber buildings, barracks, and dormitories for servants, animal corrals and stables. A frontier fortress, the castle would not have been in any way luxurious; only two of the buildings discovered in the castle's bailey evidence open fires.

Montgomery's first wife, the great heiress Mabel Talvas, described by Orderic as 'small, talkative, ready to do evil, shrewd, jocular, cruel and daring', hailed from a powerful frontier family which boasted a lengthy Frankish pedigree. The Conqueror had acted as matchmaker. His reason for doing so was to set the family up as the focus of Norman power in the region around Sées, on the Orne River, thirteen miles north-north-east of Alencon. The doyen of the brood, William Talvas (d. c. 1060), had been notorious in his day for his cruelty, much like his grandson Robert de Bellême would become in the days when the Bastard's sons vied for control. In the mid- to late 1040s, Talvas hired assassins to strangle his first wife, Hilda (Mabel's mother), and sometime later had his feudal vassal William d'Giroie blinded and emasculated for providing military support to a rival; Giroie's ears had been removed for good measure, yet the victim somehow survived his dreadful ordeal and later became a monk at the Abbey of Le Bec. His retreat must also have served as a hospice. Giroie's brothers later set an ambush for Talvas and killed him in an undisclosed but excruciating manner. Mabel also met a bad end. As part of another family feud, she was murdered in December 1077, at Bures-sur-Dives. Her head was vengefully struck from her shoulders as she emerged from her bed or bath (sources differ) by a man she had disinherited. The killer then fled to Apulia, and later to Sicily. The Conqueror despatched assassins to hunt him down. Even Sicily became unsafe for the desperado, so he fled to Syria, an indication of

William's diplomatic reach. He would much later reappear as a guide for the crusaders during the First Crusade.

Montgomery sired six sons and four daughters by the ill-fated Mabel. Of the sons, five survived into adulthood: Robert, Hugh, Roger, Philip and Arnulf. The eldest, Robert de Bellême, gained his mother's lands upon her death in 1077. He would later inherit his father's lands and titles in Normandy. The family landholdings in England were earmarked for the second of Montgomery's sons, Hugh, known as Hugh de Montgomery (sometimes Hugh the Proud). The division of land was in keeping with Norman custom and mirrored the split of the Anglo-Norman realm between Robert Curthose and Rufus. Both Montgomery's eldest sons backed the ducal side in 1088 and were never again fully trusted by Rufus, whereas the third son, Roger, known as 'the Poitevin', backtracked to side with the king. He was later trusted by Rufus to arrest Bishop St Calais and place Durham Castle under siege. The Poitevin, nicknamed as such after his marriage to an heiress from Poitou, controlled the most westerly crossing point over the River Ribble at Penwortham west of Preston. The main risks to the region came from north Wales, Northumbria, Man and Cumbria. All were still the haunts of Viking bands, as well as Welsh, Irish, Scottish and Cumbrian pirates. The Poitevin's castle motte at Penwortham is still extant. Roger also founded the Benedictine priory at nearby Lancaster, dedicated to the Virgin Mary; it still stands today, though much altered. Montgomery's fourth son, Philip, may have remained the duke's man. Arnulf's affinity is not known, but like his father he may have remained uncommitted until forced off the fence to back Rufus.

Montgomery married again after Mabel's murder. His young bride, Adelais, hailed from the Île-de-France. The wedding took place in 1080, the year Robert Curthose became reconciled with his father. Adelais made the long and arduous journey that year to join her husband at Shrewsbury on the Welsh borders, a place which must have seemed to her at the extreme edge of civilisation and where dangerous neighbours abounded. A particularly 'evil road' is said to have run across Wenlock Edge which could not safely be travelled until the early twelfth century. Adelais was nevertheless in safe hands when travelling westward. Only retainers trusted by Montgomery to wield the sword were settled by him on the Welsh borders. His castles were numerous and strongly garrisoned. In bringing a Frenchwoman to England, Montgomery was bucking a growing trend toward inter-marriage between Norman lords and Anglo-Saxon and Welsh heiresses, an indication that he, like the Conqueror, remained emotionally tied to the Continent, not to his newly won lands in England. Inter-marriage between Normans and Anglo-Saxons has otherwise been held to explain the relative ease with which the Conqueror imposed his rule on England. Bernard de Neufmarché, one of the leading rebels in 1088, had married the late King Gruffydd ap Llywelyn's granddaughter Nesta. The offspring of their union would over time come to construct a new ruling class in Wales.

Inter-marriage may also help explain why the French language never became dominant. Its endurance has been ascribed to the attentions of Anglo-Saxon wet-nurses and servants, who continued to speak in their mother tongue. Only a small minority of men and women, those attending the English court, ever conversed in French. Orderic had been the son of an English mother and a French father and had been brought up in infancy in Shropshire, before being sent to Normandy at the tender age of ten. He tells of feeling himself to have been exiled and that the French spoken at the monastery which became his home was at first unintelligible to him. Old French very quickly ceased to be the idiom of all but a tiny minority in England. Moreover, State structures which had once made England such a wealthy and well-governed kingdom came to reassert themselves. Historian John Blair (*The Anglo-Saxon Age*) says that in many ways England up until the year 1400 remained much like England in the year 1000, when Ethelred II was king.

Bellême's landholdings in Normandy over time came to comprise chunks of both northern Maine and southern Normandy, a remit which formed a flat, straggling triangle of land, with the town of Sées at its apex, and the castles at Alencon and Bellême forming the base. He also controlled the fortress town of Domfront, his westernmost bastion, which lay within the bounds of Maine. Upon first hearing the news of the Conqueror's death, having stopped overnight at Brionne, while en route for Rouen, Bellême spurred his horse and galloped back the way he had come, intent on ousting the in-situ royal troops from his castles. Those he placed in lockdown included St Ceneri, Ballon, Bellême, Alencon, Lurson, Essai, La Roche d'Ige and Domfront. He acted well within normal parameters when faced with the prospect of a hiatus in overlordship. He replaced the king's watchmen with men of his own, some of whom immediately went on the rampage. During this lull in ducal authority, his actions may have served to destabilise the southern reaches of the duchy, an echo of the anarchic days of William the Conqueror's minority. Orderic described the duchy at this time as beset by unceasing calamities.

Despite his bad reputation the Conqueror had always held Bellême in high regard, presumably for his military and administrative skills, not his somewhat devil-take-the-hindmost modus operandi. William arranged Bellême's marriage to Agnes of Ponthieu, the heir to the rich county of the same name, which lay to the north-east of Normandy. Unaccountably, the Conqueror may have come to trust Bellême more so than he did his own elder son, Robert Curthose.

*

Many distinguished knights were on hand to support Robert Curthose when campaigning at Ballon on the Maine borders in the autumn and early winter of 1088. They included Robert de Nevers (known as the Burgundian), William of Breteuil (the brother of the imprisoned rebel earl Roger of Hereford) and Ralph de Tosny (a belligerent nobleman from one of the most powerful families on the southern frontier of Normandy). Tosny in fact was a veteran of Hastings and is claimed to have spurned the honour of carrying the Norman banner that day so that he might more quickly be in the thick of the action. His half-brother William of Evreux, another Hastings veteran, also rode out with Robert in 1088. That the duke retained such a strong following after the recent setbacks in England indicates he maintained a firmer hold over the duchy than is often allowed for. His household knights are said to have been so strong they could not be opposed and carried all before them.

The fighting at Ballon occurred at the end of August and the beginning of September 1088. A young knight, Osmund de Gaspree, became an early casualty. Gaspree's death is dated to 1 September. Losses were suffered by both sides, but in the end the garrison commander, Montdoubleau, came to terms with Curthose to avoid further blood being spilt. An impressively battle-scarred ducal entourage then rode on in triumph to Le Mans, driving in and scattering remaining hostile outposts along the road. Robert quickly gained the submission of the key noblemen at Le Mans. Further reinforced by troops from Maine, he went on to capture the by now vulnerable Montgomery frontier stronghold at St Ceneri, sited on a rocky pinnacle above the winding River Sarthe, just to the south of Alencon. The castle was one of a dozen or so belonging to the Montgomery family in the region, and had in the past been the subject of much dispute and feuding between rival families. When St Ceneri eventually fell to the duke, the garrison commander Robert Quarrel was blinded and the common soldiers mutilated. These were acts of violence mirroring the Conqueror's savagery at Alencon forty years earlier and carried out for the same reason, to sow fear and enhance ducal prestige. Rough justice enacted in this way highlights a harder edge to Robert Curthose than is apparent in the literature of the times. It was, though, a brutal age, where blinding, castration and exile were accepted political expedients.[4]

*

Robert de Bellême had been among the first to rally to the ducal cause in England in 1088, and had been numbered among the five hundred or so fighting men ensconced at Rochester, placed there in a commanding role by Bishop Odo when the bishop fled to the south coast after the loss of Tonbridge. As mentioned, Roger de Montgomery's intervention had then proved to be crucial to save Bellême from Rufus' ire, when resistance at Rochester collapsed under the weight of hunger and pestilence. Part of a deal to gain his son's passport back to Normandy may have been for Montgomery to back Rufus and for Bellême to promise that he would never again oppose the king.

Montgomery's dilemma in the spring and summer of 1088 highlights the problem facing men whose families held land on either side of the English Channel. The earl had lobbied the Conqueror against dividing the Anglo-Norman realm by citing the inevitable backlash this would engender and had been proved right. After a short harrying spree, probably in support of Robert Curthose, he had, as we have seen, held back from more openly declaring his allegiance to either Rufus or Robert. Rufus' eventual persuading him to support him may have come at the price of more than just Bellême's pardon, since several other of Montgomery's sons may also have been compromised. A quid pro quo agreement may have required not only Bellême but also the other members of the Montgomery family to pledge to back Rufus over Robert in the future. Rufus' best interests would have been served by turning as many Norman landowners as possible, and then to send them off to sow discord in Normandy as a sort of fifth column. If word of this arrangement had become known to Bishop Odo, it would help explain the bishop's reference to 'horned men on the rise', and his encouraging the duke to ride south to invest the Montgomery castles at Ballon and St Ceneri and to harry Montgomery lands. It would also explain why Odo ordered Bellême to be detained on his arrival back in Normandy, and for a time incarcerated ('chained in fetters') in the bishop's dungeon complex at Neuilly l'Évêque, in north-eastern France.

Draconian measures like this speak of a growing fear of Rufus pervading the duchy after the abortive rebellion in England. The shackling of a potential turncoat like Robert de Bellême was a sensible precaution until the political climate in the duchy settled. Locking him up might also be seen in the context of the duke's need to move against the Manceaux and his marcher rebels. By enabling Robert Curthose to call the shots on the troublesome borderlands, unhindered by the threat of Bellême intervening, the duke could more effectively make his move on Maine.

More damage might have been inflicted on the family's lands and castles had not Roger de Montgomery hurried from England with Rufus' blessing to place the remaining family strongholds in a state of high alert. Through emissaries he pleaded with Robert Curthose not to press his advantage any further. His intercession succeeded in putting an end to the duke's chevauchee and gained Bellême's release sometime early in 1089. Having made his bloody mark at St Ceneri, and having handed the castle over to one of his supporters, Robert Curthose may have been glad to call a halt to the ravaging, ending a short but bloody campaign.

*

An already tense situation in Normandy worsened when William Rufus made clear he would seek to avenge himself on his brother's supporters in Normandy, raising the likelihood of a further bout of armed conflict. Rufus spoke of the great mischief that had been done to him by the Normans. Overlooking his own recent coup de main at Westminster, he considered his brother to have in no way been provoked to meddle in England. The two men may never have been close. There was an approximate eight- or nine-year difference in age, so simple sibling rivalry might be ruled out as a reason for the two brothers being at odds: land and power were at stake, the future shape and control over the Anglo-Norman realm created by their father.

The king called a meeting of his nobles at Winchester to appraise them of plans which may have been maturing in his mind for some time. Discounting more general ambition or malice, Orderic claimed the English king was focused on the dire state of the Norman Church under his brother's rule, not the quest for dominance or revenge. Orderic wrote, 'Rufus was desirous of depriving his brother of the duchy [because] ... without a just patron, the Norman church was as a sheep in the midst of wolves.' Normandy is claimed by Orderic to have bordered on the anarchic, a place where petty tyranny prevailed unrestrained. He wrote,

> The infernal furies made human beings, villages and houses, the victims of fire and slaughter ... At the sight of so many evils the impoverished clergy weeps, the convents of monks lament, and the helpless people are everywhere desolate and sorrowful. They only rejoice ... who can rob and thieve without restraint ... The respect for the priesthood, to which once all did reverence, is nearly extinct in the flood of calamities which so violently rages ... those who are plunged in the gloom of the world's troubles can neither enjoy the light of true wisdom nor extricate themselves from the snares of vice.

As with 1088, the timeline for the coming years is problematic, but it would appear that Rufus, through surrogates and the judicious use of bribes, gained control of St Valery at the mouth of the Somme estuary and was able to place a stranglehold on Normandy's trade. He could do this by using the vast taxable wealth of England now at his disposal. The *Anglo-Saxon Chronicle* for 1089 says, 'England was greatly done for by unjust taxation and many other misfortunes.' A number of Norman noblemen were likely bought outright by Rufus. They declared for him and stood ready to welcome English knights to bolster their garrisons. Their castles in the main lay within the region most accessible to English invasion. Stephen of Aumale, a cousin of the Bastard's sons, for instance, fortified his castle on the banks of the River Bresle and welcomed troops loyal to Rufus to augment its defence. Gerard of Gournai, offered up the strongholds at Gournai, La Ferte-en-Bray

and Gaillefontain to the English king. At Rufus' behest, knights
rode out from these places and ravaged ducal lands to the south
and along the marches with the Vexin. The raids may have been
spearheaded by men from Rufus' own military household, even
though the king remained in England. Robert's sphere of control
quickly became limited in the main to the lands to the south of the
looping Seine.

Among the noblemen who kept faith with the duke in the face of
this threat was his cousin William of Evreux, a veteran of Hastings,
whose family were credited with contributing eighty longships
for the invasion in 1066, so were of very high status and worth.
For his participation in the battle Evreux gained only a modest
tenancy-in-chiefdom. The reason for such paltry reward may have
been that he had not at that time gained an age to take on more
extensive landholdings. Since then he had fought dutifully at the
Conqueror's side and had been captured and imprisoned during
the siege of Sainte-Suzanne Castle, in the Mayenne region, in 1085.
Like most of the men who supported the duke, Evreux hailed from
south of the Seine. The Norman civil war had in a sense resolved into
a north-south split. Another nobleman who rallied to Robert was
Helias of Saints-Saens, one of very few northern barons wooed to
the ducal cause. To gain Helias' support Robert had to provide him
with his, Robert's, illegitimate daughter to wed, and a substantial
land dowry comprising the county of Arques and the lordship of
Bures-en-Bray. Helias' loyalty clearly came at a premium, but he
from then on became one of the duke's most loyal allies.

Rufus meanwhile concentrated on fundraising to reward his
troops and bribe more Norman notables. His soldiers in Normandy
were well-paid and equipped professionals, sufficiently fired up
and compensated to contest small-scale actions independent of
kingly oversight. So successful were they, a major mobilisation
of Norman and French forces became necessary. In a dramatic
reversal of what had occurred in England, Robert now faced a
growing rebellion. The Anglo-Norman realm was more divided
than ever before.

8

COUNT OF THE COTENTIN

Hard to gauge at this time is the status of the Conqueror's youngest son Henry, and the little we know of his comings and goings is difficult to rationalise. Immediately after his father's death, Henry had busied himself organising transport for the mass of pre-weighed coinage he would inherit. He did not have any paternal land bequeathed to him, despite a last-minute plea to his father for territory he could call his own. The reason he had the coins carefully weighed was to make sure he had not been defrauded by his father's treasurers. He appears to have been a suspicious and somewhat needy young man. The bedside conversation between father and son, as imagined by Orderic, was, 'What my father do you give to me?' To which the king replied, 'I bequeath to you £5,000 from my treasury.' Upon which Henry said, 'What shall I do with this money, having no corner of the earth I can call my own?' The king answered, 'My son, be contented with your lot, and trust in the Lord.'

Henry's reported haste when securing the money may have been down to his fear that one of his brothers might muscle in before his casks were filled and transported to safety. The mass of silver was of a sufficient magnitude to require many heavy barrels to house the hundreds of thousands of pennies, and a substantial wagon train to move from place to place until stored somewhere permanent.

He had no real reason to worry. William Rufus was by this time on passage to England, and Robert, though close by, had not yet received the news of his father's death. A man of Robert's great rank and sensibilities would in any event hardly have deigned to prise money away from his youngest brother by force. William may have provided Henry with the great tranche of cash to secure an appanage from one of his brothers. If so, Robert proved the more accommodating. The duke needed money, whereas Rufus, with a rich country to tax, had less need of a large lump sum. Robert would probably not have countenanced bartering or cajoling when approached by Henry for land; any wheeling and dealing was likely left to others. Commercial activities of all kinds were shunned by the knightly classes in medieval times. St Augustine had pronounced money to be evil and to make a profit on the lending of money a sin; he had claimed that a merchant could seldom if ever please God. Robert was a religious man who would one day take the Cross and fight in the First Crusade. Even when abroad in the east and in extremis, he had no time for quibbling and bargaining.

For a sum that has been placed at either £3,000 or £5,000, Henry gained comital oversight over the greater part of western Normandy, a landholding which comprised the totality of the Cotentin Peninsula, including the regions of Coutances, Bayeux and Avranches, the monastery at Mont-Saint-Michel, and also a title and a place near the head of the ducal council. Henry from then on witnessed Robert's charters as Henrici *comitis*, a designation encompassing the Cotentin, which if anything understates the extent of his power base, which was later assessed by Orderic as a full third of the duchy. Robert was nothing if not generous. Charters issued by the duke in the autumn of 1087 and early 1088 are witnessed by Henry in the style 'Henry, the duke's brother', but this later changed to 'Count Henry'. Henry most likely had to do homage to his brother. He was not a mortgagee, but in fee, owing the duke knights and loyalty.

The Cotentin was a discrete entity, peripheral to ducal oversight. It could be ruled without interference from Robert. There should have been no need for conflict, and it seems Robert and Henry worked well together at first. The younger brother, already possibly the more worldly-wise of the two and better educated, was able to provide the elder with advice and counsel. Robert may have been glad of a sibling confidant and advisor. There are strong suggestions in the sources that he struggled to consistently apply himself to the rigours of governance. Many years later Henry would claim his brother to have been unfit to rule. This oft-repeated assertion cannot be discounted as merely retrospective and propagandist. Henry would have been in a good position to know at first hand his brother's strengths and weaknesses. Although now coming under challenge from revisionist historians, the weight of evidence suggests Robert's interests lay largely outside of politics and administration, and that he was prone to lean heavily on others when governing the duchy.

Henry had not in fact been left entirely landless when his father died. He had royal estates in England bequeathed to him by his mother, worth in excess of £300 a year according to the Domesday Book. To petition them from Rufus, after being given leave to do so by Duke Robert, he travelled to England, delaying his journey until such time as his arrival would not be interpreted by his brother as in any way unfriendly. He had steered clear of involvement in hostilities so far, but some of the money he paid Robert for his appanage may have been used to fund mercenaries to support the ducal cause. Rufus hid any enmity he may have felt in this respect. The sources state the meeting between the brothers passed off cordially. The king promised to honour his brother's land petition. Rufus always treated his social equals courteously and he would not have made an exception for Henry; but good grace and easy words may have concealed growing anger or indifference. Instead of making the lands in question over to Henry he appropriated them for himself and, as mentioned earlier, assigned them to Robert Fitz Haimon. This was done to make good on promises of rewards made at the height of the emergency in 1088.

The jewel within the land grant was the important barony of Gloucestershire. Henry's response, when learning of his disinheritance, is not recorded in the sources, but there are indications he may have made the round trip to England from Normandy more than once in an attempt to press his claim. On his return to Normandy after one such trip he came in for an even greater shock when placed under arrest by Bishop Odo's henchmen, possibly the very same heavies who had earlier placed Robert de Bellême in an armlock before bundling him off to stew in one of the bishop's many dungeons. The fear, as with Bellême, must have been that Henry had been 'turned' by Rufus. The precise sequencing of events is unclear. Henry and Bellême may have arrived back together in Normandy from England, and therefore been taken into custody at much the same time.

Being defrauded by Rufus and then arrested and interred by Robert would have been a great shock for an already anxious and avaricious twenty-year-old. Historians differ in how they view Henry at this time. Some see him focused entirely on his own interests to the exclusion of everything else, positing that his self-serving manner grated with both his brothers; others see him as a victim of his brothers' lack of interest in him. Arguing against Henry being taken into custody immediately, some sources indicate he was for a time appointed by Robert Curthose to the castellanship at Rouen and only later rounded upon and placed under house arrest. The chronicler Robert de Torigny (d. 1186) claimed Henry in some undisclosed manner threatened the peace of the duchy, endangering the life of the duke. The historian argued Robert Curthose came to fear for his life, so was well within his rights to arrest his brother and to strip him of the earlier bequeathed lands and titles. Torigny claimed that authorities had foiled a plot to unseat the duke in favour of Henry. More recent opinion about all this is divided, and whether the imprisonment was really justified as an outcome of Henry's plotting or merely Robert Curthose seeking to marginalise his brother cannot be established with any degree of certainty. There is, though, something of a Stalinist feel to all of this.

Another man locked up at this time was Robert de Beaumont, who had crossed Robert Curthose over the ownership of Ivry Castle, located on the banks of the River Eure, thirty miles or so to the west of Paris (now a town known as Ivry-en-Battaile, for a later battle). Ivry in the Conqueror's day was famous for its stone keep, which became a common feature of all later Norman castles. Beaumont claimed Ivry as an adjunct of his castle at Brionne. Robert Curthose needed to maintain close control over both of these castles, so could not afford for either of them to open their gates to Rufus' supporters. Said to have been acting under the influence of a hostile court faction (probably headed up by Bishop Odo), the duke had Robert de Beaumont imprisoned, secured Ivry Castle and then laid siege to Brionne Castle. Between the ninth hour and sunset on some unspecified day, the duke is said to have employed incendiary arrows to set alight the timber roof of the keep at Brionne, which was located high up within the strongly palisaded hilltop perimeter walls. Threat of incineration quickly forced the garrison to surrender.[5]

The three arrests – Bellême, Henry and Beaumont – may have been part of a wider purge, the full facts of which have gone unrecorded. Only later and with great difficulty did Beaumont's father manage to prise his son from captivity. Like Montgomery on behalf of Bellême, Roger de Beaumont had to remind the Duke of his family's unblemished loyalty to the Conqueror, perhaps even reminding the duke that his son had fought at Hastings. William of Poitiers wrote of Robert de Beaumont that day finding himself in battle that day for the first time:

> He was as yet but a young man and he performed feats of valour worthy of perpetual remembrance ... at the head of a troop which he commanded on the right wing he attacked with the utmost bravery and success.

It was a strong appeal that the duke could not but accept, even if Bishop Odo and others harboured reservations. Little wonder from this point on the Beaumont family nudged themselves ever closer to Rufus. By the year 1093, Robert de Beaumont was in England advising Rufus. He would later be made Earl of Leicester, a singular honour to add to his other titles, which included Count of Meulan, Viscount Ivry and Lord of Norton. Warring with the family might be viewed as a severe miscalculation on the part of Curthose and his advisors.

Henry, meanwhile, only gained release from prison after a petition was launched by a number of western Norman barons on his behalf. A ducal charter of 24 April 1089, witnessed by 'an unusually high number' of these lords, may have marked the event. The count's release date would appear to have occurred shortly after Robert Curthose's return from Le Mans. Henry, on this basis, would have spent around six months in confinement or under close guard. Robert did not visit Henry during this time, but probably this was not through malice: the duke was away on campaign much of the time. He did, though, find time to revoke his brother's comital title. The chronicler Henry of Huntingdon wrote,

> When Robert had sold Henry part of Normandy in return for his treasure, he [later] took the land away from him ... this was displeasing to God, but He deferred vengeance for a time.

Even after Henry's release, Robert Curthose remained wary of his brother and kept him at court under close observation. However, at some point the count absconded and returned into the west. The Cotentin lay outside direct ducal oversight and remained accessible to Henry. The nobility welcomed the count's return. Henry busied himself spinning webs of loyalty and patronage with the men who had lobbied for his release. The main castles we know that were fortified by him are at Avranches at the southern end of the Cotentin and Cherbourg at the northern end. The castles at Coutances and nearby Gavrai may also have been made ready. Power-hungry and militarily active, Henry, described by Orderic at this time as 'a young bull of a man', is said to have shrewdly won over by fair words or rewards many of his father's nobles to the support of his cause. He quickly established himself as the quasi-ruler of western Normandy. In the coming struggle between king and duke it cannot have been clear what side Henry would back. What does seem clear is that having expended much of the money inherited from his father, the count was not about to give his newly acquired lands up without a fight.

*

Through proxies, bribes and the infiltration of tight-knit kinship groups, Rufus tightened his grip on upper Normandy during 1089 and the spring and summer of 1090, in particular the high land abutting the Seine and Loire rivers. He had already gained control of a number of important castles in the region including the strongholds at Aumale and St Valery, both in the modern-day Seine-Maritime department of France. The port at St Valery was also at this time under his control. The English chronicler for 1090 says that Rufus by his astuteness or by bribes secured the castle at St Valery and the harbour. From these places Rufus' knights launched attacks against the duke's lands.

In an attempt to seize back the initiative Robert rode out from Vernon Castle, located on the banks of the Seine midway between Paris and Rouen, and attacked the English king's strongholds at Eu and La Ferte-en-Bray. The attacks might be likened to spoiling raids or preventive strikes. Robert Curthose's boldness at this stage owed somewhat to the fact he enjoyed the support of the French king, who made French knights available to the duke for the defence of the duchy. The king had a duty of care, only to have been expected of a lord on behalf of a vassal in extremis, so this was not in any way remarkable. Philip is said to have invaded Normandy 'with a great raiding-army' in support of the duke. The French king and the Norman duke, according to the *Anglo-Saxon Chronicle* for 1090, together besieged the castles that had been captured or were already in the hands of Rufus' supporters.[6]

Adding to the duke's woes, the Manceaux sought to take advantage of the civil war between the competing brothers. Although suppressed by Robert's earlier occupation of Le Mans, during the same campaign which saw the fall of the castles at Ballon and St Ceneri, a bold enterprise is said to have been entered into against the Normans by the Manceaux in 1090. Robert promptly fell ill – one of several 'time-outs' he took at moments of great danger, presumably because of a stress-related illness, not lethargy and idleness, as Orderic suggests. Many 'sworn men' had by this time failed him, and several had made over their castles to Rufus. Even more damaging, Philip of France at some point withdrew his support, having been paid off by Rufus. The duke must have been at a loss whether to face north to confront Rufus, or face south to deal with the Manceaux. He was between a rock and a hard place, to use modern jargon.

Fearful now also of a pre-emptive strike by the Manceaux, he called on Fulk IV of Anjou (a former enemy and a direct competitor against the Normans in Maine and Brittany) to mediate on his behalf at Le Mans. Fulk's price for agreeing to act as peacemaker was the hand of the young daughter of Simon de Montfort and Agnes, Countess of Evreux. This was the beautiful Bertrada, a niece of the veteran campaigner William of Evreux, who as we have seen was one of Robert Curthose's key allies at the time. Bertrada, though comely, was young and inexperienced. Fulk on the other hand had been married three or four times before. When approached about the match, Evreux complained that the duke was looking to his own interests at the expense of young Bertrada's virginity; this was perhaps a ploy to obtain in a tit-for-tat manner the best deal possible for the hand of the unfortunate maiden, who remained a pawn in the ensuing diplomatic wrangle. Evreux's price for his niece's maidenhead was the restoration of a number of fiefs to him, plus the reinstatement of family estates made forfeit by the Conqueror. Much of what

Evreux demanded he gained. Fulk took Bertrada as his bride and honoured his part of the deal by nipping the revolt on Normandy's southern borders in the bud. The region remained quiescent for at least a year.

Cast by Orderic as a man of 'many reprehensible, even scandalous, habits', Fulk's marriage to the young Bertrada de Montfort became the carnal highlight of a notably lusty life. Bertrada bore him a son, called Fulk the Younger, who would one day become King of Jerusalem. Historians in the twelfth century would discern the hand of God orchestrating the pairing, not simply the affairs of men. If nothing else, the affair serves to highlight the complex dealings entered into in medieval times to fashion favourable political outcomes without recourse to warfare.

Sometime in 1095, the abused Bertrada fled from her husband and threw herself upon the tender mercies of King Philip of France. Fulk suffered from painful bunions but this did not prevent him pursuing yet another young bride. He repudiated his marriage to Bertrada. King Philip then disavowed his own wife to seduce the castaway. Orderic wrote, 'The absconding concubine left the adulterous count and lived with the adulterous king.' Described as 'a gormandiser', a burgeoning belly had never prevented Philip from cosying up to the ladies. He is imagined as 'rotting away shamefully in the filth of adultery' when casting aside his queen, Bertha of Holland, for the younger model and in 1095 he would suffer excommunication as a result. When he and Bertrada rode into any town, the bells of the church are said to have fallen silent, only to start ringing again as soon as they left. His excuse for setting Bertha aside was that she had become too fat for him to lust over. This may have been true, but Philip was also famously fat. In later life the king is said to have grown weaker with each passing day. Abbot Suger wrote that after 'abducting the Countess of Anjou, Philip could achieve nothing worthy of royal dignity … consumed by desire for the lady he had seized, the king gave himself up entirely to the satisfaction of his passion, losing all interest in the affairs of state'.

Rouen, 3 November 1090

Henry at this stage must have feared being squeezed by both brothers. He kept his fortresses in the west prepared for war against one or other of them, yet when ignoble elements on Rufus' payroll at Rouen made hostile moves against the duke, rather than wait in the wings, surprisingly, he positioned himself firmly in the ducal camp. So little is really known about how the Bastard's sons interacted we can only speculate as to what Henry's motivations were at any particular time, but danger to the existing order at Rouen posed by the growing insurgency must have played to the duke's advantage. He was able to call on all noble Normans – even the out-of-favour Henry and the count's allies in the Cotentin – to rally to his side.

The count was in fact among the first men to do so. He may have been keen to demonstrate to his brother that he remained a man to be trusted when it came to the crunch and that any plan on Robert's part to strip him of his appanage in the Cotentin would have been a mistake. Henry also needed to sustain his hard-won alliances in the west. His future lordship depended on good relations with his western neighbours, many who were the duke's loyal vassals and therefore sure to back Robert against his Norman rebels. Robert may in fact have called on Henry's support as part of a more general call to arms. Orderic claimed Robert made a treaty with Henry, which bound the latter to support him against any insurgency. Henry would have wanted to avoid Rufus gaining control of Rouen, since this would have enabled the English king to become firmly established in Normandy – an outcome as much to Henry's disadvantage as to Robert's. Rufus might have expended more of his English treasure to buy his younger brother's loyalty but may have dismissed Henry as too young to worry about.

The insurgency at Rouen erupted at the beginning of November 1090. Loss of the city to the rebels would have been catastrophic for Robert, resulting in a more general overthrow of ducal authority. Normandy's one-time capital (from around 912 onwards until 1050, when William moved his centre of governance to Caen) was walled and strongly fortified. An imposing castle defended its south-eastern approaches. The city had been the trading hub most heavily hit by the recent English embargo. Trade being so important between England and the Continent, the port city must always have been a likely flashpoint. Even when the Vikings first arrived in the 840s they had occupied an ancient city, once the capital of the Roman imperial province of Lugdunensis Secunda. A warrior king of great size named Rollo (or Rolf) had been its medieval founder. A direct ancestor of William the Bastard and his sons, Rollo was so tall and heavy no horse could carry him. For this reason he is claimed to have always campaigned on foot, becoming known as 'the ganger'. He had commanded one of several predatory Viking warbands which campaigned from bases in East Anglia against the French at the beginning of the tenth century.

After defeat by Frankish mailed cavalry in a series of bloody skirmishes in the Loire Valley, some of the Viking warbands returned westward to England and Ireland, or returned to Scandinavia, while others like Rollo's raided less well-defended coastal areas of France, entering the wide estuary of the Seine. Finding the area only lightly defended, they travelled upriver and occupied Rouen. Here Rollo established his forward base of operations for attacks eastward toward Paris. Chronicler Flodoard of Rheims describes how after another campaign waged against the Vikings by Count Robert of Brittany the Norsemen had first begun to accept Christianity. Certain coastal districts were then ceded to them, including the river port of Rouen. The conversion of the Vikings to Christianity is a common theme in France and England at this time and is likely to have been the decisive act in achieving legitimacy of tenure.

Henry arrived at Rouen Castle toward the end of October at the head of his household retinue and with other notables. Through his promptness he helped save Robert from an ignominious reverse. Street brawls between opposing factions may already have been fought out on the city's thoroughfares by the time he reached the city gates. More severe fighting had not yet ensued.

The leader of the insurgency, a man named Conan Pilatus, was the richest of Rouen's citizens, a commoner who could boast many soldiers and armed retainers. Conan had built up and maintained a private army in breach of ducal law. The ranks of his insurgent bands included professional soldiers and townspeople opposed to the duke – an amalgam later to become known as the Pilatenses. Although a commoner, Conan was uncommonly rich and notably arrogant, the type of man abhorred by the Norman nobility, whose relative poverty fuelled in them a sense of outrage. Conan has been said to have been challenging the ruling class over an increasingly influential commercial class. With winter fast approaching, Conan alerted Rufus' knights to move promptly to assist in securing the city for the king. Had this message not also reached the ears of Robert's agents at around the same time via an informant, the fate of Rouen might have been well and truly sealed.

The fightback at Rouen is well documented. With Henry's troops already in the city, further ducal reinforcements under the command of Gilbert de Laigle arrived from the south on Sunday 3 November 1090, crossing the Seine by a bridge close to where the modern suspension bridge now stands. An Anglo-Norman force of three hundred men-at-arms led by Reynold de Warenne, a castellan of upper Normandy, who had set out from the castle at Gournay, arrived at much the same time from the opposite direction, entering Rouen unopposed by the west gate, left open deliberately by Conan's supporters to allow the knights immediate entry. De Laigle's troop, meanwhile, faced stiff opposition from rioters at the south gate, which may for a time have remained closed to them. Fighting in this sector became protracted. Fear was soon abroad that the duke's life might be endangered. The situation became so fraught that Robert had to be hurried away from the intensifying melee through the east gate and then by boat to the Priory of Notre-Dame-du-Pre, a pre-arranged escape route. At the nearby hamlet of Emendreville, today an industrial district of Rouen known as Saint-Sever, a number of the duke's close associates awaited him. Commoners who hailed Robert while en route were under no illusions as to the identity of their rightful lord; they waved and encouraged his flight. In a dramatic sense the peasantry might be seen as a counterpoint to the dangerous mercantile elements within Rouen, threatening the feudal order. Orderic wrote of the episode,

> While all was in the confusion of this wild fight, and the citizens hardly knew which side to take, the duke was persuaded by his friends to make his escape with a few followers, from apprehension that he was foolishly exposing himself to perils which could bring him no honour, and to the eternal ridicule of all the Normans. He therefore went out at the east gate, and was dutifully received as their lawful sovereign by the inhabitants of the suburban village, called Mal-Palu.

Although more might have been expected of the duke in a combative sense, the Normans feared that should harm come to him at the hands of a dishonourable enemy the ducal governance might be threatened. The idea a villainous upstart like Conan could directly challenge ducal rule and succeed was abhorrent to the loyalist Norman knightly classes. Robert might have resisted the urging of his advisors and remained to lead the fight, but instead he delegated authority to Henry, who was soon back in the thick of the fighting.

The battle fought in the streets and plazas of Rouen swung this way and that. Not until Gilbert de Laigle's knights successfully overcame the opposition they faced at the south gate and broke into the city, then charged down narrow paths and passageways with swords drawn, bellowing out the ducal battle cry, did the fight swing the duke's way. So inflamed had passions become, innocent and guilty alike were butchered. On the basis that tales grow in the telling, though, we should be cautious accepting too high a death rate, and some of the killing must be laid at the door of feuding townsfolk settling scores. Very few men from Reynold de Warenne's Anglo-Norman command are likely to have been killed. He and his troop fled the city at an early stage, hiding out in woods outside the walls until nightfall, before making their escape.

Conan became Henry's prisoner. Precisely when and how this came about is unclear. Near-contemporary sources differ as to whether Henry himself may have made the rebel captive or whether Robert sometime later entrusted Henry to deal with the miscreant. Without a trial of any sort or the opportunity to confess his sins, Conan, possibly hog-tied, was taken by the count's henchmen to the top of a high tower and thrown from the parapet. His battered body was later retrieved and tied to the tail of a horse to be dragged through Rouen's already blood-soaked byways in an act designed to strike terror into the hearts of men who might still harbour treacherous intent. The tower is said to have overlooked hunting grounds to the south beyond the Seine. It had once housed Henry's late parents' nuptial suite but predictably became known from then on as Conan's leap. The river it overlooked was described in some detail by Orderic as copiously laden with fish, with numberless merchant craft coming and going, carrying produce and merchandise of all kinds, as if an abundance of wealth that was now lost to Conan and his mercantile allies. Orderic Vitalis' account of what occurred is heavily burdened with New Testament analogies. Medieval authors were targeting a religious readership who would have anticipated God's intervention being played out through the actions of men. Orderic, our main source, seeks to extol Christian virtues even when recounting dark deeds. Underscoring knightly ideals, Henry is said by him to have warded off attempts by the serpent-tongued Conan to inveigle a pardon, saying to his tempter, 'By my mother's soul, there shall be no ransom ... only swifter infliction of the death he deserves ... No respite is due to a traitor.'

Henry acted with ruthless decision – disturbingly so. Yet near-contemporary commentators like William of Malmesbury viewed Conan's end as a just outcome, swiftly executed;

Malmesbury called it 'a speedy punishment and a fitting outcome for a man so palpably guilty of treason'. Henry may have sought to emulate or even outdo his father when it came to cold-bloodedness. Other captured rebels were swept up and carried off by Robert knights as captives, in the manner of earlier Viking raiders, to be incarcerated in 'loathsome dungeons', from which many would never again emerge to look out upon their native skies. One nobleman, William Fitz Ansgar, was imprisoned until the Ansgar family stumped up the tremendous sum of £3,000. That men could take matters into their own hands in this way has been seen as evidence of a lack of respect for the duke or of his inability to rein them in, but without Rufus' blood money none of this would have taken place.

The duke was said to have been angered by the rough justice meted out by his followers; he had, it is claimed, intended merely to imprison Conan and to act leniently with other intriguers. As in the context of Earl Waltheof, capital punishment was rarely the last resort of Norman justice. Henry may even have been censured by the duke. If the count had hoped to win his brother Robert over by acting in such a draconian manner, he was soon disabused.

*

Rufus had by this time expended a vast sum but had seen only patchy reward for his outlay. His subjects had been heavily taxed to fund the Normandy campaign. From England, through intermediaries, the king now focused his attention on sowing discord in the lands still under ducal control, where William of Evreux and Ralph de Tosny (the latter sometimes referred to in the literature of the times as Ralph de Conches) were feuding over a land dispute. Evreux may have been the more able of the two to call on widespread support in Normandy, trumping Tosny's ability to attract backers. The latter nevertheless held lands around Conches, Tosny and Acquigny, as well as other fiefs scattered north of the Seine and in the Cotentin, so was not entirely without support.

Importantly for what transpired, Tosny also held land in England, having gained the English estates of his nephew Roger of Hereford after the 1075 rebellion: these included manors in Berkshire, Gloucestershire, Worcestershire and Herefordshire.

Tosny first appealed to Robert Curthose to come to his assistance, but the duke failed to respond. Tosny had rallied to Robert's side in the late 1070s, when the rebel prince had defied his father. He had also later fought alongside the duke in Maine in 1088. For Robert not to mediate in the winter of 1090/1 is therefore something of a puzzle. Historians cite it as an example of the duke's faithlessness, but there are two sides to everything; and we have, in truth, very few facts to go on. The feud between Evreux and Tosny has been described as a long-running and a nasty private war along the march with Maine. Tosny had witnessed several of the duke's charters in the early 1090s, but according to his academic biographer C. P. Lewis he remained 'ever alert to his own interests'; what is more, Tosny's wife Isobel – a woman renowned, unusually, for donning armour and riding at her husband's side into battle – egged Tosny on to back Rufus over Robert.

Petty squabbles between competing noblemen were the curse of western Europe, and Robert seems to have been reluctant to take sides. He was dealing with two men who each had calls on his loyalty. The upshot was that he lost Tosny's support, driving the nobleman into Rufus' camp. The English king was happy to back Tosny, a man with lands in England, against Evreux. Rufus despatched armed support under the command of Stephen of Aumale and Gerard of Gournay to fight alongside this new ally in Normandy. The company rode south against the duke, preparatory to a full-scale English incursion south of the Seine to be headed up by the king in person.

9

HENRY IN PERIL

During the long winter of 1090/1 Robert Curthose attempted to reassert his authority by placing the castle at Courci-sur-Dive, located in the modern-day Vienne department in the Nouvelle-Aquitaine region of western France, under close siege. Robert's attack on Courci was in support of claims to ownership made by the recently imprisoned Robert de Bellême. Putting aside any earlier reservations as to Bellême's loyalty, and perhaps now less ready to take his uncle Odo's advice with respect to the Montgomery family, the duke now actively sought him out as an ally. Bellême had in fact dutifully fought alongside Henry and other ducal loyalists at Rouen, but he had acted in a self-seeking manner in the aftermath of the fighting by taking men hostage and demanding ransoms. It might seem surprising Bellême could oppose the duke at one moment and be his ally the next. At a distance of almost a millennium it is impossible to know what drove political alignments. Bonds between lord and subject were of course permanent, but long-running vendettas like that between Tosny and Evreux were equally important in swaying loyalties. Another of these long-running feuds existed between Bellême's family and the Giroie-Grandmesnils – the result of the earlier mentioned killings in the days when William Talvas and William d'Giroie had clashed. In fact, the two clans had been at loggerheads as long anyone could remember, with the dukes of Normandy very much piggies in the middle.

The Grandmesnil family, like the Montgomerys, figure prominently in Orderic Vitalis' writing. They were the founders of St Evroult monastery, the monk's home for most of his life. Hugh de Grandmesnil had fought at Hastings and became one of the Conqueror's most trusted lieutenants. For his service, he had gained shrieval responsibilities in Leicestershire, where he held sixty-seven manors. He had also been allotted land in Nottinghamshire, Hertfordshire, Northamptonshire, Gloucestershire, Warwickshire and Suffolk. Hugh was lucky to survive Hastings. During the battle his bridle broke during one the many cavalry charges that day, leaving him powerless to control his mount, which careered toward the spears of the English. Only when a great shout went up from the enemy did the horse shy away and bolt back in the opposite direction to safety. Hugh's sons had ridden out with Robert Curthose during the rebellion of 1078–9, earning their father's disapproval for doing so. A desire to make things right the following year had seen Hugh join others to act as a conciliator between William and Robert. Hugh and one or more of his sons had again supported the duke in 1088 when ravaging royal estates in England.

Robert Curthose joined forces with Bellême at the latter's siege lines around the Grandmesnil stronghold at Courci-sur-Dive, where a great wooden tower, known as the Belfry, had been built; it could be moved on four wheels and was designed to overlook a castle's defences and overawe its inhabitants. Robert was helping Bellême target the possession of a family for whom the duke had much to thank; retaining Bellême's undoubted military skills clearly trumped earlier bonds and affiliations. Once again, as with Ralph de Tosny, Robert stands accused of faithlessness, but this time with better cause. The Belfry might have succeeded in doing its job had not the defenders inside Courci sallied out and set fire to the structure. The bravery of the squire who scaled the tower to set the Belfry alight gained scant recognition from Orderic, who claimed God's wrath had fanned the flames and that the tower was destroyed because it had been erected, by a 'tyrannical order', during the days 'when the Feast of our Lord's Nativity should have been observed'. When forced to lift the siege in the face of the mounting threat posed by Rufus' mercenaries, the ducal army scattered.

*

Unlike in 1088, when Robert failed to engage in person during the rebellion against his brother, there can never have been any doubt that the more driven Rufus would make a personal appearance in the duchy after the debacle at Rouen. The king and his barons arrived in Normandy on 2 February 1091 (Candlemas). They sailed across the Channel aboard the royal longship *Sea Snake*, just one of a number of warrior-laden vessels which must have made the crossing. A comparable craft built for Edward the Confessor is described in the *Vita Edwardi* as 'equipped for six score fearsome warriors', with 'a golden lion' crowning the stern and 'a winged and golden dragon at the prow' affrighting the sea and belching 'fire with triple tongue'. The English ships carried over with them a fortune in silver coins. Rufus is said to have valued bribes above blades.

The king made his headquarters the castle at Eu in Upper Normandy, and soon there was a sizeable army of Englishmen and Normans operating in the region. By gaining control of upper Normandy east of the Seine and the Channel ports, Rufus and his knights succeeded in preventing any invasion attempt on England from the duchy in the future: an important achievement, even if this was not an immediately likely outcome. Rufus had also placed himself in a good position to dictate the remaining moves in the developing contest between the brothers. Many Normans owing allegiance to Duke Robert now deserted him, paying court to Rufus in the hope of gain and favour. Frenchmen, Bretons and Flemings are said to have crowded the roads to Eu to make their obeisance to the English king. The duke again appealed to the French king to come to his assistance, but the entreaty went unanswered: Philip may have been temporarily deafened by the incessant jangling of the mass of English silver coinage being counted.

Striking out northward, Robert sought and confronted his brother's forces. Rufus suffered a minor military reverse, but the setback cannot have amounted to much. Rufus was a cautious commander, and military prowess could not make up for Robert Curthose's lack of support. Intermittent fighting which may have threatened the fall of one of Eu's satellite fortresses and the capture of a number of Rufus' knights was in the end halted by the intervention of the exiled Bishop William of St Calais, who played a pivotal role in what followed. Reliant now on Robert's good graces, but eager to be reinstated at Durham, the wily St Calais had grounds to do both king and duke a favour. Encouraged by him, the brothers met face to face to seal their differences. We can imagine them embracing and offering up compliments and hospitality, while keeping fingers tightly crossed. In recognition of his peacemaking efforts, on 11 September 1091, St Calais recovered his bishopric at Durham.

With Rufus in Normandy were at least three major cross-Channel landholders: Robert Fitz Haimon, Hugh d'Avranches, Earl of Chester, and Bishop Geoffrey of Coutances. The latter had, it will be recalled, been caught up in the struggle for power which had erupted in 1088 and had at that time sided with the duke over Rufus. Fitz Haimon on the other hand had remained unblinkingly loyal to England's new king throughout and had afterwards materially benefited and gained heightened favour at court. Avranches, a Cotentin lord as well as an Anglo-Norman baron, may at some stage in the past have sided with Henry over Rufus, but by 1091 he was on good terms with both men. All three of Rufus' companions held lands in western Normandy and therefore had a strong interest in a deal being fashioned which would secure their landholdings and underwrite their ability to move freely between England and Normandy without the need of a letter of passport from duke, king or count.

Hugh d'Avranches

As his name suggests, Avranches owned paternal land in the Cotentin, won by his Viking ancestors. Although closer in age to Robert Curthose, and as far as is known on good terms with the duke, he had also befriended the otherwise isolated Henry from quite early on. Avranches' meteoric rise in the Norman pecking order after 1066 indicates him to have been a considerable politician and a popular one too. In England he could boast a marcher earldom based at Chester, where he founded the city's famous abbey, and from where he terrorised the northern Welsh, earning the sobriquet 'the wolf', Hugh Lupus. Cheshire in its entirety may have been granted to him sometime before 1070 by the Conqueror, who trusted him implicitly.

Avranches had been too young to fight at Hastings but had crossed to England soon after the battle and became one of the Conqueror's right-hand men. Outside Cheshire he gained a hotchpotch of other manors once owned by the late King Harold II, shared out by the Conqueror between Avranches and the late William de Warenne. He proved to be a skilled military commander and administrator. When based at Tutbury Castle overlooking the River Dove, in as yet unpacified Mercia, he oversaw the subjugation of Staffordshire and the northern march toward Wales. Tutbury still boasts a prominent motte, upon which the ruins of a later fourteenth-century keep now stand. The earl built another castle at Chester in 1070. It may have been from here that the Norman conquest of north Wales was first planned.[7]

As with other men close to the Conqueror, Avranches had acted as a go-between for the king and Robert in 1080, after the latter's rebellion. A friend to both men, he could mediate without risk of being seen as one-sided.

Robert Fitz Haimon

Avranches' colleague Robert Fitz Haimon was the son of the loyalist Haimo, sheriff of Kent. He had gained important landholdings that had once been earmarked for Henry as well as other lands made forfeit to the crown after the '88 rebellion, some of which had been gained from his travelling companion Geoffrey of Coutances. Father and son had stood four-square behind Rufus during the debacle in 1088. Fitz Haimon and Henry de Beaumont afterwards are claimed to have persuaded Gundulf, Bishop of Rochester, to build the large stone castle we see today at Rochester, to deter any future Norman sortie down the Medway. A marriage to Sibylla, the daughter of Roger de Montgomery, had then allied him with the great marcher lords of Shropshire. He became Gloucester's first feudal baron. He and Sibylla provided the funds to build a new church for the already existing abbey at Tewkesbury. In a picture now housed at the Bodleian at Oxford, he is depicted holding an impressive sword in his left hand and the church and abbey in miniature in his right hand. Dressed in a flowing red gown over a blue dress with matching hood and sleeves, Sibylla looks on.

Although granted by Rufus the lands left to Henry by Queen Matilda, Fitz Haimon remained on close personal terms with the Conqueror's youngest son. His relationship with Rufus was closer still – a closeness leading some to wonder whether the two men were lovers. Accounts dated to the 1130s mention his grief after Rufus' passing, and make specific mention to a new cloak which he lovingly placed on the funeral bier when the king's corpse was conveyed for burial.

Fitz Haimon became Rufus' champion in south Wales. The broad outlines of the later lordship of Glamorgan began to take shape under his authority. He commissioned the great timber palisade built on a pre-existing moated hillock within the crumbling walls of a Roman fort at Cardiff. The castle which grew up there would one day become the heart of a growing medieval town and would for a time serve as a prison for one of the Bastard's sons. Remorseless incursions into Wales spearheaded by Fitz Haimon came to characterise Rufus' reign. His raiding into Wales occurred after 1088, right on through the nineties. In 1090, at an unnamed battle fought in Wales, he is even accounted as getting the better of the Conqueror's one-time ally Rhys ap Tewdwr. Earlier compacts reached with Tewdwr by the Conqueror and Robert in 1081 appear to have broken down quite early on in Rufus' reign.

*

No deal with respect to the future relations of England and Normandy was ever likely to have been seen as better than a bad deal for men like d'Avranches, Fitz Haimon and Bishop Geoffrey. Rufus would have been under enormous political pressure to come to an accommodation with his brother for the sake of stability. Robert Curthose must have come under similar pressure. In the end, quite soon after Rufus' arrival in the duchy, the duke in fact had to concede all the land already occupied and fortified by Rufus and his turncoat allies north of the Seine. This concession comprised the castles at Aumale, Gournay and Conches (Ralph de Tosny's fortress), the port and county of Eu and other lesser castles already occupied or controlled by Rufus. These grants were an immediate condition of any final agreement, made to secure Rufus' gains and prevent any future invasion bid from Normandy. They in effect drew a line in the sand between the brothers by demarcating spheres of control. Philip of France may have had a hand in the mediation talks. He is known to have been with the duke and Rufus at Caen just before the brothers sat down together to discuss the finer points of the treaty (later, in the summer, it became known as the Treaty of Caen, *circa* August 1091).

An English king (and a very rich one at that) had now come to control large swathes of upper Normandy, which may have given Philip room for pause. From Robert Curthose's perspective, the territorial concessions represented acknowledgment that a full half of Normandy and as many as twenty castles lying north of the Seine were now lost to him; the agreement in effect recognised the military status quo. Rufus had mobilised superior military and financial assets to exact a heavy price from his brother. He had won no battles; rather, bickering self-interest between noblemen and floods of English money in the form of judicious bribes and incentives, financed by English taxpayers, had weakened the duke's grip on governance and allowed Rufus' surrogates to make important political inroads.

The details of the final deal, ratified by twelve witnesses on each side were:

(1) Robert would cede to Rufus the earldom of Eu, the monastery at Fecamp, the abbey at Mont-Saint-Michel, the port of Cherbourg and the castles now held by Rufus and his supporters. These were major territorial concessions, some of which were made at the expense of Henry.

(2) Rufus would support the duke in reducing to his obedience the province of Maine and the castles on Normandy's southern borders which were still resisting ducal oversight. Robert may, as a quid pro quo, have agreed to back the English against Welsh and Scottish incursions.

(3) Rufus would additionally restore lands to such Normans as had lost them during the '88 rebellion, with the exceptions of Bishop Odo and Eustace, Count of Boulogne, neither of whom the king could tolerate regaining a foothold in England. Rufus further agreed to assign his elder brother land in England, the specifics and extent of which would be agreed at a later date.

(4) It was also agreed that if the duke should die without a legitimate male heir, Rufus should gain the duchy. In like manner, should Rufus die first, the duke would rule in England as king.

Rufus had the upper hand throughout. Robert arguably ceded to his brother too much territory. The English king may have seen his gains as the first phase of a longer campaign to reunite Normandy and England. Revisionist historians, though, question the one-sidedness of the deal, arguing the brothers were attempting to reunite the Anglo-Norman realm and were working together in a way that would be acceptable to their barons. It could even be claimed as acknowledgement that Robert and Rufus saw the reunification of the Anglo-Norman realm as a desirable goal. Crucially for what followed, Henry suffered disinheritance for as long as either of his brothers or their legitimate heirs should live. The elder brothers envisioned a Norman commonwealth that sidelined Henry. The count's academic biographer C. Warren Hollister has called him 'the great victim of the treaty'. It can be argued Mont-Saint-Michel and Cherbourg were not really in Robert's gift to give. Even allowing for the count's overreach at Rouen, Robert's contriving against Henry in his dealings with Rufus remains difficult to square. All we have to fall back on as justification is that Robert and Rufus felt threatened by their brother's popularity in Normandy and both by now feared him. The count, for his part, made strenuous objections. He accused his brothers of covetousness and of leaving him close to destitute.

The upside of the treaty was that the Anglo-Norman realm for a short time became a cooperative venture; the downside was that, because of Henry's exclusion, a further round of destructive in-fighting could not long be put off.

Mont-Saint-Michel, Lent 1091

Henry refused to be cowed. He fell back with his knights to occupy the tide-locked citadel at Mont-Saint-Michel at the mouth of the Couesnon River, near Avranches. First and foremost a Benedictine monastic site, Mont-Saint-Michel was an unassailable fastness in the eleventh century, rising to over 300 feet above sea level, and only accessible at low tide, and even then at great risk. Tides here are among Europe's most treacherous. Medieval pilgrims making their way to the site called it 'Saint Michael in peril of the sea', which was also the formal title for the lord of the mount. The structural composition of the town is held to have exemplified the society which constructed it: from top to bottom, God, abbey, monastery, halls, stores, domestic housing and, outside the walls, the dwellings of the local fishermen and farmers. In 1067 the monastic authorities at Mont-Saint-Michel had formally recognised the Conqueror's kingship over England and for this William had rewarded them with lands in England, including an island off the south-western coast of Cornwall, modelled after Mont-Saint-Michel, to become the Norman priory of St Michael's Mount.

Henry remained intent on making himself semi-independent of his brothers. He was not going to easily give up the Cotentin and his other western lands. He resolved to hit back if his brothers ganged up on him. He strengthened the garrisons in all the nearby castles and enlisted men from the local abbey complex at Caen to reinforce them. Much of this support soon dissipated, however. Noblemen and ecclesiastics in western Normandy who held lands in England and the Cotentin could not afford to get on the wrong side of Rufus or Robert. Alone of the great cross-Channel noblemen holding land in the Cotentin, Hugh d'Avranches may have expressed concern for Henry's welfare. He may also have been the one who suggested to Henry that he entrench himself at the mount and seek to brave it out. Avranches has been claimed to have acted as a brake on Rufus' worst excesses when disagreements between the brothers became overheated. Bishop Geoffrey of Coutances, no friend of Henry's, may on the other hand have encouraged Rufus to attack the count's lands and drive Henry from the region. Geoffrey's advice in the end was taken over any moderating advice from Avranches.

King and duke were both soon concentrating their forces in the Cotentin, squaring up to Henry. The precise date of the mount's isolation is unclear, but some part of the period of Lent was spent in arms.[8] When called upon to vacate the mount, Henry did not budge. Instead, he countered by launching sorties against his brothers' enveloping siege lines. Rufus based himself at nearby Avranches Castle, which may up until then have been occupied by Henry's soldiers, having, it might be assumed, been given leave to do so until the last minute by Avranches. Presumably the garrison was evacuated when Henry fell back on Mont-Saint-Michel. Robert established himself at the nearby Benedictine Priory at Genets, an old port serving the oppidum of Avranches, located some six miles to the west. Genets would have been vitally situated for supplying the besieging armies. Armed men based at Ardevron Castle guarded against Henry's garrison being supplied or reinforced. Robert is sometimes considered to have wanted to see Henry flee from the Cotentin into Brittany unmolested, but the extensive blockade would appear to argue against this.

The mount's main Achilles heel was its lack of a water supply, something which must have been known to the besieged in advance of Rufus' and Robert's arrival. Barrels of water and wine would have been stockpiled in the castle in readiness, but the supply would not outlast an extended siege.

On the Bayeux Tapestry two knights are depicted being saved by Harold Godwinsson from engulfing quicksand on the tidal flats surrounding Mont-Saint-Michel. A quarter of century later, flouting such risks, Rufus spent much of his time engaged in jousts on the sands within sight of the mount. There were also tourneys between knights from the rival camps. On one occasion, Rufus fell from his horse when struck, to be dragged along the sand by his foot. He might easily have been killed. His accidental assailant, a dumbstruck and fearful Breton in Henry's pay, was afterwards praised by the king for his prowess and enlisted as one of his own household knights: 'By the holy face of Lucca,' cried Rufus, 'you shall be my man.'

After about two weeks of close siege, the question of Henry's diminished supply of drinking water became a matter of contention between king and duke. The latter favoured making water available to ease their brother's suffering, saying it was 'the common right of mankind'. On occasion he allowed parties from the mount a free pass to bring supplies of drinking water and gifts of wine gourds back. Rufus raged at his elder brother's lack of resolve. The characters of the king and duke are here seen as boldly realised opposites. When criticised face to face by Rufus, Robert is said to have retorted, 'Should we leave our brother to die of thirst? Wherever shall we look for another if we lose this one?' There is an almost comic aspect to this. He may, though, have been remembering the loss of their other brother, Richard. As has been pointed out by Katherine Lack, Robert would have remembered the death of Richard, who had been only a few years Robert's junior, whereas Rufus, much younger, can scarcely have been old enough to have felt the loss. Historians have also speculated that the duke, as the elder son, was in a sense exerting his overlordship over both of his younger brothers: allowing supplies to be shipped to the one and fending off objections from the other.

Rufus soon afterwards abandoned the siege altogether. He is said to have withdrawn unappeased. He may have realised he had been played by Robert as a proxy bailiff, but was not the sort of man to dwell on his setbacks. William of Malmesbury considered Rufus to have been 'an eloquent critic of his own mistakes', adding that any resentment the king may have felt soon 'dissolved into laughter'. Rufus and Robert parted on good terms. Two weeks later, Henry sued for surrender. The count, according to Orderic, left the fortress 'with honour intact'. Defeat is turned into a victory of sorts by this claim, but it is likely a retrospective embellishment on Orderic's part since Henry is described elsewhere as unwillingly prised from the mount and imprisoned at Rouen. If Henry had any of his inheritance left, several wagons would have been needed to cart away the casks holding the treasure, but first of all his Norman and Breton mercenaries would have had to be paid off. Henry's money may in fact have already been fully expended by this time; bands of disgruntled soldiers may have been left to make do and mend. It is also possible Robert confiscated what remained to meet the costs of mounting the siege.

For a time after his release, the count is claimed to have eked out an existence in the manner of a landless adventurer, attended upon by just a single knight, a clerk and three squires. Henry's sojourns have been spun as character-forming, with prudence and mercy instilled through suffering, in much the manner of a holy man when sacrificing hearth and home to wander. Cast adrift by his brothers, he is held by the chroniclers to have become closer to God as a result. Much more is imagined than can have been real. The count is placed in Brittany for a while, then in the French Vexin, where he may have hoped to gain a fiefdom from Philip of France. A relatively unimportant third son of a dead king, now operating outside his brothers' orbits, his roaming across Europe passes beyond knowing, much as Robert's had in the years leading up to the Conqueror's death.

FIRE AND FURY IN THE NORTH

Why should we [the English] despair of victory,
when victory has been given to our race as if in fee by the
most High? Who would not laugh rather than fear when
fighting the worthless Scots with their half-bare buttocks?
Ailred of Rievaulx

As Henry exits the scene, Edgar *atheling*, Margaret of Scotland's brother, re-enters to play a crucial role in moderating relations between the Bastard's sons – even though, like Henry, he himself had become a victim of the Treaty of Caen. An important footnote of the agreement between king and duke had seen Edgar face expulsion from Normandy at the insistence of Rufus. Prior to this, Edgar had come to hold land on both sides of the English Channel. During the latter part of the Conqueror's life, Edgar is known from the evidence of Domesday Book to have been granted two estates in Hertfordshire. Robert had also made over to him gifts of land in Normandy. Edgar may have taken part in the recent fighting against Rufus' forces in 1090/1 at Robert's side. When expelled, he sailed from Normandy for Scotland once more, to the court of his brother-in-law Malcolm Canmore. Ousting Edgar betrays unease in Rufus' mind that his elder brother and the last living male Anglo-Saxon claimant to the English throne had allied themselves against him; even if Edgar's prospects of one day becoming King of England were vanishingly slight. The English king's insistence Edgar be dispossessed and banished has since been described as 'vindictive'; this is how the victim and his brother-in-law Malcolm Canmore must have viewed it.

With Rufus busy in Normandy locking horns with Henry, the Scots once again raided into Northumbria, punishing Rufus. Chroniclers tell of Northumbrian men, women and children fleeing to the woods and mountains to avoid the Scottish advance. The inhabitants of Durham hurriedly took refuge behind the walls of the city, carrying with them all their household goods and herding their livestock to safety. The beasts were shepherded into the town cemetery, where there was sufficient grass to feed them. Richard of Hexham described a similar raid and reported captured English womenfolk being stripped, bound and roped together, all the while goaded with spears. Scarcely a Scottish household, according to Richard, was from then on without its English slave.

Local Northumbrian forces moved to confront the invaders and for a time Durham must have been beset on all sides by rival bands. Then all of a sudden the Scots decamped and set off for home. The sacred relics of St Cuthbert gained the credit for vanquishing the invaders, but the hurried departure might more credibly be linked to the prompt intervention of English shrieval forces and a desire on the part of Malcolm's men to leg it home with their booty intact.

Bound by the terms of their treaty, which committed both men to cooperate when their common wealth came under threat, Rufus and Robert now worked in partnership to organise a military response to the Scottish attacks. Haste is indicated in the scant sources. Plans to march against the Manceaux were put on hold and other important engagements cancelled. Henry cannot at the time have posed an overarching threat to the duchy; if he had, Robert might have made his excuses to remain in Normandy. 'Rootlessness and relative impoverishment' are said to have prevented Henry from turning the situation to his advantage. By early August 1091,

Above: The coronation of King Harold in 1066 as depicted on the Bayeux Tapestry. Harold enjoyed the title 'sub-regulus' during the latter part of the Confessor's reign, militarily legitimised by his success against the Welsh.

Below: Bosham Church, near Chichester, West Sussex. Harold is portrayed on the Bayeux Tapestry entering and exiting the church before embarking on his ill-fated embassy to Normandy in 1064.

Left: The famous single-mast longships of the period made good use of favourable winds and could otherwise make a fair headway when rowed with the mast lowered. This is an original longship, known as Skuldelev 2, displayed at the Viking Ship Museum in Roskilde, Denmark.

Below: Replica longship berthed at Roskilde.

Above: The ruins of Wigmore Castle, Herefordshire. Ralph de Mortemer made Wigmore his family's home and main ecclesiastical centre of worship. Very soon after the Conquest his family came to govern extensive tracts of the Welsh borders from here.

Below: The marches toward Wales, from inside Wigmore Castle looking out into rural Herefordshire. During the early Norman period many castles were raised along the marches to keep the Welsh at bay.

Left: The Welsh warlord Rhys ap Tewdwr, the doyen of a future royal house of England. He was the victor of the Battle of Mynydd Carn in 1081, but was defeated and killed in battle at Brecon in 1093.

Below: A good example of a motte at Christchurch, Dorset, built in 1100, soon after the death of William Rufus, by Henry's great ally Richard de Redvers, who hailed from Reviers in the Cotentin.

Right: Robert Fitz Haimon and wife Sibylla. Haimon became Gloucester's first feudal baron. He and Sibylla provided the funds to build a new church for the existing abbey at Tewkesbury.

Below: Roger de Montgomery controlled the most westerly of the Sussex rapes at Chichester, beside the River Lavant. The motte remains shown here lie close by the city walls in modern-day Priory Park.

Left: Arundel Castle in West Sussex, built by order of Roger de Montgomery to control the rape of Arundel. The massive stone keep was added in the reign of Henry I.

Below: Ruins of Lewes Priory, known as the Priory of St Pancras, founded by William I de Warenne and his wife Gundrada in around the year 1081. At its height, it boasted one of the largest monastic churches in the country and housed around fifty Cluniac monks.

Brionne Castle. Standing today above the village of the same name, the great donjon of Brionne pictured here may post-date 1090 when attacked and taken by Robert Curthose. (Stanzilla, Wikimedia Commons)

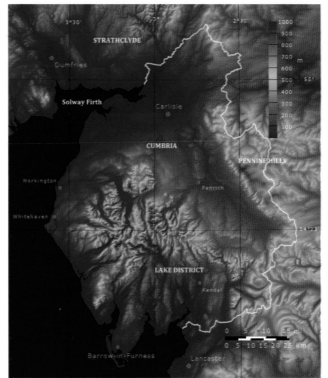

Topographical map of Cumbria, showing the proximity of Carlisle to the Solway Firth and the Scottish border. (PawełS, Wikimedia Commons)

Above: Norman door and Saxon rood at Romsey Abbey, Hampshire. The rood depicted is thought to have once been situated above the chancel of the original Saxon church. There is also a second, smaller one in the abbey. Henry I's future queen, Matilda of Scotland, was educated here in the late 1080s and early 90s.

Below: Romsey Abbey. The original abbey was founded by King Edward the Elder in 907, but destroyed by the Vikings around one hundred years later.

Above: Ludlow Castle bailey, with the great marcher castle's ruins in the background. The castle's stone fortifications were added from around the 1080s onwards and were finished before 1115, during the reign of Henry I.

Below: Inside the de Lacy era keep at Ludlow, with distinctive Norman pillars.

Above: The Varangian Guard. After 1066 the guard gained an influx of Anglo-Saxons. Anna Komnene, the Byzantine Emperor's daughter, referred to them as 'axe-wielding barbarians'.

Below: Robert of Normandy at Antioch. Robert Curthose's heroics on crusade were well publicised in western Europe.

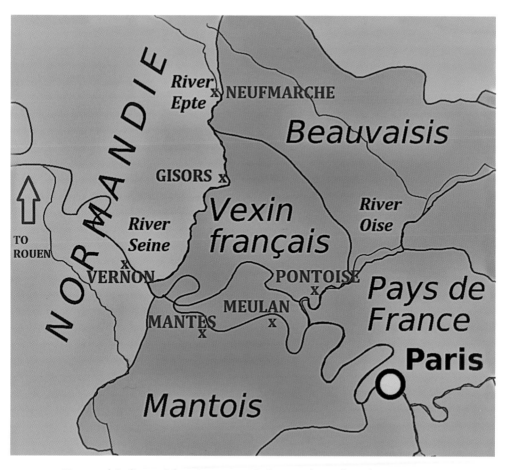

Normandy's disputed frontier zone with the French. (Wikimedia Commons)

Detail from stained-glass window at the Cathedral of Saint Corentin at Quimper, in Brittany, depicting Anselm in conversation with a bored-looking William Rufus.

Left: The Rufus Stone in the New Forest is reputed to mark the spot where the king fell mortally wounded while on a hunting trip.

Below: The New Forest with the Rufus Stone seen in the middle of the picture. We are looking south-west, the direction from which the fatal arrow is said to have been loosed.

Above: The beach at Portchester in Hampshire, beside the walls of the roman castle. On 20 July 1101, Robert Curthose landed here with an army of knights.

Below: Tomb of Robert Curthose at Gloucester Cathedral. The wooden effigy has its legs crossed to denote that a crusader sleeps below.

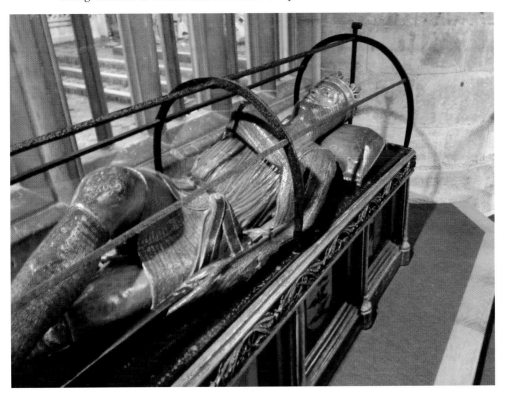

Above: Canterbury Cathedral. This perspective is from the cloisters, once the hub of Archbishop Lanfranc's medieval monastery.

Below: Christchurch Priory in Dorset, as seen from the top of the castle motte. Rufus' chancellor Ranulf Flambard was the church's first dean and it was likely he who ordered the building's construction.

Above: The Norman house at Christchurch, once the home of the de Redvers family, who were important allies of Henry I and hailed from the Cotentin Peninsula.

Below: Canterbury stained-glass window, with St Anselm in the centre, flanked by archbishops Anselm and Baldwin, and with Rufus, red-bearded, on the extreme left and a white-bearded Henry on the right.

Tinchebrai, Normandy, where the Anglo-Norman realm was reunited after a short but fierce battle. (Hamonjp, Wikimedia Commons)

Henry I (left) and William Rufus (right) set in stone at Canterbury Cathedral.

king and duke were together in England gathering their forces at Windsor. They planned an invasion northward into Scotland with a fleet (*scypfyrd*) and an army (*landfyrd*), something only previously achieved by the Roman general Agricola in the first century AD, King Athelstan in the ninth century, the Conqueror in 1072 and Robert himself in 1080.

Rufus is said by Orderic to have ambitiously assembled 'the whole military force of England' to move against the Scots. Seaways and navigable river systems, weather permitting, afforded by far the safest and quickest mode of travel for supply trains in medieval times, avoiding dangerous chokepoints on the land routes, but by the late autumn of 1091 the passage of boats up the eastern seaboard into Scotland would have been a fraught business. Arguably, the expedition should not have been attempted until the following spring. Fifty ships under rowlock and sail, laden with corn from Wessex, plus warships and other ancillary craft set off nonetheless, hugging the east coast, heading north. The king and duke rode with the *landfyrd*, halting at various points along the Great North Road, before arriving at Durham around mid-September for the formal reinstallation of the once again puffed-up Bishop William of St Calais. The bishop had travelled with them from Normandy and had then accompanied them to Durham via Windsor. His formal homecoming – a grand affair – was attended by all the great and good of Northumbria.

Durham was then as now an important pilgrimage centre. The king and duke would likely have stopped there to pray even had there not been an important ceremony to attend. A stone church built at Durham during the reign of Cnut the Great housed St Cuthbert's relics but was now awaiting demolition to make way for St Calais' new cathedral – one day to perch grandiosely above a bend in the River Wear. The conjunction of cathedral and castle now constitute an impressive World Heritage Site. How long the brothers lingered over their devotions at Durham is not known. Their prayers were in any event interrupted by disastrous news from the coast. Just four days shy of the start of the Michaelmas festivities, which commenced on 29 September in 1091, disaster struck when the bulk of the ships and crews of the Anglo-Norman fleet lying off the Northumberland coast 'wretchedly perished', presumably driven by wind or tide onto dangerous rocks near Coquet Island, then the site of a thriving medieval monastery. Locals spoke of another of the region's several saints contriving the disaster: the long-dead but easily angered St Oswy.

The Anglo-Norman expedition had been hamstrung, yet the brothers held to their task and led the land army further north. Bad weather then set in, causing many of their scurriers and outriders, caught in the wilds, to perish from cold and hunger. The initiative passed to the Scots, who occupied a strong position in Anglian South Lothian, probably on the north bank of the Tweed. The river barrier between the Scots and Anglo-Norman armies is sometimes assumed to have been the Forth (the 'great river') but the width of the Forth estuary would have prevented contact, even with an intact fleet, and a confrontation further upriver in Stirlingshire would have meant a significant overland march in midwinter, which seems unlikely to have been attempted without guaranteed supplies. It is to Rufus and Robert's credit they had not turned back before this. Rufus' aim may have been to ravage and terrorise Scottish lands but essential foraging now became the priority. Bitter weather very much favoured the Scots, who lay much closer to their sources of supply. The Scots' main advantage when fighting in their own backyard was better knowledge of the terrain, a hardy constitution and a penchant for irregular warfare. The anonymous author of the *Gesta Stephani* (*The Deeds of King Stephen*) claimed them to have been 'neither overcome by excess of cold, or enfeebled by severe hunger, putting their trust in swiftness of foot and light equipment'. The Anglo-Normans, on the other hand, now had a dangerously over-extended line of communications, stretching back to Newcastle.

Earlier agreements made by Malcolm and the Conqueror would have lapsed upon the latter's death; moreover, as far as is known Malcolm had not entered into any new arrangements with Rufus and had not visited the English court. Treaties were made between monarchs, not states as would be the case today. Malcolm would not have considered himself under any particular obligation to Rufus, whom he had never met. Through an embassy across the river led by Edgar he made this clear, saying, 'King William, I owe you nothing except war.' He nonetheless recognised a bond of kinship with Robert, saying, in words made up by Henry of Huntingdon, 'If I see Robert, the eldest son of the late King William, I am ready to pay him the homage which is due to him.'

That Malcolm saw Robert to be worthy of homage but did not feel the same about Rufus was likely both an insult and a calculated ploy to divide and rule. Robert was escorted by Edgar to the Scottish camp. During a three-day sojourn, Malcolm allowed the duke to inspect the Scottish army, telling him he wished Rufus might have met him in battle to feel at first hand 'the points of his army's spears'. The vanguard of the Scottish army on the river bank was backed up by an even stronger main body, lying over the crest of a nearby hill. Robert may have been flattered by the attentiveness of the Scottish king, but advised him to submit to his brother and become his friend; he added that the situation in England and Normandy had very much altered since the time of the Conqueror, when the two men had last met. If Malcolm had sought to drive a wedge between the brothers he had failed.

It should be seen to Robert's credit that he did not seek to take advantage of the strong position he found himself in. In subsequent negotiations – we do not really known if these were made between Malcolm and Rufus face to face, or by Robert acting for his brother and Edgar for Malcolm – the Scottish king asserted rights over the Lothian region, claiming the territory had been granted to him by Edward the Confessor; and adding that it had later been reconfirmed by the Conqueror. In person or through emissaries Rufus accepted a continuation of the agreement.

At some point the two kings must have met and embraced. The English chronicler for 1091 says 'Malcolm came to Rufus and became his man'. The scribe goes on to confirm that all previous compacts agreed between Malcolm and the Conqueror were reinstated ('in all such obedience as had been done in 1072'). Twelve unnamed villages are said by John of Worcester to have been ceded to the Scots and an annual bounty of 'twelve marks in gold' agreed to be paid by Rufus. The alliteration of twelve (villages and marks) might indicate a link between place and payment, but may also have been a chronicler's device to denote completeness. Twelve in scripture is considered to be the perfect number, symbolic of God's design: twelve disciples; Jacob's twelve sons, etc. Yet it is now thought these twelve villages really existed, and therefore still do; they have tentatively been identified as in Tynedale, a region on the English-Scottish borders stretching from the Cheviots to the Alston Moors: Haltwhistle, Thirlwall, Walltown, Knarsdale, Kirkhaugh, Melkridge, Thorngrafton, Plenmellor, Ridley, Whitfield, Elrington and Ouston. All twelve are claimed as in the past having been gifted to the Scots by Siward, Earl of Northumberland; a gift that was later ratified by King Cnut. The presumption must be that Edward the Confessor and William the Conqueror also accepted Scottish control over Tyndale. Whatever the truth of any of this, Rufus had for the time being solved the Lothian question.

The English king's knights despoiled the lands they passed through on their return southward. William of Malmesbury wrote how they plundered the north of England 'as if it were an enemy land'. Symeon of Durham, on another occasion, claimed Rufus' entourage did much greater harm than any 'court or raiding army ever ought to do in a land at peace'. The proceeds of plunder represented a hefty bonus on top of already enviable pay rates. Rufus' reputation as a generous paymaster attracted fighting men from far and wide, from places as distant as the Middle East. A scarcity of well-trained mercenaries in western Europe meant incomers could set their own pay rates and act as they pleased.

Edgar accompanied the Anglo-Norman army on its travail south. He had acted as a valuable intermediary between the two sides and his close friendship with Robert had been rekindled. Rufus may have remained wary of him nonetheless. The phraseology in the

Anglo-Saxon Chronicle, when stating William kept Robert and Edgar with him at all times, might indicate a growing fear of the pair on Rufus' part, and their sudden departure for Normandy via the Isle of Wight on 23 December 1091 is now generally accepted as signalling a breakdown in relations between king, duke and *atheling*. Robert may in fact have been aggrieved at Rufus' refusal to accompany him back to Normandy to help quell the ongoing revolt in Maine. Rufus had also failed to identify and make available lands in England that had been promised to Robert. Whatever the cause, the quid pro quo agreement made at Rouen was breached: the English chronicler for 1091 says, 'Little faith was kept in their [the brother's] covenants.'

*

Not until the spring or early summer of 1092 does Henry re-enter the historical record, when seizing control of the great hilltop fortress town of Domfront, in south-western Normandy. His activities and whereabouts up until this time remain uncertain, but his alienation from his brothers had persisted. He is claimed to have gained control of Domfront with the help of both foreign and local backers. Sited high above the Varenne Valley on a prominent sandstone escarpment in the Passais region, the citadel had great strategic potential. The fortress, which probably at the time comprised a wooden keep ringed by earthen defences, was located close to the Norman border with Brittany and Maine, on an important road network. The site has since been described as 'a vital springboard for the conquest of Normandy'.

The Conqueror had wrested Domfront from the Angevins in 1049 after a lengthy siege, before later granting the lordship to William Talvas, Bellême's ill-famed maternal grandfather. The bastion had become part of the lord's maternal inheritance and had been strongly garrisoned by him with men he thought he could trust after the Conqueror's death. Now, in a dramatic turnaround, he had been ousted to make way for Henry. Bellême's troops may have been chased off by Domfront's castellan, with the support of Breton mercenaries on Henry's payroll. The inhabitants may have also had a hand in the affair; they are claimed to have suffered ill usage at Bellême's hands and are said to have 'thrown off his yoke'. An Englishman named Achard, Henry's one-time jousting master, was one of his enablers in the spring of 1093, and was later rewarded by Henry with lands in Berkshire. Domfront had been the most westerly of Bellême's strongholds and the closest to Henry's appanage in western Normandy. The ruins to be seen today include the castle ramparts, casements and keep, and give a good impression of the stronghold's size.

The count's seizure of Domfront might best be seen as round one in a campaign to regain what he felt remained rightfully his. He did not rest on his laurels. From Domfront he soon seized back large chunks of his former lands in the west. Church records from Domfront suggest he was an exacting taskmaster, who coerced the local peasantry to work on strengthening the castle defences and building a new stone donjon. His heavy-handed rule may have been no less severe than Bellême's had been. Henry also renewed his alliances with the great men of the region: Hugh d'Avranches, Roger de Mandeville and Richard de Redvers, to name but three. The grouping that coalesced around the count at this time has been described by Hollister as a 'court in waiting'. One grant of a castle which he made to Avranches, made as 'in fee to a Vicomte', has been held to indicate Henry was acting in the manner of 'a duke of the west' – not merely the out-of-favour brother of a duke.

Robert Curthose and Robert de Bellême now worked together to bring about Henry's downfall. Henry meanwhile ravaged ducal lands, assisted by members of the Giroie family, who, as we have seen, were long-time enemies of Bellême's. The sources suggest Henry acted much in the manner of a foreign despoiler, but things did not always go his way: the Giroie castle at St Ceneri soon fell to Bellême when the garrison bolted upon hearing the fake news that their commander was dead. Bellême, the instigator of the ruse, ordered the castle to be sacked and invited the monks from a nearby monastery to join in and take away what they liked. They promptly arrived and carried off the withered arm of the named saint, a priceless relic. Elsewhere, Robert Curthose captured and destroyed a newly built Giroie castle at Montaigu which had been raised illegally in the face of a ducal proscription. He also had a castle built at Chateau Gontier in the Pays de Loire and garrisoned it with loyal knights to counter Henry's raids. This freed him to campaign further south, where a continuation of internecine conflict and general lawlessness on the borders with Maine threatened to destabilise the region. He is said to have ridden out at the head of the *exercitus Normanniae* (the whole Norman army). That he was free to do so argues against his authority in the region as undermined by Henry's actions and Rufus' blood money as has so often been claimed.

Nor did Robert rely overly on Robert de Bellême. Part of the deal struck to evict Robert Giroie from Montaigu was to cede back to him lands forfeited in the 1060s by the Conqueror; and, puzzlingly to a later observer, this transaction appears to have disadvantaged Bellême. For the duke to gamble on losing Bellême's support at such a critical time indicates that having augmented his support he was well positioned to do so. The episode has been seen by one of the duke's biographers, William M. Aird (*Robert Curthose, Duke of Normandy*), as the workings of a deliberate policy on the duke's behalf to exert ducal control over two feuding subjects, and has also been described by him as expertly handled. On this basis, it is tempting to imagine Robert had at last come to grips with the realities of power, and had learned important lessons in playing his noblemen against each other, without recourse to the advice of men like his uncle Odo. True or not, his actions helped restore some order in the region and may have helped prevent a later anarchy erupting after the death of Bellême's father, Roger de Montgomery, on 27 July 1094. Bellême benefited incrementally from additional land revenues, becoming an even more powerful adversary. The duke's earlier assertion of authority might be seen as a timely warning shot to deter the Lord of Bellême from any untoward power play. Montgomery's second son, Hugh, gained his father's English estates and titles and became the second Earl of Shrewsbury. He would come to pose a similar political and military threat to Rufus as did Bellême on occasion to Robert Curthose.[9]

*

1092 was notable for a great fire which consumed London, but 'fire and fury' also played out in the north of England when Rufus invaded Cumbria in breach of the agreements made with Malcolm the previous year, the curtain raiser for a further round of Anglo-Scottish bickering and bloodletting. Cumbria was at the time under Malcolm's loose control, said to have been 'not possessed by right, but subjugated by force'. When Rufus gained the throne, the region remained under the mantle of a shadowy Scottish surrogate named Dolfin. There is a case to be made that Dolfin embodied the last man standing from a fast-vanishing Anglo-Danish dynasty in the north of England, clinging on with vice-like tenacity to the region as a proxy ruler, owing allegiance to the King of the Scots. Dolfin's father had likely ruled the region in the late 1060s, and Dolfin's brother might have been Northumbria's ill-fated Earl Waltheof. His remit included the wild and barren Stainmoor, where the last Viking King of York, Eric Bloodaxe, had met a grisly end. Bounded geographically by the sea, the Solway Firth, lakes and the Pennines, Cumbria was too remote and underpopulated for either the Scots or English to maintain close control over. In the past it had acted as a buffer zone of sorts. A worry that the Scots would fall on York via the Stainmoor Gap is thought to have been the reason why the Conqueror sited Richmond Castle and its castellan Alan Rufus of Brittany as a watchdog.

Cumbria had once been part of the post-Roman entity of Rheged and later had become annexed to the Kingdom of Strathclyde. At its heart lay a jewel, the gently meandering Eden River, nestling safe between forbidding hills. Given the region's questionable status up until the eve of the Conqueror's death – Carlisle and its environs were not included in the Domesday survey – Rufus' move risked triggering a war and also put at risk agreements reached the year before in Lothian, where the neutrality of Cumbria may have been an agenda item. Although provocative, his action has been applauded by future historians as an attempt to curtail the continuation of Scottish rule over Cumbria through proxies. He has been described as operating well within his rights when campaigning to restore what has been called the historical frontier with Scotland. The annexation has been described by his biographer Frank Barlow as among the king's most notable achievements. In fact, Rufus lays claim to have taken a more hands-on approach to the Scots than any King of England since Athelstan in the first half of the tenth century.

The English king arrived in Cumbria at the head of an army and camped at Carlisle, a largely desolate place, laid waste by the Vikings two centuries earlier. Dolfin and his adherents were driven out from the region across the Solway Firth to Galloway in a series of unrecorded actions. Rufus then had a castle built at Carlisle from the abundance of stone available from the walls of the original Roman fortress and strongly garrisoned it. The *Anglo-Saxon Chronicle* for 1092 confirms the king ordered 'a great multitude of churlish folk, with women and cattle, there to dwell and till the land'. These would have been 'un-free' men and women, who may have had little choice in the matter; in other words they were forcibly resettled. Athelstan (d. 939) had once done the same on Wessex's borders with the Cornish. Transplantation during Rufus' reign may also have taken place on the Welsh borders in and around Brecknockshire in modern-day Powys, and Ireland would suffer similar indignities under later English kings.

After the turn of the year, Rufus fell seriously ill. He was rushed from the Midlands to Gloucester, where he lay in a febrile state throughout the whole of Lent. Monks from various infirmaries nearby ministered to him. Rumours spread the king was dead or dying. Anticipating death, Rufus, as his late father had done, ordered all his political prisoners to be released and all his outstanding debts forgiven. He also made new land grants to the Church: the *Anglo-Saxon Chronicle* says that many monasteries in England benefited, but that the king afterwards revoked the grants. Rufus believed God to be punishing him for sins, which historians ever since have been happy to believe were considerable. He made a full confession to Bishop Anselm of Bec, who happened to be attending the royal court at the time. Anselm also administered the last rites, so dire did the king's prospects seem. Rather than die and face God's opprobrium for neglecting the oversight of His Church, Rufus insisted the bishop accept the vacant see of Canterbury. After Lanfranc's death three years earlier, the archbishopric had been left without a spiritual head – a cause of great admonishment for the later chroniclers. Another vacant see, Lincoln, was bestowed on Rufus' chancellor, Robert Bloet: his nomination is dated to March 1093.

Described as the most original and widely attractive theological and devotional writer in western Europe, Anselm, sixty years of age in 1093, definitely had the intellectual stature, even if not the ambition, for the posting. An essentially modest and unworldly man, he might have doubted his ability to hold down such an important position. He once wrote, 'My life terrifies me.' At first he resisted accepting the offer; when he did finally grasp the pastoral staff, he had to be half dragged into church to hear the singing of the *Te Deum* which proceeded his election. Whether this reluctance was genuine or a form of etiquette has been the subject of some debate. Hesitancy to undertake the primacy of the Church of England might also be explained through fear of serving under a ruler like Rufus, a king who in the past had maintained a tight royal hold over ecclesiastical appointments and who would not be dictated to by the Church authorities. Anselm spoke of fearing to become 'an old sheep tied to a young bull'. Robert Curthose is said to have encouraged Anselm to accept Rufus' offer, which begs the question whether Robert was also for a time at his ailing brother's bedside. None of the sources make mention of it, but they may have thought it unnecessary to do so. As heir to the English crown, and with his brother close to death, making the journey would have been a prudent thing for the duke to have done. Edgar was definitely back in Britain, variously at Gloucester or travelling to consult with King Malcolm and escort the Scotsman back through England.

Upon hearing of the English king's ill health (possibly from Edgar), Malcolm had been quick to seek an advantage. The loss of control over the Cumbrian borderlands the previous year had been a blow to Malcolm's prestige and security. The *Anglo-Saxon Chronicle* says he 'asked for the covenants which were promised him', and that he was then summoned by Rufus to attend upon him at Gloucester. Safe conduct was assured and Edgar may have arranged for a number of English hostages to be sent to the Scottish court as guarantee. The Scottish king was now in his sixties and intent on making a stately progress as befitted a monarch. Either then or on the return leg, he took time out to attend the laying of foundation stones for the new cathedral to be built by William St Calais at Durham (an event dated to 11 August 1093). Malcolm may have been peacefully asserting himself in the region to gain a degree of political leverage for his coming talks with Rufus. Through intermediaries, he had already likely continued to press his case for Rufus to keep to the letter of their agreement made the previous year, as well as to restore Cumbria to Scottish control. Northumbrian escorts in his party may have considered Malcolm's lording it in England to have been provocative. The Scotsman also took time out to visit his two daughters: Edith (Robert's goddaughter) and her younger sister Mary. Both were at the time being brought up and educated in southern England, where up to seven years may have been spent by them, variously at Romsey Abbey in Hampshire and Wilton Abbey in Wiltshire.

The monastery at Romsey had been rebuilt around the year 1000, after its earlier destruction by the Vikings. By the 1080s it had become famous for its schooling in literature and languages. Wilton was likely favoured by the royalty for the same reason, and, unusually, the town there constituted a barony in its own right: the only others were at Shaftesbury, Barking and Winchester.

By the time Malcolm arrived at Gloucester, Rufus had recovered from illness. Appropriately for a religious audience, it was at Easter that he first showed signs of recovery. As mentioned with regard to the grants made to the monasteries, he enjoyed no sustained epiphany: as well as reneging on land grants, he backtracked on all the good laws he had promised. He also sought to undermine King Malcolm by placing unreasonable demands on him and declined to treat with the Scotsman face to face unless as part of an elaborate submission to be witnessed by the attendant English northern nobility but not by any of the Scottish king's followers. Although taken aback, Malcolm refused to be cowed, saying he would only do homage within his own borders, as had been the custom for Scottish kings time out of mind. Anglo-Scottish relations took a nosedive.

It might seem surprising that Rufus undermined Malcolm in this way, and we have no good reasons for him doing so. Maybe he was egged on by northern noblemen at court, one of whom may have been the aggressive and ambitious Robert de Mowbray, Earl of Northumbria, whom we last came across when riding out with his uncle Bishop Geoffrey of Coutances in 1088, and who had ten years earlier been at Robert Curthose's side at the Battle of Gerberoy. Rufus may well have sought to impress his northern barons by supporting pleas that he should act uncompromisingly and not give ground when in talks with the Scots. Malcolm's ostentatious progress through England, plus a later alleged cosying up to Alan Rufus of Richmond with respect to a possible marital alliance, may also have been held against him. Rufus had earlier banned any match between the two Scottish princesses at Wilton and any of his northern barons. Alan Rufus controlled all of the important routeways into the heart of England across the Pennines; marriage for him or one of his sons to a Scottish princess would have been out of the question. However, by the time Malcolm had reached Gloucester, Alan was dead of natural causes, so fears along these lines may have abated. It is also possible that Rufus might have had the eldest of the daughters, Edith, in mind for himself, and may possibly have been angered to receive news the girl had taken vows while at Wilton. Another possibility is that he pressed Malcolm too far with respect to the girl's future marriage arrangements by insisting he play the lead role in arranging a future husband for her, on the basis she was as much an English asset as a Scottish one.

Although a fiercely combative man, Malcolm Canmore was a known quantity of noble lineage who had integrated his English-speaking borderers into the Scottish mainstream. The adoption of knight service and the building of castles in Scotland had aped southern practice during Malcolm's reign. Some historians even consider the king to have gone out of his way to extinguish Scotland's essentially Celtic character, in part achieved by eliminating Macbeth, a violent warlord who has in modern times, courtesy of the Bard, come to characterise undiluted Gaeldom. Malcolm defeated Macbeth at Dunsinane Hill in 1054, later killing him north of that place in the wilds of Aberdeenshire on 15 August 1057, at Lumphanan in Mar. Having been snubbed by Rufus, and having gained no concessions, Malcolm returned to Scotland in the late autumn of 1093 an angry man. He had both daughters in tow, taken from Wilton for their better security north of the border. Rufus granted the party safe passage through England, boasting he would not detain through trickery a man he could defeat in battle at any time he liked. Malcolm took the comment as a declaration of intent: he raised an army in Lothian, re-crossed the border and attacked Northumbria east of the Cheviots, placing the Anglo-Norman motte-and-bailey fortress at Alnwick under siege – surely a precursor to a more penetrative raid into Northumbria. The English chronicler for 1093 says, 'King Malcolm returned to Scotland. And soon after he came home, he gathered his army [and two of his sons] and came harrowing into England with more hostility than behoved him.'

The Battle of Alnwick, 13 November 1093

The castellan at Alnwick, Gilbert de Tesson, had been the Conqueror's standard bearer at Hastings, so was not the kind of person likely to yield without a fight. Lands overridden by Malcolm's troops were given over to plunder and rapine... but this time, unlike on the several occasions before when the Scots had invaded Northumbria, an Anglo-Norman army stood ready and waiting to intervene. The fighting men of Northumbria, led by their earl, Robert de Mowbray, were soon mounted, massed and ready at Bamburgh, sixteen miles north of Alnwick, but just half a day's ride away. Their attack, made on St Brice's Day, took the Scots completely by surprise and resulted in a swift and bloody outcome.

The encounter at Alnwick might be better described as a running fight rather than a battle. If a circle of spears formed to protect the Scottish king, it must have been quickly overrun. Under normal circumstances, Malcolm would have sought to avoid a set-piece run-in with an English army. Flight or parley were better options for him and his commanders. Launching opportunistic chevauchees across the border to ravage and intimidate was one thing; to fight a full-scale battle, especially against a better-arrayed and armed set of opponents, was another. We might imagine the Anglo-Norman knights fighting from the saddle at Alnwick, lances held overarm or couched. The fearsome mounted cavalrymen on the Bayeux Tapestry give a good indication of what some at least of Mowbray's knights might have looked like in battle, although the kite-shaped shields on display on the tapestry may by the end of the eleventh century have been reengineered to be curved and shorter, done to facilitate fighting on foot, which over time had become more prevalent.

The Scots were no match for the English on the day. Cistercian abbot and writer Ailred of Rievaulx, writing about a different encounter, claimed the Scots' main attribute as soldiers was an irrational contempt for death. Some sort of kilt or covering may have been worn by them. Ailred wrote that only those Scots who had become like the Normans (therefore reasonably well apparelled for war) would be grouped around their king, whereas the mass of near-naked Scots would stand on the flanks and to the rear of the army, roaring out their battle cry: 'Albannich, Albannich!' Ailred mentions them 'presenting their naked hides to the opposition in battle, protected only by a light, calf-skin shield'. Bravery was all very well, but when the common Scottish soldiery lowered their spears to contend at close quarters with the Anglo-Normans, they also faced decimation to arrows and crossbow bolts. Ailred relates how 'southern flies [arrows] swarmed forth from the caves of their quivers and flew like closest rain'.

Adding credence to the assertion the Scots were surprised by the arrival of Mowbray's relief force, Malcolm is claimed to have been unarmed when killed by the thrust of a spear or lance. The *Anglo-Saxon Chronicle* says the Scots were 'trapped and surprised', presumably between the ramparts of the castle and their escape route. The Scottish king met his death on a ridge about a mile north of Alnwick, some way from the main fighting; a Gothic stone cross (erected *c.* 1774) marks the spot. We can imagine Malcolm ringed by his bodyguard, watching on as the disaster unfolded someway distant. The bulk of the Scottish army may have been destroyed on the banks of the River Aln, where swirling waters acted as a brake on further flight. Geoffrey Gaimar reckons on 3,000 Scots killed, which, if accurate, would tell us the approximate size of the Scottish force, including ancillaries and non-combatants – few Scots are claimed to have been left alive at battle's end.

*

The killing of the Scottish king may have been done in cold blood and not in the heat of battle. His death later attracted cautionary words from Geoffrey Gaimar, who says in his *L'estoire des Engleis* that Malcolm was killed 'whether it was right or wrong to have done so'. The Scottish king's killer, Arkle Morael, was sheriff of Northumbria and Mowbray's honorary steward. He may also have been related in some way to Malcolm (a familial or fraternal closeness, perhaps like Robert of Normandy through baptism). An affinity between the two men made the deed all the more shocking for contemporaries. Another knight, Geoffrey de Gulevent (the belcher), also had a hand in the slaying of the king. The precise manner of Malcolm's death (though undisclosed) was later claimed to have been so shocking that even the most hardened Normans were discomfited: 'a whiff of dishonour' is said by Frank Barlow (*William Rufus*) to have tainted the victory at Alnwick.

Honour for a Norman nobleman was hard won but easily lost. The dishonourable killing of a fellow knight might attract the wrath of a king. An example of something similar had occurred at Hastings, when one of William the Conqueror's knights had hacked at the dead or dying King Harold's thigh. William branded the culprit a disgrace for perpetrating such a dastardly and shameful act and stripped him of his knighthood. Rufus, perhaps an even more chivalrous man than his father, would no doubt have reacted similarly had the killers of the Scottish king been on hand when he was informed of the event. Monks at Durham, meanwhile, took a nationalistic and moralistic tone, describing Malcolm's death as a divine punishment for his attacks on Northumbria.

The king's death removed the main source of opposition to Mowbray in the lands between the Tyne and Tweed, allowing the earl to exert wide-ranging, semi-independent control over the region. To be fair to Mowbray, Northumbrian earls had always in the past had to act with a high degree of independence and did not necessarily look to the English king for any sort of sign-off for their actions. The distances involved meant they had to look out for themselves, not rely on their liege lord to rush north at the head of an army.

Malcolm's eldest son and heir, Edward, was among the few who managed to fight his way out of the enveloping cordon and make it back across the Scottish border, but soon afterwards he succumbed to his wounds. Of the Scottish royal family present at the battle, only the king's second son, another Edgar, a Scottish prince (not Edgar *atheling*), managed to escape unscathed. Because there were no Scotsmen left alive to remove the body of their king, two local Northumbrians were co-opted to place Malcolm's body on a cart and take it to Tynemouth for burial. The king's remains were then later moved to Dunfermline Abbey. Queen Margaret of Scotland died within a week of her husband, on 16 November; her death was said to have been through grief at having lost both Malcolm and her eldest son so suddenly. In point of fact, she had been seriously ill for some time, so the devastating news may simply have hastened her end. John of Worcester wrote,

> Margaret, queen of Scots, was so heavily affected with sorrow that she suddenly fell into a serious sickness. Without delay, she summoned the priests, entered the church [Dunfermline Abbey], and having confessed her sins to them, caused herself to be anointed with oil and strengthened with the heavenly viaticum, beseeching God with the most earnest and heartfelt prayers, that He would not suffer her to live longer in the world of trouble. Nor was it very long before her prayers were heard.

Before her death, Margaret had charged Turgot, the prior of Durham, to take charge of her younger children – Edith was then aged just thirteen, Mary ten and David just nine. There were also elder brothers alive: Edmund, Ethelred, Edgar and Alexander. The first three, plus the late Edward, had been named after the kings of old from the Wessex royal line, indicating an awareness on Margaret's part of their dynastic importance south of the border.[10]

*

A period of civil war broke out in Scotland after Alnwick. Multiple claimants to the throne vied for pre-eminence. The Scottish crown was first claimed by the late Malcolm's brother Donald, who became Donald III of Scotland, commonly known as Donalbane, meaning Donald 'the fair', probably in his late forties at the time he gained the crown. His reign signalled a change of emphasis and a reaction against the clique of English advisors and courtiers who remained at large in Fife after the death of Queen Margaret. Donalbane had spent much of his youth in the Hebrides and had as a consequence been subjected to Celtic and Norse influences. His accession presaged a backlash against English manners and customs and was welcomed by a patriotic native Scottish nobility, men and women described as deeply shocked by the killing of King Malcolm and Prince Edward. He may even have attempted to reinstate the traditional Gaelic Tanist system of inheritance, whereby the worthiest and wisest of the male relatives of a chieftain or king (not necessarily the eldest son) might be elected by the people. Rufus in the meantime backed the late King Malcolm's son Duncan over Donalbane. Rufus had known Duncan intimately for much of his adult life. Made a hostage in the Conqueror's day, Duncan had been freed and knighted by Robert Curthose in 1087. By 1093, he displayed all the attributes of a Norman lord.

Promising to do homage to Rufus, Duncan, the self-styled 'heritably undoubted king of Scotia' raised a small army of mercenary knights and Northumbrian infantry, the latter drawn to his cause after his marriage en route north to Ethelreda, the daughter of Gospatric, Earl of Northumbria, and the sister or half-sister of the elusive Dolfin of Cumbria and the late, much-lamented Earl Waltheof. He then invaded Scotland, drove out Donalbane and was crowned Duncan II at Scone. Before crossing the border into Scotland he made sure to secure divine aid from the Northumbrian St Cuthbert (d. 687) by gifting the saint the long-lost lands of Tyninghame (the hamlet on the Tyne) in East Lothian, where the church and village had once been destroyed in the year 941 by Olaf Guthfrithsson, a belligerent Viking King of Dublin and York. The restoration of these lands is contained in Scotland's earliest charter. He also bestowed land on Dunfermline Priory, the foundation of his late stepmother Margaret of Scotland. Duncan knew his quest for kingship to be dangerous and needed all the help he could get, even if of an invisible kind. That Duncan aspired to be a warrior king is given added credence by his single-faced seal, which shows a mounted knight with lance and pennon.

Anglo-Norman knights who accompanied him across the border would have been viewed by the Scots as foreign interlopers. His reign has been described as brief and stormy. Viewed as a Norman surrogate, a Scottish insurgency soon arose against him. The *Anglo-Saxon Chronicle* for 1094 says the Scottish king's rebels that year 'killed well-nigh all of Duncan's men'.

Duncan managed to escape with a few survivors. Later, during a hiatus in the violence, a reconciliation of sorts was arranged. Duncan agreed to break with his Anglo-Norman allies and embrace mainstream Scottish traditions. This fragile pact soon broke down and the twenty-two-year-old king was driven out of Edinburgh. On 12 November 1094 he met his death at the Battle of Mondynes, twenty miles south of Aberdeen, in north-east Scotland. His opponents that day were forces loyal to the resurgent Donalbane. The place where Duncan fell is said to be marked by a large standing stone in a field at Mill of Mondynes. He was later buried on the Isle of Iona.

Underlining the tenuous strands of loyalty operating north of the border, Donalbane had somehow managed to attract the support of the late queen Margaret's second son, Edmund (Donalbane's half-brother), who became co-regent of Scotland for a time and was also named Donalbane's formal heir. Notably it is Edmund, not Donalbane, who is claimed to have ordered the death of the unfortunate Duncan. For this he is said to have later done penance. When close to death, he is alleged to have asked for the fetters he wore while imprisoned to be buried with him still attached, so that his guilt might remain on show after death as it had been in life. Rufus meanwhile arranged for the late Malcolm's daughters Edith and Mary to be brought back to England, to be again placed under the care of the nuns at Wilton Priory. His facilitator may have been Edgar *atheling*. The fate of the girls, those dynastic jewels, would have been of immediate concern to all of the Bastard's sons as well as to their uncle Edgar.

In 1097, the final episode of the power struggle in Scotland played out when Edgar *atheling*, tasked with the guardianship of his namesake the late Malcolm's son Edgar of Scots, invaded Scotland.

The two Edgars are said to have won that land from Donalbane in a fierce fight. The Scottish prince was crowned King of Scotland shortly afterwards; said to have been enabled to possess the land of Lothian and the kingdom of Scotland 'by the gift of Lord William II, king of the English and by paternal heritage'. English troops, courtesy of Rufus, fought in the front line of the invading army, which was likely commanded by Edgar *atheling*. This decisive campaign has been seen by some modern-day historians as a second conquest in Britain. The new Scottish king afterwards owed fealty to Rufus. In effect, he became an English surrogate.

Submissive by temperament, King Edgar is characterised by the medieval historian Ailred of Rievaulx as a 'sweet and lovable man, who employed no tyranny, no harshness, no greed against his people, but ruled his subjects with the greatest charity and benevolence'. This description should be treated with caution. The king acted with studied sternness on occasion: Donalbane suffered blinding on his orders in 1099; what is more, the mutilation may have been bodged for the ex-king afterwards died of an infection. One of Edgar's first acts was to make over two counties previously under Scottish control to the see of Durham. These were the counties of Berwickshire and Coldinghamshire. The grant may have been insisted upon by Rufus, a clever way for the English king to buttress Northumberland from the attentions of later generations of Scots. Rufus demanded from King Edgar no overt rendering of service or payment, just sixty shillings a day to be paid for his keep when attending the English court. At Easter 1099, the Scottish king carried Rufus' sword at the symbolic crown-wearing ceremony in Westminster Abbey – a great State occasion, and so memorable an event that Geoffrey Gaimar featured it in his *L'estoire des Engleis*. When totting up Rufus' achievements, the placing on the Scottish throne of a line of pliant kings (Edgar's successors Alexander and David were also English allies) should be accounted at the top; but it should not be forgotten that Rufus' sword-arm in Scotland had been the other Edgar, the *atheling*, whose claims to the English crown, for some, had never really gone away.

II

TURNED BACK
THROUGH INTRIGUE

Although Robert Curthose had assisted his brother Rufus when negotiating with Malcolm Canmore in 1091, the favour had not been returned when the duke flexed his muscles in response to the separate threats posed to the duchy by their brother Henry and the resurgent Manceaux. During the summer of 1093, having fully recovered from his illness that year, and having sent King Malcolm packing, Rufus had busied himself striking deals with a number of Continental magnates. The strength of Robert's hold on Normandy, backed by the French, must have given the king reason to pause during a year made difficult by illness and military and diplomatic threats from the Welsh and the Scots. He may even have feared an invasion from the Continent (and not one necessarily sponsored by Robert; there were other Frenchmen who eyed the rich prize of England). Rufus pinned his hopes on winning over the Continental Normans with bribes and promises and in this way isolating his brother. In what must be seen as a response to all this wheeling and dealing, a delegation from Normandy presented Rufus, then still at Gloucester, with a draft renunciation of the Rouen peace covenant, telling him his brother Robert would act on it unless Rufus, described as 'forsworn', travelled to Normandy to clear himself of acting faithlessly. Not only had Rufus failed to make good on the conditions of the agreement, he was now in clear breach of faith by having attempted to bribe the duke's subjects and close neighbours. Robert threatened to brand his brother a perjurer and said he would disavow the Rouen agreement unless Rufus travelled to Normandy to face a judicial hearing.

Which of the brothers had the upper hand at this point is moot! The duke appears to have been calling the shots. Rufus' response was to amass even more money to fill his travelling chests. Raising money in heaps would hardly have been necessary had reconciliation with Robert been his uppermost consideration. The heavy financial demands he placed on both his secular and ecclesiastical subjects served to undermine an already shaky relationship with Archbishop Anselm, who sought to capitalise on the king's overtures for money by raising the subject of reform as a quid pro quo. Part of Anselm's reform agenda was the forced imposition of celibacy on the clergy. Proponents of this have since been described as 'religious radicals'. In typically down-to-earth manner, Rufus took the side of married clerics over reforming bishops. Many of the former had dependent children. Draconian reform was seen by them as a personal disaster, something Rufus could empathise with.

Historians from our less religious modern age, like Rufus' biographer John Gillingham, support the stance the king took as practical and compassionate. At the end of one presumably heated argument with Anselm, Rufus rebuffed the archbishop's reluctant offer of money, saying, 'Clear off, I now have enough of my own.' When the archbishop later offered to bless the king's endeavours in Normandy, Rufus again spurned him, telling him, 'I utterly abominate any blessings and spew them from me.' Anselm would later distribute the sum earmarked for the king's war chest, said to have been £500, to the poor, stating in his defence, 'If I had promised nothing or too small a sum, the king could have appeared to have had a just cause for anger; but if he had accepted it, I might have suffered great harm and been suspected of simony.' Simony has been defined as a deliberate act or a premeditated will and desire to sell things that are spiritual, by the giving of something temporal – in other words, cash for favours.

A few years later, Anselm would break with Rufus. The reasons are explained in a letter to the Pope, penned by Anselm in the winter of 1097; it has since been called 'a virulent indictment of Rufus rule from an indignant churchman's perspective'. He wrote,

> I have been archbishop for four years, living uselessly and in immense and horrible tribulation to my soul, so that every day I would rather die outside England than continue to live there … I saw many evils which I ought not to have tolerated, but was unable to correct as a bishop should. The king treated churches badly after the deaths of their prelates. He harassed me and the church of Canterbury in many ways … refusing to restore those estates he had given to his knights … against my wishes he gave away others as it suited him.

Anselm also mentioned unprecedented heavy services imposed on him, adding that 'the laws of God and of canonical and apostolic authority were flouted [by the crown], and many other wicked practices indulged in'; these practices are undefined, but were presumably to do with specific aspects of the clashes between Church and State that became a feature of these times.

Whereas the late Archbishop Lanfranc had been able to hold his own in arguments with the two Williams, Anselm was of a more fragile temperament. Historians in the past have assumed the prelate was driven into exile by Rufus, but modern historians like Gillingham consider it more likely he insisted on leaving the country, despite protestations from his contemporaries, the king included. William of Malmesbury, for instance, wrote of Rufus' arrogance and of his arbitrary wielding of power for power's sake in his dealings with Anselm; Malmesbury claimed that Rufus saw himself as master of both Church and State, modelling himself on the uncompromising style of his father. Pressure on the relationship between king and archbishop had been building for some time. Both the first two

Norman kings expected a good return in the form of cash and knights from the Church as the price of royal support. They also expected the Church to back State policy without raising difficult questions. Many churchmen must have given way under pressure from the crown or simply adopted workarounds, but not Anselm.

From Rufus' perspective, the archbishop was attempting to undermine his sovereignty. Emma Mason has suggested Rufus' pushing back should be viewed as 'upholding the traditional right of the monarchy against an increasingly pugnacious revolutionary', which is an interesting take on how Anselm might be seen. The archbishop had attempted to hold his ground by insisting he qualify his oath of allegiance to the king, saying that he would only uphold the king's writ if in accord with the word of God. Today, Anselm is claimed as a role model for Archbishop Thomas Becket, who more famously opposed Henry II. As has been pointed out by Mason, it is telling that the one short-lived attempt to secure Anselm's canonisation was instigated by Becket, an indication of how influential Anselm was to a future generation of priests.

After a delay of around six weeks due to bad weather, Rufus made the crossing to Normandy. He attended a series of meetings with his brother and a jury of twelve noblemen at Rouen. Predictably, the panel found Rufus culpable of not making good on his warranties. Rufus left the hearing in high dudgeon. The English chronicler for 1094 claims there was 'much dissension' between the brothers. The escalating crisis gained additional momentum when Rufus' newly won Flemish allies were reported as mustering to honour their financial compact with the king – as near to a declaration of war as one could get in medieval times. The Bastard's elder sons were now right back where they had started three years earlier.

*

Rufus concentrated his forces in the modern-day Seine-Maritime region, where he enjoyed substantial support. He once again made his centre of operations the castle at Eu, a stronghold described as 'the gateway to Upper Normandy'. Rufus acted with munificence when making royal funds available to his theatre commanders. He is said to have benefited from having 'keener followers and greater riches'. He allowed his troops license to plunder and loot almost at will. He is once claimed to have declared his soldiers would follow him even through raging seas, and this was probably true; they knew that if they were taken prisoner they would be ransomed without delay and probably gain a bonus. With such men fighting at his side, Rufus soon captured the important castle at Bures-en-Bray. This was likely the initial action of the campaign but the king's aggressive campaigning had placed Robert Curthose very much on the back foot, with hostile garrisons springing up all around him. David Hume wrote of the 'frank, open, remiss temper of Robert [being] ill-fitted to withstand the interested, rapacious character of William Rufus'. Robert's options were narrowing.

Among those who switched sides to back Rufus at this time, having presumably been incensed by the duke's recent show of largesse to the Giroie family, was Robert de Bellême. By the summer of 1094, Bellême's castles at Le Houlme and Argentan were now strongly garrisoned by Rufus' men. Le Houlme's command devolved upon a hoary veteran of the Battle of Hastings named William Peverel. Once a great favourite of the Conqueror, Domesday Book records Peverel holding 162 manors in Nottinghamshire and Derbyshire, including Nottingham Castle. Although a soldier of proven ability, Peverel could not in the end prevent Le Houlme falling to Robert's forces when attacked. The duke afterwards took a heavy toll of prisoners. When assaulted by knights under the command of Philip of France, the castle at Argentan also promptly surrendered. King Philip can no longer have been in receipt of English subsidies and must have again backed his Norman vassal. He is said to have netted a large number of Rufus' knights at Argentan, including the commander of the garrison, Roger the Poitevin, who had escorted Bishop William St Calais to trial in 1088.

Roger was the epitome of an Anglo-Norman lord of the time (to recap, he was the third son of the late Roger de Montgomery and a younger brother of Robert de Bellême and Hugh, Earl of Shrewsbury). In the feudal pecking order he might be likened to Count Henry, dependant on his brothers and the whims of others, awaiting the 'main chance'. The loss of Argentan to Philip of France came after just a single day's campaigning. Roger might have been expected to have put up more of a fight when defending the castle. His conduct has since been described as 'pathetic', but Philip was Roger's Continental overlord with a more direct call on his subject's loyalty than Rufus could match. His readiness to submit to the French was in this sense a feudal necessity. The capture of these castles and also of a significant number of Rufus' knights represented a major coup for the Franco-Norman axis.

Putting a superstitious gloss on events, English chroniclers saw the reverses as divine retribution for Rufus having insulted Archbishop Anselm. In an attempt to break the deadlock, Rufus called for even more money to prosecute the war. His chief financial administrator, Ranulf Flambard, summoned a muster of the English feudal levy. Each man received a sum of money from his local district. This yielded in total £20,000, of which the crown promptly appropriated half. The levies were then sent home. These men might have served in an emergency to face an insurgency or foreign invasion, but for services overseas professional soldiers were needed. The money gained bought Rufus many additional mercenaries and bankrolled untold bribes. Yet even with this additional injection of funds, Rufus remained holed up for a time in the castle at Eu, hemmed in by enemies. Precise dates are lacking, but by mid- to late summer it appears Alencon (another of the Bellême strongholds) had also fallen to the French. Once again Philip took hundreds of Rufus' knights captive, only for them to be promptly ransomed back. The king might have remained stuck at Eu had not relations between the French king and Duke Robert suddenly broken down.

The falling-out is said to have occurred at Longueville, located in the modern-day Seine-et-Marne department. Chroniclers write of nameless intrigues afoot. The *Anglo-Saxon Chronicle* for

1094 says Robert joined forces with the French king and both marched on the castle at Eu, which was held by Rufus in person; their plan was to lay siege to the castle, but at Longueville Philip 'was turned back by intrigue', halting the campaign. That Philip had again been bribed seems the most likely explanation, but there may have been other reasons for him to hold back his support: by keeping the brotherly rivals evenly matched and at each other's throats, Henry included, the Conqueror's sons could not gang up against him – something he may have feared. All three in the duchy under arms at the same time posed a threat to his authority. A year or so younger than Robert, Philip was already, according to Orderic, 'sunk into age and infirmities in all the corruption of his foul adultery' – a reference to his affair with Bertrada de Montfort. Philip may have come to rue his decision when Rufus and Henry opportunistically allied themselves to attack the now weakened Robert Curthose (*c*. early autumn 1094).

The union of the younger brothers marked a dramatic turnaround from what had gone before, but working together was one thing, and combining militarily another. The ducal army was too well posted to allow for the concentration of their forces. The *Anglo-Saxon Chronicle* confirms that Henry, his blood up, could not go through Normandy to join forces with Rufus 'in peace'. Even though set upon and betrayed, Robert, militarily, had gained the upper hand. How this had been achieved is not really explained, but mounting problems for Rufus on the Scottish and Welsh borders must have played a role. Rufus was campaigning in Normandy while all the time looking back over his shoulder across the Channel.

At Rufus' request Henry took ship from Barfleur on the north-eastern corner of the Cotentin Peninsula, a move undertaken to outflank the ducal forces and to place him in better readiness to travel back to England should it become necessary. Travelling with Henry were his household knights as well as his and Rufus' ally Hugh d'Avranches, Earl of Chester, with additional soldiers, many of them Bretons. Their planned disembarkation point may have been the coast near Eu, where they would have joined forces with Rufus, but at some point the plan must have changed (either because of bad weather or because they were redirected by Rufus) to make landfall at Southampton. Rufus' position in Normandy had by now worsened further. For reasons which remain obscure, he had lost the support of a number of his key Norman castellans. Ralph de Mortemer and William d'Eu, to name but two, had switched sides to back Robert Curthose. William d'Eu would later pay dearly for his intransigence.

Rufus and Henry met face to face in England at the end of December 1094. Bad weather may have prevented Rufus from crossing the English Channel until quite late in the year. Their meeting is confirmed by a grant made by royal charter signed at Bermondsey, [11] which was attested by 'Henry the king's brother'. No other title is afforded him. While Rufus remained behind in England to deal with a major Welsh insurrection and also the first rumblings of trouble up north, Henry was given 'great treasures' and tasked with coordinating the harrying of Robert's lands in Normandy. In conflict with later reports claiming Henry from then on often fought against Robert, the count's arrival back in the duchy proved to be no great game changer. Some part of Rufus' money may well have been spent on mercenaries but more may have been earmarked for building works at Domfront, where an eighty-foot-high keep, curtain walls and a new priory were erected by Henry within the space of just a few years. The phrase 'feathering one's own nest' comes to mind – and this is something which, Henry, in his mid-twenties, would now focus on to the exclusion of all else.

*

The problems mentioned as brewing in the north of England occurred sometime shortly after the death of King Duncan at the Battle of Mondynes on 12 November 1094, when Robert de Mowbray, Earl of Northumbria and the victor of the Battle of Alnwick, made what appears to have been a dramatic bid for independence. Described by Orderic as 'daring and crafty', with features at once 'melancholy and harsh', the earl, said to have been a giant of a man, emerges from the mists of time as an altogether sinister character. His uncle Geoffrey of Coutances' death in February 1093 had now established him as one of England's most powerful barons. Mowbray's inheritance amounted to his uncle's 280 manors in the west of England and in the Midlands, which, when combined with his existing earldom of Northumbria, made him into the sort of nobleman who in fifteen-century terms would be classed as 'an over-mighty subject'. Mowbray had also married well, to Richard d'Laigle's daughter Matilda, the niece of Hugh d'Avranches, Earl of Chester. The d'Laigle family had in the past usually supported Robert Curthose as their overlord and may have remained at odds with Rufus. Whatever the truth of this, the marriage helped Mowbray extend his remit in the north of England and facilitated the forging of new alliances and linked him in a familial sense to the most powerful Norman families in England. Hubris after Alnwick may also be factored in.

When Mowbray failed to attend three summons to court in the spring of 1095, having earlier been charged with the theft of the contents of some Norwegian barges on the Tyne, Rufus (after ordering the Norwegian owners to be compensated) marched an army north by way of Newcastle and Morpeth to confront the miscreant. Mowbray had in advance of this been charged with wilful disobedience; he had become, in medieval speak, 'a contumacious vassal'. It must be noted that Mowbray had not been granted safe conduct by Rufus, so in a sense the king may have been looking for an excuse to confront the earl.

At Morpeth an attempt to ambush and kill Rufus, likely engineered by Mowbray, was betrayed by Gilbert de Tonbridge from the Clare family: this is the same man who had once before, in 1088, had a nasty run-in with Rufus; it will be recalled that he had briefly held out at Tonbridge Castle against the king and had suffered an inconsequential wound and had afterwards to be pardoned. Mowbray's best knights at this time are said to have either switched allegiance back to Rufus or were captured and interned. With Clare at his side, Rufus marched on Tynemouth, just to the north of Hadrian's Wall, where Mowbray was holed up. Rufus captured the town after a two-month blockade, netting many prisoners – but not Mowbray, who managed to escape to Bamburgh by boat. Rufus ordered a castle to be built on the windswept headland at Tynemouth before heading on to lay siege to Bamburgh Castle. Described as surrounded by waters and marshes and other impediments, Bamburgh, although without a keep, was inaccessible to an attacker. It is not clear when the fortress became sufficiently strengthened to justify the label castle, but it must have been before 1095: when Mowbray hid out there, Bamburgh had become known as 'the old castle' – presumably to differentiate it from 'the new castle' on the Tyne, built by Robert Curthose in 1080. Not until a later reign did the work commence to construct the massive structure we see today.

Rufus ordered the erection of a separate siege castle at Bamburgh, known as the Malveisin (bad neighbour), to overawe Mowbray's stronghold and to starve the garrison of supplies. The king left others to progress the siege; he needed to ride south to consult more widely with respect to the conspiracy that Mowbray had raised against him. The intractable earl, after allegedly hurling abuse from the castle walls at the men below who had betrayed him, managed again to escape capture by boat to Newcastle, accompanied by thirty knights. Gillingham claims Mowbray to have overestimated the strength of loyalty he could expect from his followers once the king had settled on personally conducting the campaign against him. Yet it was several weeks before he was brought to book, after having had to be dragged from the confines of St Oswy's Church at Tynemouth, and then threatened with blinding if he did not order his young wife to yield up the keys to Bamburgh Castle. He did, and, sensibly, she did as she was bid.

The Mowbray insurrection of 1095 might at first glance appear to have been just another Northumbrian rising, but there may have been deeper issues at stake, even a plot hatched to topple the king in favour of his cousin, Stephen of Aumale, the son of Adelaide of Normandy, the Conqueror's sister, who had died five years earlier. Aumale and Mowbray had the backing of Hugh de Montgomery, second Earl of Shrewsbury, England's most powerful man after the king, the second son of Roger de Montgomery and Mabel Talvas and the younger brother of Robert de Bellême. So wide-ranging did the conspiracy turn out to have been, Rufus is said to have ordered the facts to be suppressed. Orderic Vitalis wrote,

> Earls and [many other] men of the highest rank [who were] privy to and promoted the treasonable conspiracy [were pardoned] ... Rufus was unwilling to bring them to a public trial lest their exasperation be increased and they might be provoked to a general rising against the government, and much loss, destruction and grief should be occasioned to the community.

Only men known to have played a direct and leading role in the rebellion were targeted for retribution. A brief reign of terror ensued. Rufus' reputation as a ruthless tyrant who indulged in binges of disinheritance, killing and physical mutilation can be traced back to the bloody aftermath of the 1095 revolt. The king had by this stage been goaded too far by baronial scheming and clerical pushback. Rufus had shown leniency to all but the main ringleaders of the rebellion against him in 1088, but he now realised that he had failed to stamp out dissent. He would not make the same mistake again.

William d'Alderi, a kinsman of the king, was hanged; as we have seen, this was an unusually draconian outcome. Rufus had now crossed one of his father's red lines by executing a fellow Norman nobleman outright. William d'Eu, who had abandoned Rufus for Robert Curthose the year before, was forced to fight a duel with the king's champion, Geoffrey Bainard. Eu came off worse. His guilt having been proven by God's intercession in strengthening

Bainard's sword arm, Eu was blinded and emasculated – forms of reprisal suggested by Hugh d'Avranches, whose sister, Eu's wife, had allegedly been abused by the culprit. Another plotter, Roger de Lacy, the son of the late Walter de Lacy, was disinherited and exiled. His immensely strong and important castle at Ludlow was made over to his more loyal brother Hugh de Lacy, who became a major player along the marches with Wales. Hugh de Montgomery, arguably the most powerful of the plotters, had become a man too strongly entrenched to arrest or attack. Instead, he faced a hefty fine. He was lucky not to have suffered a worse fate.

Hugh had been a close confederate of Mowbray's. Rufus is said by Orderic to have 'spoken privately' with the earl, but only took him back into his favour after a fine of £3,000 had been paid. Mowbray on the other hand suffered a life of incarceration at Windsor, dying a captive in fetters several decades later. His estates in the north-east were broken up and made over to men who had remained loyal to the king. Other men's estates were also seized. An example is the de Merley family, occupants of the motte-and-bailey castle at Morpeth, which had fallen to Rufus after Gilbert de Clare's defection. The de Merleys had supported Robert Curthose in 1088. Their castle at Morpeth was ordered to be destroyed on Rufus' orders after the 1095 rebellion. A smaller one was later built by the family on the site. Given that Mowbray, William d'Eu and the de Merleys had all been allies of the duke, it is not beyond the bounds of credibility to imagine Robert Curthose had been on the margins of the plotting.

Described by Orderic as 'deprived of the consolations of marriage and long exposed to deep suffering', Mowbray's wife, Matilda, whose prestigious family needed to be kept on side, was pardoned by the king. She later had her marriage annulled by Pope Paschal II. Rufus did not appoint a replacement earl of Northumbria, preferring to keep a tight rein on the region's affairs himself; in the process he benefited from the income accruing from the honour. Arkle Morael, the killer of King Malcolm Canmore, bargained for his life by incriminating others and later became a refugee on the Continent; he is said by Orderic to have grown old in exile, 'poor and detested'. The historian here is making a moral point as much as an historic one. Rufus appointed Ivo de Vescy, one of his loyal knights, to become Alnwick's castellan. Vescy became the first Baron of Alnwick, and from then on owed twelve knights for the king's service when required. Aumale remained in Normandy throughout and could not afterwards be brought to account. The Count of Holderness, another Odo (Aumale's father and Rufus' uncle), did get his comeuppance, losing all his English lands and suffering either imprisonment or exile. William of St Calais, who had been a close associate of Mowbray's for many years, had also, as in 1088, been implicated in the plotting. He died on 2 January 1096, allegedly because of fright that he had been found out. Fearing the worst, he is said to have simply dropped dead. In reality he had been ill for some time, but the shock of the king's summons may well have hastened his end. He is said to have been warned his death was near by a monk named Boso who had seen a vision in which St Calais was cast adrift in a vast and horrible wilderness, where stood a lofty house made of iron, with a door constantly clanging open and shut.

12

THE CALL FROM THE EAST

While Rufus was squaring up to confront Robert de Mowbray, there came a real game changer for the Bastard's sons, when the Byzantine Emperor Alexius I despatched envoys from Constantinople to appeal to Pope Urban II for military support to fight the Seljuk Turks, a race described by him as barbarians on the confines of Asia, now threatening to invade the heart of Europe. Alexius enjoyed good relations with the west, and with Urban II in particular, so could expect his plea to get a fair hearing. The Byzantine military had been worn down by unremitting warfare and were now struggling to hold back the tide of Turkish attacks, let alone recover territory already overrun. Although the Turks were the main threat to the Eastern Empire, the Normans of southern Italy had also in the past posed problems for them; moreover, new threats had appeared in the northern Balkans. In 1071 the Byzantines had suffered twin defeats: one to the Normans at Bari; the other to the Seljuk Turks at Manzikert, in modern-day Turkey. Ten years later in the autumn of 1081 the Normans and their allies under the leadership of Robert Guiscard, Duke of Apulia, had defeated an imperial army at the Battle of Dyrrhachium, near present-day Durres on the Balkan coast, a defeat described as 'every bit as severe as that at Manzikert'.

The heavy strain of war had by 1095 left the Byzantine coffers empty, the imperial currency debased, and the system of tax collection broken. The emperor's call for help was very much a last roll of the dice for a regime in dire straits and in fact teetering close to the edge of collapse. The intensity of Turkish infiltration into Anatolia, and Norman and Serbian inroads elsewhere, had seriously disrupted movement and communications in the marches of the empire.The call, however, was for a Holy War to oppose the specific threat of Islamic expansion. A minute penned by the Bishop of Arras in November 1095 at Clermont, in the Auvergne region of France, where Pope Urban II first called for volunteers to crusade, stated, 'Whoever for devotion alone, not to gain honour or money, goes to Jerusalem to liberate the Church of God can substitute this journey for all penance.' In a speech recounted by Orderic, Urban called upon history to inspire the public:

> Let the deeds of your ancestors move you ... and let the holy sepulchre of the Lord our Saviour, which is possessed by unclean nations, especially incite you ... oh most valiant soldiers and descendants of invincible ancestors, be not degenerate, but recall the valour of your progenitors.

This great open-air-event was attended by thirteen archbishops and 225 bishops. Among them was Bishop Odo of Bayeux. Pope Urban is said to have exhorted the princes of the west, with their subjects and warriors, to maintain firm peace among themselves and to give full scope to their military ardour against the infidels. He called for battalions of European knights to avenge the sufferings of Christians.

Liberating the Holy City became the main focus, even if, from the Emperor Alexius' position, the freeing of other important cities like Nicaea and Antioch were equally important objectives. His appealing to latent piousness and warrior fervour was a clever move. Those attending at Clermont are said to have bought in and cried out as one, 'Deus Vult' (God wills it).

Urban II was a tall, unassuming man of great piety, learning and eloquence, who knew how to hold an audience. When inciting his listeners to aspire to undertaking manly achievements he invoked the memory of Charlemagne, a man Urban credited with having destroyed the kingdoms of the pagans. We do not know the exact words spoken by Urban II, but one version, penned more than a decade later by a monk named Robert of Rheims (often known as Robert the Monk), described Urban addressing the Franks as a race from across the Alps chosen and beloved of God, whereas the Turks (who are referred to by the author as Saracens) he denigrated as an accursed race, utterly alienated from God. Pope Urban is said to have recounted the horrors committed by the infidels against Christians, and of the dismembering of the Eastern Empire – called by him 'the kingdom of the Greeks'. Territory so vast had been lost to the invaders, he claimed, that it would take two months to cross. Robert the Monk described in detail Pope Urban's call to take the Cross and the spontaneous cry of affirmation. He also wrote in gory detail of the charges made by the Eastern Church against the Turks, including the desecration of churches, the torture of Christian men and the defiling of Christian women.

It was not the first time the papacy had justified holy war. Leo IV and John VII in the ninth century had absolved from all sin those men who fell fighting the Vikings and the Muslims. A full half-century before the First Crusade, Norman troops had been fighting in Sicily for the Eastern Empire against the Saracens. Notable among them had been William 'Iron hand', whose nickname is traced by historians to his single-handed killing of the emir of Syracuse at the Battle of the Olivento River in 1040.

*

Among those stirred into action to heed the call was Robert Curthose. The appeal for him to embark on crusade may have been a way to win military glory to rival his father. The need to match up to the Conqueror must have driven each of his three sons in varying degrees. The threat to Normandy posed by Rufus and Henry and the recent loss of Bellême's support may also have influenced the duke. It has been argued he may have sought to cut his losses and travel east to avoid the pressing issues dogging him at home. This suggestion is now coming under a revisionist onslaught, and rightly so. Although a state of war existed between Rufus and Robert, the duchy may have been more peaceful than at any time since 1087. The main fighting within the Anglo-Norman realm, as we have seen, had occurred in Northumbria in 1093 and again in 1095. Rufus had been the man more threatened in 1095, not the duke.

Of greater relevance in the context of the First Crusade is that the Conqueror's sons' forbears had boasted an impressive record of religious service. Their great-grandfather, Richard II of Normandy, had pledged money to restore the Holy Sepulchre in Jerusalem and had in 1026 funded the travel of several hundred pilgrims. Their grandfather had died as a pilgrim at Nicaea on 2 July 1035 while en route back from the Holy City. Even the first Richard, Count of Normandy (d. 996), known as 'the fearless', had been noted for acts of piety and ensuring that Church lands were protected and in some instances even restored to them. His reign is said to have been one where monasteries flourished and a period of extended peace and tranquillity was enjoyed by his subjects. Rather than taking the Cross from a position of weakness, there is a good case to make that the duke did so from a strong sense of religious obligation.

In his mid-forties, wiser and more mature, Robert Curthose now enjoyed great prestige. The military leaders of the First Crusade were by and large princely rulers, men of high rank and resources who could afford to pay the immense costs of maintaining an army and journeying across eastern Europe to the Holy Land. Robert might have struggled to find the necessary money had he not decided to mortgage Normandy to his willing brother Rufus for the considerable sum of 10,000 marks – by no means a giveaway. English taxpayers in the end funded the duke's expenses in much the same way as they had earlier bankrolled Rufus' campaigning in Normandy. Robert's crusading was in this sense a cooperative venture across the Anglo-Norman realm.

Monasteries were the main source of loans for other men. Count Alan IV of Brittany, who had married again after the death of the princess Constance, exchanged land with the abbey of Sainte-Croix de Quimperle for money to fund his expenses. No interest was charged on the money advanced by monasteries to aspirant crusaders, but the Church gained a profitable income from hypothecated land in the meantime. If the crusader failed to return from the Holy Land, monasteries were within their rights to take ownership of such lands. The same would have been true of the dukedom of Normandy. Duke Robert's death on crusade would have left the duchy under Rufus' control as the new duke, gaining him at last the same title as his father: King of England and Duke of Normandy. However, it should not be assumed this was an outcome Rufus desired; the First Crusade, in the wider context of the times, was very much a family undertaking. The *Anglo-Saxon Chronicle* twice states that Rufus and Robert became reconciled prior to the latter's departure. Societal and religious developments in the late eleventh century persuaded western European families to respond positively to the call from the east. The Norman royal family in this sense needed to be represented on crusade, much as any other. Already a knight of renown, Robert of Normandy was the obvious candidate. The Normans in 1095 acted no differently from other European royal houses when eschewing material considerations, leaving wives and children, pledging land and taking on loans.

A strong cast of powerful, determined men and the enthusiasm evoked in them by the idea of crusade undermines any notion that the duke sought to escape the strains of leadership and pressure from his brothers, or indeed that Rufus acted in any way other than generously in backing Robert – although gaining Normandy must have been a potent lure. Other notable Soldiers of Christ among Robert's wider family and court circle included Bishop Odo of Bayeux (his uncle); Stephen of Aumale (his cousin); Stephen, Count of Blois (his brother-in-law, married to Adela); Alan IV of Brittany (his brother-in-law, married once to Constance); Robert II of Flanders (his cousin); and William, Ivo and Aubrey de Grandmesnil (the sons of Hugh de Grandmesnil, his old ally). All of these men were motivated by high ideals and many would have had to borrow money to make their dream into a reality. The First Crusade has been called a great stirring of hearts, not an excuse for the fattening of wallets.

Nor was the crusade an undeclared desire for conquest – at least, not at first; not until much later did a desire for conquest take precedence when motivating men to make the journey east. If acquisition of land had been a primary incentive, Henry, the only one of the Bastard's sons to have been left landless at the time of William's death, and who had since then on occasion struggled to maintain a toehold in the Cotentin, might have been expected to put himself forward to fight the Turks. Historians in the past have puzzled why he did not! One suggestion is that Rufus needed Henry on hand to keep an eye on Normandy while Rufus was in England, and he made a point of preventing the younger man from travelling. Supporting this idea, the king also discouraged many of his regular knights from crusading, fearful of the drain in manpower this might occasion. England was in fact underrepresented in knightly terms on the First Crusade. The *Anglo-Saxon Chronicle* entry for 1095 laments that, in a year of grievous famine, men and money were wasted fighting in Wales (Christian against Christian) while Crusade beckoned.

Rufus himself may well have been attracted to the idea of crusading, but the heavy responsibilities of governance and the many unresolved issues simmering on the frontiers of the Anglo-Norman realm precluded it. The notably irreligious Robert de Bellême appears never to have contemplated taking the Cross. After the death of his father he was now an even more powerful landowner in Normandy than before. Robert's decision to go east must have opened up great opportunities for him. The duke's conciliatory treatment of Robert Giroie had almost certainly alienated Bellême from the duke, and the death of his father, Roger de Montgomery, had removed all paternal constraints. Montgomery had died at Shrewsbury Abbey sometime the year before. He might otherwise, like Odo, have taken the Cross, hopeful to die in the Holy Land. Better to be reconciled to God, before death he had donned a monastic habit and taken vows. He was probably then in his mid-sixties. After his father's death and Robert Curthose's departure on crusade, Bellême was free to exploit his new-found relationship with Rufus to the maximum. For Henry, also, Robert's leaving must have seemed something of a boon. The count now had a more secure base in the Cotentin and had at last gained the tenurial security he craved. At some point, Rufus formally made over the counties of Bayeux and Coutances to his younger brother.

Rufus travelled to Normandy at the beginning of September 1096 with the money for the loan. The mass of coins, weighing three tons or so, had to be transported across the Channel by ship in sixty-seven barrels. This caretaker offer, eagerly seized upon by the English king, was contracted for either three or five years (the sources are contradictory). A papal representative acted as facilitator. The money invested represented approximately a quarter of Rufus' annual income. The tax to pay for it amounted to around four shillings per taxable unit of arable land. Compared to earlier taxes to pay off Vikings or to maintain battle fleets, this was not overly expensive. Even so, because the Church was not exempted from the tax, much fuss was made by the Church authorities, who accused Rufus of preferring to buy control of the duchy rather than fight for it. They claimed Rufus was squeezing the Church more than he squeezed his barons (the term they used was 'milking the church'). Normandy is said by the English chronicler for 1095–6 to have been redeemed by heavy and 'manifold taxes' on the English, which added to the misery of a people already suffering the effects of hunger and homelessness. Abbots were forced to strip the gold and silver from precious objects like reliquaries, altar furnishings and shrines.

The man held accountable for executing this war tax on the king's behalf was the previously mentioned Ranulf Flambard.

His sobriquet Flambard meant torchbearer. William of Malmesbury described him unflatteringly as a man who skinned the rich, ground down the poor and swept other men's inheritances into his net. According to Orderic, Flambard was addicted to feasts, carousals and lusts, and was cruel and ambitious – 'a prodigal to his own adherents, but rapacious in seizing the goods of other men'. He has been described more recently by his academic biographer J. F. A. Mason as a man devoid of spirituality, secular, innovative and ruthless. He had served the Conqueror as a financier, and during Rufus' reign he is said to have become 'the manager of the whole kingdom'. He held down the roles of treasurer, keeper of the king's seal, chief justiciar and procurator, while also directly managing the affairs of a number of abbeys and bishoprics.

Flambard was the dean at Twynham in Hampshire when the construction of hugely impressive Christchurch Priory Church first commenced, and in 1099 he was made Bishop of Durham, replacing the late and equally worldly, not to say slippery, Bishop William St Calais. He had to pay Rufus £1,000 for the honour of Durham. Robert Bloet had earlier, in 1093, also made payments to Rufus when made Bishop of Lincoln. Thomas, Archbishop of York had tried to block Bloet's consecration on the grounds that Lindsay (roughly, modern-day Lincolnshire) lay within his diocese. The chronicler known as Hugh the Chanter alleged Bloet gave £3,000 to intervene on his behalf (Henry of Huntingdon reckoned the amount to have been £5,000, which would have been an enormous sum). The king gave Thomas the abbeys of Selby and St Oswald in Gloucester to compensate him for the loss of Lincoln. In the end it all came down to money and property. Rufus had no wife or son to act as regent and appears to have taken most of his high-ranking noblemen with him on campaign in Normandy, so needed a man with Flambard's drive and experience to administer the country in his absence – and had to keep him firmly on side.

King Philip of France is also claimed to have been among those who volunteered to join the crusade, but when he pressed the Pope to have his interdict lifted to allow him to travel he was denied.

The king, known to future historians as 'the amorous', was still living in a state of sin with his runaway mistress, Bertrada de Montfort. From the Church's point of view it was important for participants in the crusade to be free from any encompassing sin, not to be up to their necks in it. Although a dent to the king's prestige, the ban can have represented no great loss for the crusader armies. A heartfelt desire for the French royal house to be represented on campaign did nevertheless drive Philip to push for his brother Hugh of Vermandois (known as 'the great' – for his great wealth, not his deeds) to join the expedition. As with the Norman royal family, French representation was important. Hugh had once been an ally of the Conqueror. In 1085, he had helped William ward off a threatened Danish invasion of England that year, fomented by Robert the Frisian. It is said Vermandois only agreed to take part in the crusade after witnessing an eclipse of the moon on 11 February 1096, claimed by soothsayers to herald a great apocalyptic event – something he felt he had to be a part of. Entrusted with the golden standard of St Peter while in Rome, the highest honour the Pope could bestow on a layman, in messages to the Eastern Emperor Hugh is said to have styled himself the supreme commander of the Frankish army.

Crusading offered a practical and sure way of avoiding dying unshriven, allowing men of violence to engage in war and be armoured spiritually as well as physically. Some of the men who set out on crusade went to great lengths to atone for past sin in advance of travelling. In some instances this was insisted upon by the Church. A vassal of the excommunicated Holy Roman Emperor, the famously rich crusading knight Raymond of Toulouse, for example, gained leave to go only after he had made repairs to all of the religious foundations he and his men had wrecked in the past. Other men made hefty donatives to the Church and made sure to settle any outstanding disputes with neighbouring monastic foundations. Stephen of Blois, the husband of the Conqueror's daughter Adela, made a gift of woodland to the Church, so that his wife and children would be watched over while he was away. Past sins may have weighed heavily with Robert Curthose of Normandy too. Orderic claimed it to have been on the advice of the duke's chaplain and other churchmen 'he left the government of his dominions to the king of England' and decided to take the Cross and join the pilgrimage to Jerusalem. For men like Robert, rather than the heady thrill of combat, it must have seemed a once-in-a-lifetime opportunity to divest his soul of mortal sin, a considerable burden for still militarily active men in their forties, fifties and sixties.

Helias de la Fleche, Count of Maine, was another man who hoped to join the crusade. Helias had purchased rights to Maine from his cousin Hugh V and had been at war with Robert Curthose for some considerable time over control of the county, but he was willing to let bygones be bygones if enabled to accompany the duke on crusade. When he asked Rufus to recognise his claims to Maine and refrain from making an attempt to annex the county while he was away, the English king replied that Helias could go wherever he wanted but that he, Rufus, was going to have whatever his father had had, and that included Maine. Orderic likened the Manceaux at this time to 'a flock of sheep terrorised by [English] wolves'. Helias threatened legal appeal. Rufus countered with a threat of war. Neither outcome materialised.

The English king soon after this became embroiled with problems on the borders of Wales, Brittany and Flanders. He delegated the hounding of Helias to his newly acquired and highly recommended enforcer Robert de Bellême. Helias at this point abandoned any thought of crusading and the count later came to an understanding with Rufus, perhaps because many knights from Maine did in fact accompany Robert Curthose on crusade, leaving the county weakened at a crucial time. There was also a strong Breton and Flemish contingent in Robert's crusading army. Among the Bretons was the Conqueror's old enemy Ralph de Gael, the one-time Earl of Norwich and the victor of the Battle of Dol de-Bretagne in 1076. How well (or not) he interacted with Duke Robert is not known, but there is a case to make that he was putting many miles between himself and Rufus. The English king afterwards had to contend with outbreaks of banditry on the Breton and Flemish borders. Loss of the Duke of Brittany and the Count of Flanders to the crusade in fact served to destabilise these regions, as some of the resulting brigandage spilled over into Normandy.

*

The mark of the crusader, as everyone knows, was a six-inch-by-six-inch red cross – the accepted symbol of Christianity – usually stitched or pinned to the crusader's tunic, either on his breast or right shoulder, sometimes tattooed on his brow. Some of the more fanatical types are claimed to have had themselves branded. As a device, a red cross was simple and stylish. Pope Urban knew what he was doing in making the emblem so distinctive. It made the crusaders conspicuous, a badge of pride. A basket of red textile crosses, made available at Clermont, allowed churchmen to help themselves for onward distribution. This became the typical pattern as the papal mission moved from place to place, engaging with the populace of northern Europe more directly. It was also necessary for those who took the Cross to take a crusader's vow. Making vows was something European knights were well used to doing, in particular when performing homage as vassals. They knew the vow to be morally and spiritually binding, more so than any secularly contracted agreement.

The potent lure of pilgrimage, the quest for adventure when journeying to Jerusalem, 'the navel of the world', had been a long-standing obsession for many. For young, underemployed knights who were up for a challenge, the frisson of excitement at the thought of combatting the hated and much-vilified Saracens would have been a welcome distraction from the normal round. Commentators have in modern times suggested pent-up sexual tension to have played a part; others, in more banal fashion, have pointed out that gross national product had outstripped population growth in the late eleventh century, yielding surpluses, which allowed the project to be well funded. The numbers of pilgrims and knights were swelled by an unexpectedly good harvest. Up until 1095, there had been several years of drought with consequent poor crop yields, but that year any shortages were made good with more grain to spare. Fulcher of Chartres wrote that, 'with God disposing, peace and a vast abundance of grain through all the regions of the earth ... [none of the pilgrims failed] on the way for lack of bread'.

One version of Urban's speech at Clermont, written by Robert the Monk, makes reference to the warlike yearnings of the Franks and the Normans:

> Listen and learn! You, girt about with the badge of knighthood, are arrogant with great pride; you rage against your brothers and cut each other in pieces ... the Holy Church has reserved a soldiery for herself to help her people, but you debase her wickedly to her hurt ... you who await the pay of thieves for the shedding of Christian blood – as vultures smell fetid corpses ... lay down the girdle of such knighthood, or advance boldly, as knights of Christ, and rush as quickly as you can to the defence of the Eastern Church.

Making the presumption that the killing of a Christian was damnable, whereas the slaughter of Muslims and Jews in large numbers was a righteous outcome, has since been described as 'perpetuating the abuse of Scripture and rhetoric'.

An unsavoury aspect of crusading, not always recognised, was the rabid anti-Semitism it invoked, in part down to the need for money: usury was forbidden by the papacy, whereas no restrictions were placed on Jewish moneylending. There had been no pogroms against the Jews in western Europe since the seventh century, but this suddenly changed after the First Crusade was announced. Not only was slaughtering Jews a way for the unscrupulous to have their debts written off, the killing of Jews may for some have been seen as a valid extension of the crusading mission. The renowned crusading knight Godfrey of Bouillon forcibly demanded tribute from the Jews in Mainz and Cologne to raise the cash for his crusading ambitions. In the summer of 1095, a number of Jewish settlements along the Rhine were savaged by German and Frankish knights. Poorer pilgrims, part of the so-called People's Crusade, led on by the fanatical Peter the Hermit, later looted the already depleted homes and merchant houses of these same Jews. The following year, another group led by Father Folkmar terrorised the Jewish communities in Magdeburg and later at Prague. Rouen's Jews were also targeted but gained a degree of protection from Rufus, who appears to have facilitated reconversion to Judaism of many Jews earlier browbeaten into renouncing their faith to avoid being robbed or worse. This may have come at a price; ability to reconvert came at a premium, enriching the king.

The first crusading contingents left from the Auvergne in November 1096, a year after Pope Urban's sermon at Clermont. Others followed at regular intervals the following year from April onwards. The routes taken by the various armies varied: some took ship from southern Italy; others marched overland through Hungary or Dalmatia, suffering dreadful ordeals along the way but all the while said to have been buoyed up by their faith. They made up a mass of ethnicities: Frankish, Norman, German, Greek, Spaniards, Italians, Britons and Gallic peoples, as well as many others. It was as if all of western Europe was represented. The armies were also a mix of nations. Robert Curthose's Norman contingent, 'strengthened with their inherited Viking courage', are said to have formed only a nucleus around which assembled men of every type, skilled in military action. As to the overall numbers involved, we have little certain to go on. Near-contemporary accounts speak of logistically impossible hundreds of thousands when describing the corpus of crusaders and pilgrims who met the 'Call from the East'. Modern-day estimates err down toward the 60,000 mark, with most of them unarmed pilgrims and civilian supernumeraries and therefore highly vulnerable. One chronicler wrote, 'What then can we say? This is the Lord's doing; it is marvellous in our eyes.'

13

BEHOLD THE FRANKS

The first great clash between crusaders and Turks occurred at Nicaea, where Robert Curthose's grandfather Robert the Magnificent had died almost sixty years earlier. Once a Byzantine-controlled city, Nicaea in the year 1097 was held by soldiers under the command of the local Seljuk sultan, Kilij Arslan. In defiance of the Byzantine Emperor Alexius' request that they await the main crusading armies, the earliest arrivals from the west, part of the roughly 20,000-strong People's Crusade, occupied the Greco-Christian suburbs of Nicaea on the eastern shore of Lake Iznik to the south-east of Constantinople. French and German knights accompanying the pilgrims managed through surprise to capture one of Kilij Arslan's castles at a place called Xerigordon. The Turkish response was swift and brutal. After an eight-day siege, Xerigordon fell back into the sultan's hands. All of the captured crusaders who would not immediately convert to Islam were slain. The throng of mainly unarmed pilgrims were then set upon a few weeks later at a village called Dracon. Adult survivors were again given the option of conversion, but clerics and infants were despatched without recourse to convert. One priest found at prayer was decapitated where he knelt. Many thousands are said to have been killed. The dead bodies were heaped into pyres, and later the sun-bleached bones were crushed to make mortar to fill in the cracks in the walls of the Turkish fortifications.

When the chronicler Fulcher of Chartres later passed this way, accompanied by Robert Curthose and Stephen of Blois, he noted the severed heads and bones of the dead remained scattered over the landscape: 'The Turks [had] destroyed all those who were ignorant of the arrow.' For many this was the first jarring proof that the Byzantines had lost control of not only Jerusalem but much else too. The arrival of Robert and Stephen was headlined by the chronicler Guibert of Nogent: 'Meanwhile, two men arrived, the most celebrated for deeds of arms and the wealthiest counts, whom we have already mentioned, accompanied by many knights, whose arrival filled the whole army of the Lord with joy: Robert, Count of Normandy, and Count Stephen of Chartres.'

By this time the various crusading contingents had placed Turkish-held Nicaea under siege. They employed state-of-the-art weapons of war: battering rams, wooden siege towers and stone-throwing artillery called mangonels. The emperor provided them with wood, nails and rope. With Nicaea completely surrounded by the great host of westerners, attempts by Kilij Arslan's horsemen to raise the siege were easily countered. The Turkish horse archers operated best in open terrain. The hilly and wooded nature of the countryside at Nicaea disadvantaged them. Stout walls and a robust defence nevertheless prevented a swift outcome in favour of the crusaders. On one occasion we know about, a knight from Robert's command, who found himself isolated after an abortive assault, was shot dead by Turkish archers lining the walls. A device with sharp iron claws was then lowered by chain to grip the corpse and lift it over the battlements. The stripped cadaver was hung from a noose in full view of the besiegers, either as a deterrent or simply for the devilment of it.

Only when the perimeter walls were breached by the slow process of undermining (this was work carried out under cover of a massive engine of war, said to have been commissioned at great cost) did the Turkish garrison at last surrender. A Byzantine army, not a crusader army, then called the shots and occupied the city. The Turks would only surrender to the imperial forces, not to the westerners.

They rightly feared a massacre should the crusading armies gain entry into the city. Fulcher of Chartres wrote that the Turks 'slyly' returned the city to Alexius, fearful of the dire consequence should the crusaders storm it. Even after the city's fall, the crusader knights were not permitted to enter in greater numbers than ten at a time. Gifts of money, horses and women from Alexius were needed to pacify the western leaders when denied the gory fruits of war. Fulcher mentions the emperor giving the leading crusaders 'gold, silver and mantles', and the common foot soldiers copper coins.

Alexius was setting the agenda. After the fall of Nicaea, he mapped out the route to be taken by the crusaders south to Jerusalem, and he highlighted the towns and cities which would need to be secured on the way. Rather than proceed deeper southward into Anatolia with his own forces, Alexius' plan was to march northward to deal with mounting problems on his frontier with eastern Europe where Cumans, Hungarians, Alemanni and Serbs were ravaging the Danube Valley. He did, though, promise to ensure the western army remained provisioned throughout, and that he would come to their assistance in extremis. A number of recipients of Alexius' largesse now threw in the towel, happy to have been compensated but daunted by the prospect of the long road south. Some of them enlisted in the Byzantine army, motivated more by a lucrative career than crusading.

The Battle of Dorylaeum, 1 July 1097

When heading south on the road to Dorylaeum, the remaining crusaders split their forces to better facilitate foraging. However, in doing so they attracted a Turkish attack on the foremost unit. Kilij Arslan's cavalry had been tracking the westerners, remaining all the while at a safe distance but determined to avenge their earlier losses at Nicaea. Kilij Arslan's sobriquet meant, in old Anatolian Turkish, 'sword-bearer', or 'lion with a sword'; he was a worthy challenger, but one who appears to have underestimated the fighting acumen of the Franks and Normans. His cavalry comprised a mix of light and heavy horsemen, with the former, the horse archers, predominating. These were lightly attired men on squat, fast central European horses, described by a contemporary as 'swift as eagles, with hooves as solid as rock'. The heavy cavalrymen, all armoured, rode slower, more robust horses. The horse archers each carried two bows and thirty arrows in a leather quiver, whereas the heavy cavalry wielded lances as their primary weapon, with maces as backup. There were also troops of mounted javelin-men. Fulcher of Chartres confirms Arslan's army to have been a fully mounted force, whereas the crusaders comprised a mix of mounted knights and infantry.

When a gap of around three miles opened between the crusader vanguard and the main body, the Turks launched an impromptu ambush on the foremost unit, which comprised the combined forces of Bohemond of Taranto, Robert Curthose of Normandy and Stephen of Blois. Guibert of Nogent wrote, 'For two days they marched in two separate divisions. One contained Bohemond, Robert of Normandy, and Tancred, together with a large contingent of knights; the Count of Saint-Gilles, Duke Godfrey, the Bishop of Puy, Hugh the Great, and the Count of Flanders were leading the other group through pathless territory. On the third day, an innumerable, terrible, and nearly overwhelming mass of Turks suddenly rushed upon Bohemond and his men.' The crusader knights were quickly driven back under a hail of arrows behind the phalanx of their supporting foot soldiers. The infantry had quickly formed up in a 'tight-knit' defensive formation. Fulcher of Chartres, who was there, wrote, 'The Turks, with clashing of weapons and shrieking, fiercely let loose a shower of arrows ... stunned and almost dead and with many injured, we straightaway turned our back in flight.'

Guibert of Nogent added that the Turks attacked 'suddenly and swiftly, hurling javelins, and fighting in their usual fashion by fleeing as they fired arrows into the breasts of their pursuers'. Robert Curthose and Bohemond kept things together in the front line of the fighting. Robert is said to have been inspired to fight by 'the exemplars of his noble lineage'. Accounts mention him and Bohemond as prominent throughout. Guibert of Nogent wrote,

'The count of Normandy, properly mindful of his father's military valour and noble ancestry, performed mighty deeds of arms, fighting off the enemy, and offering a fine example of resistance to our momentarily frightened army.' Any lingering doubt after the debacle at Rouen that Robert had lost the nerve to stand and fight and hold his ground was banished from men's minds by the bravery he displayed when rallying his troops.

Having so quickly lost many of their horses to Turkish flight arrows, the riderless knights of the vanguard for several hours formed a human shield, behind which lighter infantrymen engaged the swirling Turkish host with crossbow bolts, arrows and spears. The non-combatants are said by Fulcher, who was one of them, to have huddled together 'like sheep in a fold, trembling and terrified'. Their makeshift camp had its rear partially protected by marshy ground and a river, which proved immensely important in preventing them from becoming surrounded on all sides, as well as providing the fighting men with drinking water, preventing dehydration. Guibert of Nogent wrote of this aspect of the fight, saying, 'God was also present, so that the women who had accompanied them stood by their men, constantly bringing water to refresh the knights. Indeed, their encouragement and advice did more to make the men more tireless and inventive than the water did to refresh them.' Robert and Bohemond continued throughout to hold things together against the onslaught. Fulcher tells how they raised their men's resolve by shouting, 'Stand fast together and trust in Christ and the victory of the Holy Cross.' That the crusaders held out long enough to be relieved by the main body of crusaders, earlier recalled by a messenger sent by Bohemond, was afterwards seen as miraculous, spun as a sign that God was unwilling to see the crusade 'brought to nought to the dishonour of Christianity'. There were, however, two notable losses: Bohemond's son William, plus an unnamed great-nephew of Geoffrey of Conversano, the Lord of Brindisi, Robert Curthose's host while in Calabria.

*

The crusading armies reached the major communications hub of Antioch on 30 October 1097 and immediately set about placing the strongly and extensively walled town under siege. During the advance on the city there had been hard fighting by Robert Curthose's 2,000-strong command to force a crossing of the River Orontes to the north of the city. There had also been hair-raising mountain crossings to navigate. One 'cursed mountain', the highest point of the Taurus range, cost the crusaders heavily in lost animals and their packs when plunging over cliff faces. The knights are said to have 'wrung their hands, overcome with fear and shock'.

Antioch's great size and extensive defensive perimeter – the thick walls were studded with more than three hundred watchtowers – made it impossible to mount an all-enveloping siege. Dating back to the reign of Justinian in the sixth century, the stout walls defended Antioch to the north, south and west, while mountainous terrain, more strong walls and a great fortified citadel shielded the city to the east, enabling the garrison to launch sneak attacks from higher ground on the crusaders below. Only the northern and north-western gates to the city could be blockaded with any degree of security. Carefully sited wooden fortresses were built by the crusaders from timber shipped to the Syrian coast from Cyprus to deny the Turks access to pasture for their animals and the ability to sally out to skirmish. The largest of these, known as the *Malregard* (Bad Overseer), was sited to prevent any spoiling attack made by the Antioch garrison from the high ground to the north-east.

The main city gates further to the south remained unblocked. From one of these, known as the Bridge Gate, agile Turkish horse archers on occasion sallied forth to pester the encamped knights on the west bank of the Orontes. Albert of Aachen wrote, 'Morning, noon and night ... there were these sudden attacks, sallies [and] scenes of carnage.' Described by another eyewitness, Raymond of Aguilers, as 'hit and run attacks', the main cost to the crusaders appears to have been in horses. There were some notable casualties as well: Archdeacon Adelbaro of Metz, for example, was seized in an orchard near one of the city gates and beheaded. To serve as a better place of safety and respite, the crusaders erected a fort nearby. Another construction undertaken was a bridge of boats across the Orontes to open up better communications with the coast, where lay the crusaders' main line of supply from Cyprus.

Despite the crusaders' best efforts, the Turks in Antioch remained partially supplied throughout the siege. Within the city, a mix of nationalities and religious orders resided, lorded over by an allegedly 5,000-strong Muslim garrison. Distrustful of the majority of Christians living within the city – Greeks, Syrians and Armenians – 'the maddened Turks' are said by Fulcher of Chartres to have killed a number of them and dumped their decapitated heads over the walls to discomfort the crusaders. One Greek religious leader was regularly hung upside down from the walls and the soles of his feet beaten.

As the siege dragged on, extensive ravaging for supplies on the part of the crusader armies served to denude the surrounding land of produce. After Christmas 1097, famine loomed. Fulcher wrote, 'In the year of our Lord 1098, after the region all around Antioch had been wholly devastated by the multitude of our people, the strong as well as the weak were more and more harassed by famine.' Particularly hard-hit would have been the horses, numbering in their thousands, which needed plentiful water and hay each day. The crusaders had enjoyed an abundance of supplies at the start of the siege but these had not lasted long. According to Matthew of Edessa, one in five crusaders died from starvation. Non-combatants fared even worse. Sorties to secure additional supplies attracted ambush. The crusaders by wintertime were suffering greater distress and hardship than the citizens of Antioch, but were nonetheless tightening their grip around the city. Crisis of supply did in fact for a time come close to bringing a halt to the campaign, explaining the importance the crusade leaders placed on maintaining communication with the coastal towns at St Symeon and Alexandretta, where intermittent supplies were unloaded for shipment into the interior.

Robert Curthose at some stage led a contingent of the army which occupied the coastal town of Latakia to the south, presumably to open up a new convoy route. Ralph of Caen wrote of the citizens there appealing to the crusaders for military support. Having only recently fallen into crusader hands, the port, like those to the north, was also supplied from bases in Cyprus. At least two fleets, a Genoese of thirteen transports and an even larger English one, were by this time operating to ferry supplies and a steady stream of reinforcements, but not yet in a quantity sufficient to feed the still substantial crusader host. When the worst of the winter hit, the galleys were prevented from putting to sea altogether.

Respite from the soul-sapping misery of the siege lines at Antioch would have been welcome for a man of Robert's advancing years. He had been away from Normandy for the best part of a year and a half, much of the time travelling along unforgiving, dusty roads and making camp under the stars. At first he and his comrades had travelled by way of the Via Francigena, the ancient routeway that had for many years borne the pilgrim traffic from northern Europe across the Alps to Rome, arriving at the eternal city in December 1096. Unedifying rivalries between the supporters of the two contending popes had deterred some of his fellowship from continuing any further. Lawlessness in Rome was everywhere apparent. Even the lowliest of pilgrims had stood the chance of being attacked and their few possessions stolen.

Having left Rome behind, Robert and his entourage had travelled down into southern Italy and had overwintered in Calabria, where they are said to have suffered a severe winter. The more driven and headstrong Count Robert II of Flanders had hurried his contingent across the eastern Mediterranean from the port of Bari, whereas Robert and Stephen decided to settle and in doing so gained reproof from future cloister-bound historians. Remaining in southern Italy over the winter was a much more sensible option than attempting to make the fraught passage across the Adriatic; it was foolhardy for the Flemish count to have done so. Fulcher wrote of the opposition of local sailors, and adds that the previous year Hugh 'the Great' of Vermandois (King Philip's younger brother) had attempted the passage from Bari to the Balkan Coast in October but had been caught in dreadful storms. Only a few of his ships, Vermandois' included, had survived the crossing. Robert of Flanders on the other hand was granted a period of fine weather, so his recklessness paid off.

Robert Curthose may no longer have been a young man, but Bishop Odo of Bayeux was older still and while in Calabria his health may have been failing. At Christmas 1096, the bishop is said to have left the Italian mainland and travelled across the straits to Sicily to visit the Norman ruler of the island, an old friend known as Roger the 'great count'. If the two men did in fact meet up is not known. Odo died on 6 January 1097 at Palermo, shortly after his arrival. He may have hoped to have held on to life long enough to continue the crusade and to die at Jerusalem. If Odo accompanied Robert to avoid being left behind to the tender mercies of Rufus, as has sometimes been posited, the desire to see the Holy City before he died would have been the more pressing imperative. Odo has been described as a 'prince-bishop on a grand scale'. His energy and leadership had likely underpinned the conquest of England – even if he later sought to take undue advantage. Robert had lost a loyal and irreplaceable advisor and advocate.

Not until Easter Sunday 1098 had Robert and Stephen's army embarked from the port of Brindisi, yet even with the worst of the winter behind them some men and women (four hundred according to Fulcher) had lost their lives when one of the boats of the fleet foundered. Quick to make a moral point, Fulcher wrote how the corpses of the drowned each bore the mark of the cross miraculously imprinted on the shoulders, a sure sign of their salvation. The remainder of the fleet successfully made it to the port of Durazzo, in modern-day Albania. From here they – the last of four sizeable armies to have set out eastward – travelled overland along the Via Egnatia into Bulgaria and onward to Constantinople. Even then there was scant respite for the travellers: Alexius can never have anticipated such an enormous throng arriving on his doorstep, and by the time Robert and Stephen's army arrived he had become guarded in his dealing with the crusaders, and probably for good reason. Bohemond of Taranto, an earlier arrival, is claimed to have nurtured designs on toppling Alexius and the higher echelons and taking the empire for himself. Rumours of this may have reached the emperor's ears. By the time the Norman contingent arrived, few among the crusader knights present were welcome to enter the city for fear they might run amok. Instead they were forced to make camp outside the city walls, where they purchased supplies at open-air marts.

*

Robert's extended stay at Latakia may in fact have been the first time since his spell in Calabria that he been able to relax his vigil. However, he may have overstayed his time on the coast. There is mention in the sources of his absence becoming resented by men on the front line at Antioch. It is possible ill health delayed him. Whatever the cause, it is to his credit he re-joined the main army outside Antioch at the beginning of February 1098, in time to take command of the siege. Bohemond was away doing battle with a Turkish relief force, fighting what has become known as the 'Lake Battle' (9 February). The author of the *Gesta Francorum* wrote,

> Bohemond, protected on all sides by the sign of the Cross, charged the Turkish forces, like a lion which has been starving for three or four days, which comes roaring out of its cave thirsting for the blood of cattle ... The other troops, seeing Bohemond's banner carried ahead so honourably, stopped their retreat at once, and all our men in a body charged the Turks, who were amazed and took flight. Our men pursued them and massacred them.

Around this time Stephen of Blois quit the crusade altogether; at the peak of his privations he had written home to his wife Adela complaining of 'enormous torrents of rain ... and excessive cold'. He said that many crusaders had feared the heat of the Syrian sun, and so were quite unprepared for a hard winter. Stephen had earlier described Antioch as 'a city great beyond belief, very strong and unassailable'. He had informed Adela that he had been chosen to coordinate the various facets of the campaign – a role which must have played to his strengths, of which he was proud. To homesickness was added the brutalising effect of campaigning in extreme conditions, and at some indeterminate point he possibly suffered a complete emotional collapse.

Albert of Aachen claimed Stephen, like many others who deserted at this time, was afraid of failure and of suffering an abject death at the hands of the Turks. News of a large enemy relief force approaching Antioch may have triggered his flight. As an even sadder footnote to this unhappy affair, when Stephen eventually arrived back in France it was, as briefly mentioned in chapter three, to an angry reception from his wife Adela, who is said to have been deeply aggrieved that her husband had broken his vows to march on the Holy City. Stephen's letters to Adela up until then have been described as forming 'a uniquely intimate insight into the experiences of the Crusade's great leaders', and confirm the trust he placed in his wife as his regent while he was absent. (See appendix 1.) Among her many duties that we know of are the commissioning new churches and strengthening bishops – dealing with misbehaving nuns even gets a mention. She toured the county, settled land disputes and even engaged in a recruitment drive to identify and encourage potential crusaders. She was not unique in doing so; many other noble women at this time took it upon themselves to undertake duties which in the past had been in the male domain.

When Stephen returned to France, he is said to have carried back cartloads of treasure: jewels, icons and maps which he housed at Chartres. Adela is claimed to have berated him for not making good his pledges; if she refused him sex is of course not known, though stories abound of their lovemaking being interrupted by her unprompted criticisms. William M. Aird points out that the image of the princess persuading her husband 'to redeem his reputation through action' has become an enduring motif of the crusader movement and the passions it aroused. It may also be the case Stephen faced the possibility of excommunication. He did return to the east, and took part in the lesser crusade of 1101. He was killed at the siege of Ramallah in May 1102.

The Battle at Antioch, 29 June 1098

Antioch finally fell to the crusading armies after eight months of siege and at least two major relief attempts by the Turks. The city was not taken by storm in the end; instead, bribes made by Bohemond to a traitor within secured covert access. On the night of 2/3 June 1098, twenty chosen men were able to cast their rope ladders unopposed, scale the walls and unlock a nearby postern gate, allowing the crusaders unopposed access to the heart of the city. Soon the streets of the city thronged with crusaders, swords drawn and bloodied. Bohemond's great purple banner is said by Fulcher to have 'furled and unfurled' as if buffeted by the winds of war. The capture of the city had come hot on the heels of news of the approach of yet another relief army from Mesopotamia and Syria, described by the Muslim chronicler Ibn al-Qalansi as 'an uncountable force', much larger than any yet faced by the crusaders. Led by Kerbogah of Mosul, the secular sword-arm of the Sultan of Baghdad, a man described by the crusaders as diabolical and more recently as 'a self-seeking atabeg', the news of this army's approach triggered Bohemond's audacious commando raid on the postern gate. Kerbogah is claimed to have taken a common-sense view of the crusaders' attributes, telling his soldiers they faced men of flesh and blood like themselves; the only difference, he told them, was that the crusaders were impure and uncircumcised, so at a disadvantage.

Alexius' army had marched south to reinforce the siege, but had unaccountably turned back. News that the Byzantines had left the crusaders to their fate filtered through to Antioch (likely spread by Kerbogah's agents). This led a number of other prominent crusaders to follow Stephen's example and flee to the coast. Among them were a number of Robert's noblemen, including two of the Grandmesnil brothers, Ivo and Aubrey, who later became known as 'the rope dancers of Antioch' for their daring escapade in letting themselves down to safety outside the city. Now besieged themselves, the remaining crusaders faced a rapidly deteriorating situation. They are said in the *Gesta Francorum* to have 'eaten the flesh of horses and asses'. So terrible did the famine become, the men and women are said to have boiled and ate fig leaves, vines and thistles, while others 'stewed the dried skins of already long ago consumed animals'. Muslim sources speak of the common soldiers feasting on carrion.

There is an element of Hollywood about what happened next. Spurred on by the miraculous finding on 14 June of a fragment of metal, alleged to be a piece of the holy lance that had pierced Christ's side while on the Cross, the crusader knights rallied around Bohemond as their leader and prepared to fight to the death. Albert of Aachen says Bohemond persuaded them 'it would be better to die fighting than to succumb to a cruel famine'. Held aloft at the head of the army, the newly recovered holy lance head served as a victory sign and a morale booster. Robert Curthose commanded the third in line of six divisions of knights, each of approximately 120 men. The date of the battle was 29 June 1098. It is claimed that all in the army had fasted for three days beforehand. Not only did this serve as a religious purgative, it must also have helped eke out supplies.

Guibert of Nogent, who later spoke face to face with veterans of the crusade, provides us with a ringside account of what occurred. He wrote that as the knights rode out of the city gate, the churchmen within maintained a barrage of prayer. Hugh of Vermandois, with his vanguard of archers, was, Guibert wrote, the first into action. His men drove back a blocking squadron of enemy horsemen, while the main body of the crusader army remained close behind. Keeping the Orontes River on their right flank, they rapidly advanced against Kerbogah's array. When Kerbogah saw the host emerging from the Bridge Gate, he is said by Guibert to have exclaimed, ominously, 'Behold, the Franks!' A nearby soldier named Amirdal, famed for his martial prowess, replied, 'Either flee now or fight well; for I see the standard of the great Pope advancing.'

Robert of Normandy may have been the man who suggested this bold frontal assault, mirroring his tactics at Gerberoy two decades earlier. Two hundred knights remained in Antioch as a reserve. The rest thundered forth to do battle. After a hard fight, during which Robert Curthose and Godfrey of Bouillon had a hand in beating off a fierce enemy flanking attack, the Mesopotamians were routed. One notable casualty of the fight was the late Roger de Montgomery's youngest son, Philip. The fleeing enemy horsemen are claimed to have set the grassy plain on fire, a pre-arranged warning to their camp guards to grab their food and belongings and take to their heels. Ibn-al-Qalanisi wrote, 'The lords of the pedigree steeds were put to flight, and the sword was unsheathed upon the [Muslim] foot soldiers who had volunteered for the cause of God.'

A fierce desire for survival and the potency of their cause had given the crusaders a decisive edge. Robert Curthose's heroics at Antioch were well publicised in western Europe. By this stage the crusader army had put three separate Muslim armies to flight. We can only imagine how such tidings were received by Rufus and Henry. Did they feel an immense pride in their brother's achievements; or did they, being only human, betray envy and a hint of remorse that they had not set off into the east with him to win undying glory at the sword's edge.

*

The Holy City was first sighted by the crusaders on 7 June 1099, almost a full year after the battle at Antioch. It fell to the crusaders five weeks later on 15 July. A period of fasting had been imposed before the assault. There had also been a series of religious processions round the circuit of the walls, as if done in some manner to undermine them; this was a job better left to Robert Curthose's great mangonels, hefty catapults designed to hurl rocks, and sometimes the corpses of men or animals – even, on occasion, the heads of prisoners – over the walls of the city. Guibert of Nogent provides us with an impassioned sketch highlighting Robert's low mood after the failed first attack:

> As God is my witness, I have heard, from men renowned for their truthfulness, who were present in the divine army, that after their unsuccessful assault upon the walls of the city, you would have seen the best of the knights who had returned from the walls striking their hands, shouting angrily, lamenting that God had deserted them. And I also learned, from sources no less reliable, that Robert, count of Normandy, and the other Robert, prince of Flanders, met and shared their mutual grief, weeping copiously, and declaring themselves the most wretched of men, since the Lord Jesus had judged them unworthy of worshipping His Cross, and of seeing, or rather of adoring His tomb.

When the final assault came, heavy missile fire from the mangonels 'shot in' the attack, enabling siege towers to be wheeled into place largely unmolested and for the knights to breach the walls and enter the city, where a savage slaughter ensued. Robert commanded the artillery arm while the rest of his Norman contingent assaulted from the north-west, opposite the Damascus Gate.

It is not known whether Robert took part in the well-publicised slaughter spree that followed. The bodies of dead Muslims and Jews are claimed to have later been piled up above head height as grim, festering mounds outside the walls. Godfrey of Bouillon, a noted anti-Semite, left the scene of the massacre at an early stage to pray at the Holy Sepulchre. Other leaders, like Robert may have followed suit. The capture of Jerusalem for the duke – the senior prince in the crusading army and also the most politic and arguably the least contentious of the leaders – represented a momentous personal achievement for him, something his brothers could never equal militarily, and of which even his late father would have been proud. Even his sometime critic Guibert of Nogent says, 'The duke had expiated his sins through perseverance and heroism: [so] vigorously [had his courage been] displayed in the army of the Lord.'

For Robert Curthose the accolades did not end there. At the Battle of Ascalon, fought on 12 August 1099, the final encounter of the First Crusade between crusaders and Muslims, the duke again distinguished himself. A relief force from Egypt had arrived too late to prevent the fall of Jerusalem, but now posed a serious threat to its ongoing occupation by the crusaders. The enemy army comprised a mix of Seljuk Turks, Arabs, Persians, Armenians, Kurds and Ethiopians. Godfrey of Bouillon led the left wing of the crusader army and Raymond the right; the forces of Tancred (a grandson of Guiscard), Robert of Flanders and Robert Curthose of Normandy formed the centre. The crusader right flank appears to have skirted the coastline. There was little room for manoeuvre. The crusader's steady advance triggered a spoiling attack from an unnerved contingent of Ethiopians. Crucially, the main body of Seljuk cavalry held back and awaited events. Once this Ethiopian 'forlorn hope' had been driven off, Robert Curthose and Tancred launched a largely unopposed charge into the enemy camp, capturing the Fatimid commander's standard – a silver device topped with 'a golden apple'. Robert is credited by Robert the Monk with making directly for the vizier's standard bearer and displaying the same derring-do heroism as before at Gerberoy and Antioch:

The Count of Normandy, a soldier without fear, was the first to join battle along with his column, aiming for the part where he could see the banner of the emir (which they call 'standard'). He slashed a path through the squadrons with his sword, creating carnage; when he reached the standard-bearer he knocked him to the ground at the emir's feet and took the standard. The emir was lucky to escape.

Robert later presented the trophy to the patriarch of Jerusalem, to be displayed in the Church of the Holy Sepulchre, a sacred place dating back to the fourth century.

Elsewhere, an attempt to turn the crusader's left flank was beaten off by Godfrey of Bouillon. Up to 10,000 Muslims are said to have lost their lives in the slaughter that followed, but such enormous losses should be heavily discounted. The city of Ascalon remained under Fatimid control and would not be captured by crusading forces until over half a century later in the year 1153. Many Muslim participants, rather than being put to death, fled the battle and sought shelter there. Raymond of Toulouse was offered the governorship of the city by the inhabitants, but he was denied by Godfrey of Bouillon, who feared a Frankish state emerging, which would have broken the oath he offered Alexius to respect the ownership of Byzantine possessions. After a number of earlier disagreements, which had seen Bohemond remain behind at Antioch, this later spat between the leaders caused a terminal breach in relations; in effect, the squabbling brought the First Crusade to an end.

A great exodus of knights occurred in the autumn of 1099. Alexius warmly received the leaders at Constantinople. Robert Curthose was among those who refused the emperor's offer of a commission in the imperial army, but some of his knights may have stayed on in Alexius' service. He may have been gifted with treasures while at Constantinople, but according to his academic biographer Kathleen Thompson, unlike many other crusaders, Robert 'entertained no designs for personal profit' and 'honoured his commitments to the emperor without seeking any financial reward'. Robert had been the crusader who had relinquished the greatest dominions of any prince to attend the crusade, and, to his great credit, 'he had', in the words of David Hume, 'all along distinguished himself by the most intrepid courage, as well as by that affable disposition and unbounded generosity which gained the hearts of his soldiers, and qualified the prince to shine in a military life'. Peter Frankopan (*The First Crusade*) says that with his fellow knights he had achieved 'one of the most astonishing feats of endeavour in history'. As an example of the privations he must have suffered, on the advance to Jerusalem, after capturing Maarat an-Numan, hunger levels had forced the crusaders to slice the buttocks off dead Muslims for sustenance. Many others had by this time died en route or deserted. Less than one in ten knights who set out from Constantinople had in the end stood beneath Jerusalem's walls on the eve of the final attack. An older and more hardened Robert travelled westward back to Apulia, where he again overwintered. He arrived back in Normandy toward the end of 1100, exhausted, triumphant... and married!

14

AN END AND
A NEW BEGINNING

Rufus spent much of his time in Normandy while Robert was on crusade. He was immediately accepted without question as an overlord to rule the Normans. In the words of his biographer Frank Barlow, this was because he 'represented the dynasty'. He did not take the title duke, nor did he submit to the French king as his vassal; as a caretaker landlord, he had no need to. He is claimed to have maintained better order than his brother, but the truth of such an assertion remains subjective. Gaining Normandy did not bring any great improvement in Rufus' circumstances. Exerting control there proved no easier for him than it had for Robert. Moreover, during the years his elder brother was away Rufus also faced a major fightback by the Welsh in the wake of a crushing defeat they had recently suffered.

In the spring of 1093, while Rufus lay ill at Gloucester, a memorable victory had been won by the Anglo-Normans over the Welsh at Brecon. Much of Powys had been overrun by the invaders. During the battle, Rhys ap Tewdwr, the Welsh king once feted by the Conqueror and Robert Curthose in 1081, made a heroic uphill charge against a strongly entrenched Norman position, only to be killed outright. *The Chronicle of the Princes of Wales* recounted, 'Tewdwr, king of Deheubarth, was slain by the Frenchmen who were inhabiting Brycheiniog [Brecon].' Gerald of Wales adds that the Welsh warlord had been betrayed by his own troops. The spot where Rhys met his death is said to mark the later site of Brecon Priory (now the Cathedral Church of St John the Evangelist).

The scale of the slaughter meted out at battle's end was said to have been significant and to have presaged the end of an ancient line of kings and heralded further impetus to Norman penetration westward into Dyfed and Ceredigion. Those who fell, Gerald wrote, 'represented 'the best men of the kingdom of the Britons'. John of Worcester went even further when writing that 'from that day, kings ceased to rule in Wales'. Gerald and John were writing much later and with retrospective insight, but even at the time the fight at Brecon may have been seen as momentous. The victor of the battle, Bernard de Neufmarché, ordered the building of a priory at the confluence of the Usk and Honddu at a point still known as Rhyd Bernard. It became a daughter house of Battle Priory in West Sussex. His original motte and a later stone castle stand nearby.

The following year a major Welsh fightback erupted. When in sufficient numbers and desperate enough, the native Welsh could sweep all before them. Much gained by the Anglo-Normans was quickly lost. The attacks began in Gwynedd, where in a short space of time all the castles erected by the Norman lords to the west of the Conwy River were carried by assault and the island of Anglesey recovered. An army despatched by Rufus to win it back was defeated at Coed Yspwys in East Gwynedd in the spring or summer of 1094. The victor at Coed Yspwys, a Welsh warlord named Cadwgan Bleddyn, demonstrated the invaders were beatable when surprised or attacked in sufficient numbers. Hugh d'Avranches' cousin Robert of Rhuddlan was among the prominent victims of Coed Yspwys, killed by Welsh javelins when attempting to prevent Cadwgan Bleddyn's seagoing marauders from re-floating their boats off the Great Orme, a serpent-like headland of Carboniferous limestone near Llandudno. Rhuddlan is said to have launched himself into the fray before donning his armour – if true, an indication he and his men had come under surprise attack. That he counter-attacked single-handed seems less credible. Rhuddlan's body fell into the hands of his enemies. His head was severed from the neck and hung from the mast of one of the Welsh longships and a Norman pursuit was only halted when the head was taken down and thrown into the sea.

Among the lords who had in the past ridden out against the Welsh with Rhuddlan, and who may have been with him at Coed Yspwys, were Robert Fitz Hugh of Malpas, William Malbanc of Nantwich, William Fitz Nigel of Halton, and Hugh Fitz Norman of Mold. All were notable marcher castellans. Fitz Norman's bolthole at Mold Castle in modern-day Flintshire remains the epitome of the Norman frontier motte, beset on all sides by enemies. Like many other Norman strongholds of the period, Mold was built upon an existing prehistoric earthwork. Dominating the surrounding landscape, it stood 100 feet above the plain. Very much in the front line against the Welsh, it would hold out until the middle of the following century when the warlord Owain of Gwynedd finally captured it.

Castle building had continued apace in Wales during Rufus' reign, not only in the north but also in the south and along the marches. North and west of Carmarthen, castles sprung up like grim sentinels and their remains still litter the landscape, a reminder today of an oppressive occupation. A motte-and-bailey castle existed at Cardigan by 1093, five years into Rufus' reign. Evidence that Rufus took a very hands-on approach to the campaigning in southern and Mid Wales is indicated by the fact three of his four stays we know about at Gloucester occurred in 1093, the year the Normans made their greatest gains in the future principality. A similar daunting structure was built the same year at Carmarthen, and another was sited at Pembroke, probably at much the same time. Arnulf de Montgomery, one of Roger de Montgomery's younger sons, captured Pembroke after arriving there by sea in the manner of his Viking ancestors. More robust stone castles would follow in the early 1100s. An anonymous

Welshman bewailed, 'Our limbs will be cut off and our liberty and self-will perish.' Norman tyranny is cited in an extract from a work by the Rhygyfarch (d. *c.* 1099):

> The People and the priest are despised
> By the word, heart and deeds of the Frenchmen.
> They burden us with tribute and consume our possessions.
> One of them, however lowly, shakes a hundred natives
> With his command, and sacrifices them with his look.

There were setbacks, however. Montgomery Castle had come under fierce attack from the Welsh in 1093 and the Norman garrison was largely wiped out. There were problems further west as well. Throughout Gwynedd, Norman castles were taken or destroyed. Further to the south, in Ceredigion and Dyfed, only Pembroke Castle may have been left in Norman hands. Rufus' castellan there, Gerald of Windsor, described as 'a stalwart, cunning man', managed to hold on to the castle against all odds, despite the desertion of fifteen knights from the garrison, who fled under cover of darkness. Windsor successfully fooled the Welsh into thinking Pembroke remained strongly defended by dressing common soldiers up as knights. He also had any surplus food thrown from the battlements to show that the castle remained well provisioned, which of course it was not.

Gerald's successful defence of Pembroke may have encouraged Rufus to launch a major foray into the west when returning from Normandy the following year. He had landed at Arundel and had held his Easter court at Windsor, before setting off at the head of a large army to campaign in the north of Wales. His enemies fell back to their Snowdonian mountain fastnesses, avoiding a set-piece encounter. The English chronicler says Rufus stayed in Wales from midsummer until August but lost many men and horses – presumably to ambushes or to accidents in the dangerous terrain. He may have been further outwitted by the previously mentioned Cadwgan ap Bleddyn, a man the same age as Robert

Curthose, a one-time enemy of Rhys ap Tewdwr and the victor of Coed Yspwys, who had been elected by the men of Powys to be their king. The Anglo-Normans in the end were forced to cut and run. Rufus ordered a spate of castle building on the frontier to hold back the high tide of resurgent Welshmen.

*

After his reverses in Wales, the security of Normandy's frontiers once again became Rufus' main focus, in particular the disputed Vexin. The king famously boasted that he would have all his father had had and more. Given the somewhat wasted condition of the French king, both physically (he had grown inordinately fat) and spiritually (he remained under papal interdict), a campaign in the Vexin seemed an attractive proposition. Rufus dug deep to buy the services of local knights in great numbers, putting further strain on English taxpayers. Robert de Bellême gained overall military command of the Anglo-Norman army. Henry also joined the cavalcade. Now once again in possession of his Cotentin appanage (recouped, it was said, 'by influence or by arms': some of it in fact regained through grants made by Rufus), the count rode at his elder brother's side. Others in the king's entourage included William d'Evreux, Hugh d'Avranches and Walter Giffard, who had now been made Earl of Buckingham. A papal plea for peace in Europe while the western armies were away on crusade was ignored by Rufus.

As early as 1095, an advanced base of operations (a *point d'appui*) had been established by Rufus at Gisors, the capital of the Norman Vexin, protecting a strategic gateway for the French into the duchy. This must have been taken from the French by force, since the town had been made over to Philip of France sometime after the turn of the decade as the price for securing French support against Rufus. Robert de Bellême, described by Orderic as 'a skilful engineer', oversaw the construction of a motte-and-bailey castle at Gisors, to act as a counter-weight to the nearby French fortress of Chaumont, which lay to the east of Gisors. Fighting at Gisors while the work progressed claimed many casualties and captives on both sides. Anglo-Normans taken by the French were promptly ransomed by Rufus for cash, whereas the cash-strapped French could not always afford to make similar outlays. In typically chivalrous and magnanimous fashion, Rufus often eschewed payment altogether, allowing his prisoners their freedom on the promise they did him due homage and never again raised arms against him. When criticised and warned that some of these men might renege on their promise, he countered, saying, 'All true knights would honour their word ... if not, they would suffer public opprobrium.' Faith in men keeping their word betrays a touching trait in Rufus that William of Malmesbury noted as one of the king's better attributes; it made the king, in the chronicler's opinion, 'Caesar-like'.

Building work at Gisors was time-consuming. Rufus was not the sort of man to let grass grow under his feet. In February 1098 he left the construction site and struck southward back through Normandy into the still-disputed county of Maine, where its count, Helias, had also been building castles. Helias had quickly constructed a castle at Dangeul in the north-east of Maine as a bulwark against any attack by Rufus toward Le Mans along the Sarthe Valley, or from one or other of Bellême's numerous marcher castles. Rufus may have hoped that by launching his offensive so early in the year he would catch the Manceaux off guard, but he was foiled when news of his approach elicited a prompt response from Helias. The latter posted defenders to dispute river crossings and to disrupt the passage of Norman cavalry through defiles and wooded areas. Making little headway, Rufus abandoned the campaign and fell back on Rouen. Bellême had earlier than this joined the king on the southern borders, ostensibly to strengthen the defence of his own castles and recruit troops against any counter-strike from Helias. Matters might have stabilised had not Helias toward the end of April fallen into a Bellême ambush and been captured. When brought before Rufus at Rouen, the king (as was his wont) treated Helias respectfully, and held him prisoner under light guard at Bayeux.

The capture of Helias changed the dynamic in Maine. The Angevin ducal heir, Geoffrey Martel (known as 'the younger', to distinguish him from a more renowned ancestor), occupied Le Mans with a strong force on behalf of his father Fulk IV. Geoffrey is said by Orderic to have been a more popular figure than his father, and he is claimed to have acted as a brake on Fulk's worst excesses as a ruler. Rufus marched against Le Mans in June 1098, reaching the city via Alencon and Coulaines. The king's host was accounted greater in size than any other ever seen north of the Alps. Comprising archers and crossbowmen, as well as knights and a strong engineering section, its strength is imagined by one chronicler as 50,000 men. A separate, more reasonable assessment, made by Geoffrey Gaimar, claims Rufus had with him 1,700 household knights and around 3,000 other soldiers, the latter 'summoned by writ'. Robert de Bellême separately mustered as many as 1,000 knights. The total force was, on this count, just shy of 6,000 men. Such a formidable array arriving in the county inclined waverers among the Manceaux to support Norman rule. Rufus may have been seen as the lesser of two evils when weighed against the Angevins.

The king nevertheless failed on his first attempt to take Le Mans. The reason was a breakdown in supply. Such a very large army needed to be continuously provided for. The yield from the old harvest (in 1097) had all been used up and the new harvest had yet to be brought in. Retreat back into Normandy in the end became inevitable. Despite this, chance yielded Rufus the advantage when four high-ranking Angevin castellans and 140 other knights fell into his hands at the end of a period of otherwise inconsequential fighting at Ballon. Such a hefty haul of notables forced the Angevins to the negotiating table. The various parties hammered out an agreement which left Helias with comital authority over Maine, but under the overlordship of Rufus. Fulk and Geoffrey were content to see Helias reinstated, even if achieved by yielding overlordship. Rufus immediately set plans in place for a victory march into Le Mans to emulate his father's grandiose takeover in 1063. Such a high level of success on Normandy's southern borders had eluded Robert Curthose. Discounting the planting of a surrogate king in Scotland (sometimes referred to as a second Norman conquest in Britain), the subjugation of Maine has been described as Rufus' first real conquest and was something for which he was immensely proud.

*

In late September 1098, after another unsuccessful sortie into Snowdonia, Rufus launched his long-awaited chevauchee into the Vexin. Reports speak of 'fire and pillage' wrought, with many knights captured and the French stronghold of Chaumont placed under siege. The early rounds went to Rufus, but in fierce fighting afterwards his army suffered a severe mauling. Great numbers of men and warhorses lost to crossbow bolts made the difference: 'Native wild dogs and carrion crows' are said by Orderic to have gorged themselves on the fallen horses of the Anglo-Normans. The chronicler reckoned on seven hundred mounts lost. This may be an exaggeration, but whatever the number Rufus had clearly suffered a major setback. The Norman retreat from Chaumont for many had to be done on foot, a sorry replay of the Conqueror's reverse at Mantes in 1087.

Rufus' defeat had come at the hands of the heir to the French throne, Louis (later to become Louis VI), known in his forties as 'the fat'. In 1098 he held the Vexin as an appanage from his father Philip. Unfortunately for Rufus, he had clashed with the younger, slimmer version of Louis. It was said in *The Life of King Louis the Fat*,

> In his youth, growing courage matured his spirit with youthful vigour, making him bored with hunting and the boyish games with which others of his age used to enjoy themselves and forget the pursuit of arms [and] how valiant he was in youth, and with what energy he repelled the king of the English, William Rufus, when he attacked Louis' inherited kingdom.

Rufus travelled back to England at Easter 1099. At Whitsun he held the famous crown-wearing ceremony mentioned earlier in the context of King Edgar of Scotland's carrying the sword of state in grand procession. Later in the year he was back in Normandy. He hurried there from the New Forest, via Southampton, and famously braved rough seas to make landfall and then to march his men, many of whom must have been gathered while en route, through Normandy into Maine to relieve his garrison at Le Mans, once again placed under siege by the Angevins. Rufus was nothing if not imperturbable and immensely energetic, a man willing to take great risks. However, this was to be one of his last; he was to take the ultimate risk a year later when deciding to go ahead with a planned hunting party in the New Forest despite warnings not to do so.

A Deflected Arrow?

England's New Forest is very old, but in 1066 was new to the Normans, whose kings claimed it as their own. Though now less extensive, it still comprises a vast swathe of dense woodland, interspersed with remnants of heathland waste, the result of land clearances in the Bronze Age, much of which later became rough grazing land for horses and ponies. It is said there are still glades, moors and marshes deep within the forest scarcely changed since the time of the Conqueror. Game animals such as deer, boar, and pheasant were in the late eleventh century protected by the king's keepers. Poaching attracted severe punishments. The most prized trophy animal was the hart, an adult red deer with well-developed antlers. Stalking horses would lure the deer herds into the range of waiting bowmen during the hunt. The horses were led on by men on foot who crouched to remain concealed from the deer throughout, so as not to startle them.

As in warfare, there was a degree of danger involved when hunting. The Byzantine Emperor Basil I (d. 886) had been killed when a stag's antler became caught in his belt, dragging him across the ground for a mile or more. The Conqueror's second son, Richard, had died in the forest, seemingly hit by a low-hanging branch when on horseback. Robert Curthose's son Richard FitzRobert also died nearby in a hunting accident of which no details survive other than John of Worcester's claim that he was struck by an arrow. Given these precedents it is little wonder Rufus' own sudden death on the late afternoon of 2 August 1100, while hunting in the forest near Minstead, attracted no immediate suspicion of foul play – even though, when compared to the other members of the royal family who died there, he was far and away the more seasoned huntsman, therefore unlikely to have taken undue risks or positioned himself in the way of a potential crossfire of arrows.

The manner of Rufus' death was variously reported. William of Malmesbury wrote that the king was found unconscious and speechless, near to death in the forest. This might be taken as a heart attack or stroke. He would not have been the first King of England to simply drop dead. The *Anglo-Saxon Chronicle* entry does, though, state the king was killed by an arrow while hunting, loosed 'by a man of his'. Other accounts add embellishments. There is mention of a deflected or carelessly aimed arrow striking Rufus, and of the king attempting to break off the arrow's shaft, only to stumble forward to fall face down – the effect being to drive the arrowhead deeper into his body.

If an assassination had been attempted, as has sometimes been claimed, the shooter would likely have been a sure marksman, a gamekeeper or the hunt's chief marksman. Standing at close range to the king, some twenty yards or so south-west of the New Forest's Rufus Stone monument – reputed to mark the spot where the king fell – a skilled bowman when targeting Rufus' bulky chest would likely have been assured of a mortal strike. A crossbowman might have better aimed for the side of the king's head to gain an even surer kill. A remote forest glade at sunset would have been a good place and time to rid the land of a man claimed by the chroniclers to have 'become abhorrent to God and man', but the fact that nobody at the time raised the likelihood of the king having been murdered makes such a bid less believable. Rather than an assassin at work, churchmen saw the hand of God at work directing the fatal arrow. Eadmer of Canterbury wrote, 'The just judge, by a death sharp and swift, cut short his [Rufus'] life in this world.' John of Worcester linked Rufus' death and the other earlier royal deaths in the New Forest with the destruction by the Normans of a number of Anglo-Saxon settlements there, including several churches, demolished by the Conqueror to render the land fit only for 'the habitation of wild beasts', not men and women.

The English chronicler dates the killing to the morning of the 2 August; other accounts say it was late in the day. The devil, 'in a horrible form', had made an impromptu appearance in the forest the day before and had, it was said, spoken at some length about the king's evil lifestyle and imminent death. Discounting this cooked-up guest appearance, William Fitz Haimon may have got word from some other source – allegedly a monk who had suffered a nightmare about the king's impending death – that something was amiss, and warned Rufus to be careful. Rufus, as would be expected, brushed off the warning. Rufus was probably no less superstitious than other laymen of the period, but he had little time for the more commonplace religious tropes. He once questioned the usefulness of trial by ordeal. Eadmer of Canterbury recounts a story of fifty Englishmen accused of crimes against the forest laws all being found innocent after an ordeal of holding hot irons. When told the verdict, Rufus exclaimed, 'What's this? God's a just judge? Damn him I say who believes that after this! I swear by the face of Lucca that from now on matters that can be bent by any man's nod shall be brought before my court, not God's.'

It was later claimed that on the eve of his death the king had a troubled night's sleep and, as a consequence, rose unusually late, delaying the timing of the hunt until late in the afternoon. Did he also by now fear a threat of some sort, or was he, as has been suggested by Barlow, merely hung over after drinking heavily into the early hours?

John of Worcester says the king's accidental killer was Walter Tyrell, Count of Poix, whom he claims was hunting in the forest at the time, possibly part of the king's immediate entourage.

Tyrell by his own later account immediately fled to the Continent when realising the king was dead, saying he feared becoming a scapegoat for the killing. Throughout his life, and even when at the point of death, he continued to deny being anywhere near the king on the fatal day. In large part it is because of this that the question of an assassination has never really gone away. We will never know for sure who pulled the fatal bowstring (if, indeed, a bow and arrow was the agency for Rufus' death), but if it was an assassination the finger points to Henry as the killer's paymaster. As Conan's killing had demonstrated, Henry could be a violent and unpredictable man and was highly ambitious. But was he up for fratricide? On balance, it seems unlikely. Jim Bradbury considers Henry 'suspected but not convicted'. Better attested is that as soon as Henry got word the king was dead he spurred his horse northward to Winchester via Romsey to seize the royal treasury. From there, he hurried 'with all speed' to London. Haste was an inevitable outcome of impatience to be crowned and does not in itself signal guilt. The future king knew he had no time to lose. His brother Robert Curthose might return from crusade at any time.

Little formality was shown when disposing of Rufus' corpse. Transported back to Winchester on the back of a cart (done, according to Orderic, in the manner of 'a dead boar' loaded up after having been 'stuck through with arrows'), the remains were hastily interred beneath the tower in the Old Minster at Winchester on the day immediately after the killing. This was a time before the concept of laying in state had been established and there was no such thing as a post-mortem or coroner's report. We should not make too much of the lack of decorum shown: the dead king cannot simply have been thrown into a hole and covered over. Robert Fitz Haimon is said to have been at the graveside with the Bishop of Winchester, and is reputed to have placed his best cloak over the king's bier when travelling to Winchester in an attempt to dignify the event. The king had, though, died unshriven. Priests may have considered him to have been as good as damned anyway, no matter how elaborate a ritual was performed.

Henry was by this time too taken up with arrangements for his coronation to bother to attend the funeral. If not an orchestrated coup, the future king opportunistically turned it into one. Hollister defends his subject, saying it would be anachronistic to call Henry a usurper. The historian held that any ambitious person would have done the same in Henry's position. Possessed with innate intelligence as well as advisers of sagacity, Henry, claimed Hollister, responded to the news of Rufus' death 'with alacrity'. But he was to an extent chancing his arm, and he knew it. When William de Breteuil suggested the coronation should be put on hold until Robert Curthose returned from crusade, so keyed up was Henry that he drew his sword and threatened to kill him. The chronicler William of Tyre claimed Henry even went so far as to spread the word that Robert would in fact never return from crusade. Henry must have known and weighed up the risks he was taking, but felt the prize to be worth it. With no time to lose and with Archbishop Anselm on the Continent in exile, Henry's crowning was carried out by Bishop Maurice of London on Sunday 5 August 1100, just three days after Rufus' death.

Ranulf Flambard a week later became the scapegoat for all the supposed evils of Rufus' regime. Packed off to the Tower of London, he became the first of many political prisoners to face incarceration there. Henry's coronation charter condemned Rufus and Flambard for various misdemeanours, in particular their rabid tax regime and the sequestering of Church revenues. How bad a man Flambard really was is an open question. As with the late king, his poor reputation owes much to the Church's abhorrence of him. Orderic held the minister to have been cruel and rapacious, a charge echoed by William of Malmesbury, who described him as 'a plunderer of the rich and a destroyer of the poor'. The nineteenth-century historian E. A. Freeman considered Flambard to have been a 'malignant genius', but more recently, in the works of historians like R. W. Southern and David Bates, Flambard attracts more a nuanced analysis. Bates, for example, claims the bishop to have diligently served the king's political agenda as what we term today a senior civil servant or minister.

Notable among Henry's relatively small clique of supporters at the start of his reign were the Beaumont brothers: Robert, Earl of Meulan, and Henry, Earl of Warwick. Both had been close allies of Rufus. The Clare family was also closely aligned to Henry and the supposed killer Sir Walter Tyrell was their brother-in-law. Having held Tonbridge for Duke Robert in 1088 and backed Robert de Mowbray in 1095, Gilbert de Clare cannot really ever have been fully trusted by Rufus, so it is surprising that he, his brother and Tyrell were members of the king's hunting party on the fatal day; it is a conjunction and circumstance that has fuelled conspiracy stories regarding the king's death ever since. The Clares would become among the most powerful noblemen in the land after the accession of Henry; yet Gilbert's academic biographer Richard Mortimer contends that they were not overly conspicuous among the new king's supporters at court, which might raise additional questions in a conspiracy theorist's mind. Other noblemen who allied themselves to Henry were Robert Fitz Haimon (Rufus' close friend) and Hugh d'Avranches (Henry's long-time ally). This quorum has been described by Hollister as 'an election of the people'. The historian caveats his words by saying it was neither a better nor a worse quorum than those that had formed before.

Fitz Haimon became a witness to Henry's coronation charter. When Robert Curthose's supporters in England rallied to the ducal cause the following year, Fitz Haimon was mentioned as one of the few barons to remain loyal to the king. Hugh d'Avranches was in fact lucky to still be alive and able to support Henry. Hubris mixed with malice had done for his colleague and namesake Hugh de Montgomery, Earl of Shrewsbury, a year or so earlier when the pair had been ravaging north-west Gwynedd and the isle of Anglesey. Their cruelty to the inhabitants – a mix of Welsh and Norse – had attracted a heavy riposte from one of western Europe's most feared warlords, Magnus Olafsson. On an unidentified beachhead near Beaumaris on Anglesey, his Vikings held the Normans to a bloody accounting. Hugh de Montgomery was killed when struck in the eye by a missile, hitting the only unprotected area of the earl's body. Tradition says Magnus hurled the fatal dart. In this fast-vanishing heroic age, leaders almost always killed other leaders. (For more on the battle, see Appendix 2.)

For Henry there was now nobody of sufficient military weight in England to oppose him: Breteuil had been harangued and threatened and Avranches, Haimon and the Beaumonts fully backed him. Of those who might still have opposed him, Robert de Bellême had inherited his late brother Hugh's lands and titles in England and was now therefore a great cross-Channel landowner, but was either out of the country or on the Welsh borders. Of the two, Bellême would likely side with Robert Curthose over Henry – the issue of Domfront remained open. Another great cross-Channel landowner, Henry's cousin William de Mortain, was in Normandy at the time. He was Robert de Mortain's eldest son by Maud, the daughter of the late Roger de Montgomery, so was also the nephew of Robert de Bellême. He is said to have harboured a dislike of Henry which dated back to childhood. Described by William of Malmesbury as displaying 'shameless arrogance' and by the *Hyde Chronicle* as 'incorrigibly turbulent', he demanded from the king the reinstatement of the county of Cornwall and also demanded he be made Earl of Kent (his 'full' uncle Odo's old stomping ground).

In an attempt to bring another potentially problematic vassal on side, Henry offered one of his bastard daughters to William II de Warenne, but Archbishop Anselm later blocked the marriage on grounds of consanguinity.

Even without men on hand to directly oppose him, Henry's acceptance as king at Westminster was made conditional upon him signing off on a charter of rights. This was not a hastily drawn up wish list, but one that has been described by R. W. Southern (*Western Society and the Church in the Middle Ages*) as 'a substantial body of baronial liberties', of sufficient substance to later inspire the Magna Carta. A new beginning was hoped for by the barons of England.

*

The key man missing from the coronation on 5 November 1100 was Archbishop Anselm. Henry had not dared await his passage back from Normandy, especially since the churchman might be accompanied by the duke at the head of a large army. The archbishop was in the end seduced back to England by an undated letter in which Henry asked to be forgiven for arranging his crowning and consecration while the archbishop was absent. Tellingly, Henry is said to have waited until he was fully established on the throne before doing so. In this way, it is claimed, he was able to prevent the pushy Anselm from making undue ecclesiastical demands on him. Henry also urged the archbishop to avoid travelling through Normandy, fearful that the prelate might shift his support to Robert Curthose should he come across him. He told Anselm to be wary, that enemies were intending to rise up. Henry by this time must have been informed his brother was alive and en route back to Normandy, doubtless to be hailed as a hero.

One of Henry's early moves was to appoint Rufus' chancellor, William Giffard (d. 1129), the elder brother of Walter, Earl of Buckingham, and once the Conqueror's chief clerk, to the see of Winchester, which had lain vacant since 1098 – a sore point for the Church authorities during the latter years of Rufus' reign. Henry's action in appointing Giffard in the traditional manner, by first receiving his homage and then investing him with the pastoral staff in what Southern terms 'the old style', inevitably became a bone of contention with Anselm. The so-called investiture controversy between Church and State, which sought to deprive monarchs of the right to homage and powers of investiture, was still at its height.

Another early move was to wed. Henry chose as his bride Edith of Scotland, the by now twenty-year-old orphaned daughter of the late Malcolm Canmore, and the sister of Scotland's new king. It will be recalled she was also Robert Curthose's goddaughter as well as the niece of Edgar *atheling*. These familial links in no way invalidated the marriage, but there remained more than just a lingering suspicion that Edith might have taken the veil while in England and was therefore already a bride of Christ in God's eyes.

After Malcom Canmore's death at Alnwick, Edith and the other members of the old Scottish royal family had been brought back to England by Edgar and placed under Rufus' protection. Malcolm had brought them back to Scotland after his falling-out with Rufus that year. Her precise whereabouts after returning to England remain uncertain. Her early schooling, as we have seen, had taken place at Romsey and then at Wilton. It had been from Wilton that her father had taken her in 1093. On her return to England in 1094, she had likely been ordered back to Wilton Abbey by Anselm, who referred to her at that time as 'the lost daughter' of the late Scottish king. Whether she did in fact resume life in cloisters is not known. Orderic says William II de Warenne at some point made a play for her hand in marriage, but was rebuffed when told the maiden's hand was 'reserved for a loftier bridegroom' – whether this was Christ or one of the Bastard's sons is not made clear.

After the death of his father in 1088, Warenne had inherited very substantial lands in England as well as his father's title to the earldom of Surrey. Marriage into the Scottish royal family would have been a major coup for an ambitious man closely related to the king. Through pride, Warenne is said to have rarely attended court. His marriage attempt on Edith may not have gone down well with Rufus, who would have feared an alliance linking a powerful Anglo-Norman family to both the Scottish and the Anglo-Saxon royal houses. When Edith later became engaged to Henry, a jealous Warenne ridiculed the king by calling him 'stagfoot' – an insult linked to Henry's penchant for hunting stags, though also perhaps an allusion to his notorious rutting with any woman of childbearing age he came across. William Warenne remained after this more closely aligned to Robert Curthose than to Henry, albeit he switched back his allegiance when it came to the crunch.

Henry had by this time fathered a brood of illegitimate children by numerous premarital consorts. Hollister says Henry fathered twenty-two to twenty-four known bastards, more than any other English king. This was positive in a martial and diplomatic sense – natural sons were typically loyal, supportive and unambitious, and natural daughters helped facilitate the forging of marriage alliances with neighbouring princes and powerful subjects – but it took a heavy toll on his marriage. After the birth of a daughter and son to the queen he had no more to do with her, though he went on to sire five more children by a long-term mistress, with whom he must have spent much of his leisure time; that is, when not chasing stags. There is anecdotal evidence to suggest Matilda may have been frightened of Henry, unwilling to cross him or stand up to him. Wife-beating may have been commonplace behind closed doors, as it still remains today.

It seems that Archbishop Anselm in 1100 still considered Edith a nun, and on one occasion he called her 'a runaway nun'. The queen elect met with Anselm and told him all that had happened to her when a girl. She claimed her aunt Christina at Romsey had wished for her to become a novice, but that she had refused to do so. Even so, Christina had insisted Edith wear a veil while in cloisters. The princess was, she alleged, in great fear of her aunt at the time, and only accepted what she termed 'the piece of black cloth' to be placed over her face to avoid a beating. Even though too young to have been preyed upon sexually, her aunt instilled in her the dread of being seized and ravished by some Norman paramour, saying she feared her niece might be swept off and married against her will. When Edith later moved to Wilton, freed from her aunt at last – Christina is said by William of Malmesbury to have grown old at Romsey – the princess came to see the sense of this pretence.

William of Malmesbury wrote, 'In order to have a colour for refusing an ignoble alliance, which was more than once offered by her father [King Malcolm], she wore the garb of the holy profession.' A jury of bishops debated the ins and outs of Edith's freedom to marry and in the end concluded she had never taken any vows in a formal sense, nor had she been at any time pledged to the cloister. She was therefore free to marry Henry, who, it appears, had already become well known to her. Had Henry once been one of those Normans who haunted Romsey and Wilton's cloisters, hoping to catch the eye of the princess?

On 11 November 1100, just six days after Henry's coronation, Anselm performed the wedding ceremony and crowned Edith queen at Westminster Abbey. It was a popular marriage, especially with Londoners, who may already by this time have come to know and love their new queen. With echoes of how the English would one day come to laud Princess Diana, Edith was called by them 'the common mother of all England'. Although christened Edith, she became formally known after her marriage as Queen Matilda, sometimes Maud or Mold; these Norman appellations would be passed on to her own daughter, her first child of the union. Choosing Edith to wed was an astute move on Henry's part. Children from the marriage would have the blood of the Conqueror flowing through their veins and would also share a direct hereditary link stretching back to Alfred the Great and the royal houses of Scotland and Wessex. Some consider the 'true history of England' to have begun with Henry I and his marriage to Edith. Their pairing has been described as giving the Norman dynasty in England the best chance of surviving into the future. Only the most extreme of ethnically challenged Normans, of whom there must still have been a few, saw the marriage as tainting the Norman royal line. They disparaged the pairing, dismissively referring to the queen using the archaic Anglo-Saxon royal name Godgifu, or Godiva, or simply Gifu. They joked that Henry should change his name to Godric.

Edith/Matilda enjoyed a large dower settlement and later controlled a number of important abbeys, including those at Waltham, Barking and Malmesbury. At the latter place she became the benefactor of our greatest medieval historian, William of Malmesbury. She also held lands in the Midlands and pursued her charitable interests there and further afield. The plight of lepers in particular became a trademark mission for her – once again there are echoes of the Princess Diana. Diplomatically and culturally, Henry's young queen also shone, proving to be a very competent regent when Henry was abroad. Through her patronage, rather than her husband's, the English court became a centre for the arts, attracting musicians, writers and artists.

15

TINCHEBRAI

Robert Curthose's triumphant return to Normandy in September 1100 for a time marked a settled and prosperous period of his life. Honoured at home and abroad as a war hero, he was also acknowledged as supreme lord of the Normans. During his second extended stay in Apulia he had courted and won the hand of Sibylla, the daughter of Count Geoffrey of Conversano, a cousin of Bohemond and the sister of one of Robert's close colleagues on crusade, who had died at the Battle of Dorylaeum. Sibylla's attractiveness and intelligence are well attested in the contemporary literature. This was likely not the usual formulaic praise heaped on dignitaries of high moral standing, although she was undoubtedly this too. Orderic claimed her to have been 'endowed with many virtues and ... loved by all who knew her'. It may have been when Robert had overwintered in Apulia on the way to the crusades that he first set eyes on his future bride. Orderic says it was a love match and not a diplomatic pairing – this despite the duke's acceptance of a substantial dowry, noted by the chronicler as a great quantity of gold, silver and other valuables, sizeable enough for Robert to at least in part redeem the duchy from his brother Rufus should he wish. Count Geoffrey must have hoped that any grandson by his daughter would one day become the Duke of Normandy and also possibly King of England.

If richer materially, the duke may nevertheless have been weakened psychologically by the terrible sights he had witnessed in the Holy Land. Chroniclers of the day did not write directly about mental trauma, even though they must inevitably have come across men and women sorely afflicted by the horrors of war, who on occasion required refuge and compassionate care. To those Robert came into contact with he may have seemed a complex man, prone to dark moods. Some returning crusaders sought the palliative attentions afforded by religious orders and renounced a life of violence altogether. Robert's fellow crusader Rotrou of Perche sought to become a lay brother at the Abbey of Cluny; although he did not go so far as to take holy orders, religion shielded him to some extent from the unruly affairs of men. It is possible Robert might have entered such an establishment had he not married. Rotrou had fought at the siege of Antioch and is reputed as one of the first of the crusader knights to scale the rope ladders into the city on 3 June 1098; he also fought in the foremost division in the subsequent battle outside the city walls. Like Robert Curthose he had fulfilled his vow to reach Jerusalem, and had witnessed the carnage accruing from the city's storming.

Normandy was now at peace, but Maine and the Vexin were potential war zones. Neither, though, were of any immediate interest to Robert Curthose upon his return. He was disinclined to engage in any expansionary campaigning. He quickly accepted Helias of Maine's retention of comital authority over the county and ordered the Norman garrison, placed at Le Mans by Rufus, to be recalled. Robert declared, 'I am worn out by years of toil; the duchy of Normandy is sufficient for me.' Whether or not Rufus, had he lived, would have accepted a return to an unstable status quo is questionable. He had been at the pinnacle of his power before his untimely death in the New Forest and young enough to entertain an appetite for further aggrandisement. He is rumoured to have set his sights on the French throne – or, failing this, biting chunks out of the bulky, well-seasoned rump of Aquitaine; or even invading Ireland.

Robert may have been cajoled to act against Henry without delay by more ambitious associates who now gathered around him: men like Robert de Bellême, William II de Warenne and William de Mortain. All three of these men were at loggerheads with Henry. To seal a reconciliation of sorts, Robert re-granted Bellême the stronghold at Argentan, as well as hunting rights at Gouffern to the south-east of Caen, and authority over the bishopric of Sées. Other men who showed the duke loyalty upon his return to Normandy were most likely also well rewarded. If Robert had lost something of his warlike edge he retained his generosity. The important castle at Gisors, for example, was entrusted by him to a worthy knight named Thibault de Payens, who had been in post as military and civil governor of the surrounding region since 1075. Orderic claimed Robert committed the fortress to Thibault simply on the basis of the latter having once shown the duke a kindness. This strikes a confirmatory chord with the open-handed man we know the duke to have been, even if the story was meant as an insult by Orderic; a reference to Robert's supposed squandering largesse.

Outside his immediate family and close compatriots, the role of inciter-in-chief with regard to confronting Henry likely fell to Rufus' ex-chancellor, Ranulf Flambard, Bishop of Durham, who, after making a dramatic escape from the Tower of London, had by February 1101 become firmly ensconced in Normandy, and was now at Robert's side as the duke's chief advisor. The Tower had not yet become the darkly forbidding place it later became. Flambard's regimen there was relaxed by later standards. He enjoyed extensive freedoms within the confines of the donjon. At some point he might have been rehabilitated by Henry and reinstated at Durham, but he was unwilling to take the chance. He knew Henry to have inherited his father's uncompromising attitude toward men who once conspired against him (Bishop Odo is a prime example). Despite being overweight, Flambard contrived to climb by rope from a window in the Tower. Nursing badly skinned hands and a number of painful bruises after falling heavily, he managed a successful getaway. At the coast he took ship for Normandy and was well received at the Norman court. Fearing the escape to be part of a wider plot to dethrone him, Henry heavily fined the keeper of the Tower for negligence.

Invasion plans orchestrated by Flambard on Robert's behalf were soon well underway; they involved the commissioning or commandeering of sufficient warships and transports to ferry the duke's knights and horses and the many and various materials of war across the English Channel. According to the *Anglo-Saxon Chronicle*, two hundred ships were commissioned and assembled at Le Tréport, at the mouth of the River Bresle, on the Normandy coast. While the work was progressing, Robert toured the duchy with his young bride, making stops at Henrician-aligned strongholds like Domfront and Mont-Saint-Michel and other centres of his brother's once extensive south-western appanage. This was done to re-establish ducal overlordship and to show off his bride. There are nevertheless reports of clashes between opposing knights. A number of western castellans must still have held out against Robert. It seems Henry, though in England, still retained influence in the duchy.

Meanwhile, Henry placed England's armed forces on high alert and declared his brother, 'lately returned from the east', to be an 'enemy of the state' – an ominously modern statement. The declaration was made in parallel to an alliance drawn up between England and Flanders, dated to 10 March 1101, whereby Robert of Flanders, Curthose's recent crusading companion, pledged to provide armed support to Henry, up to a number of 1,000 knights; but in the end, when the brothers squared up to one another, the Flemish duke appears to have held back from declaring himself. Henry's army of knights and archers concentrated at Pevensey, where an invasion fleet might most likely make first landfall, as had been the case in 1066 and again in 1088. Henry was appraised by spies of the concentration of his brother's fleet at Le Tréport, directly opposite the Sussex coast. He instructed his raw English militiamen how best to counter a Norman mounted charge. His aim was for them to mirror the verve and solidity of Harold II's fighters when battle had been joined at Hastings. Assisting the king was Gilbert d'Laigle, Pevensey's new castellan; this was the same man who had once fought at Henry's side at Rouen when combating Conan's insurgency, now one of Henry's most trusted lieutenants in England.

Did Robert ever ponder the pros and cons of waging a war with his younger brother? The cons were that Henry was now firmly established in England and enjoyed the support of the Church; he had been consecrated king in the sight of God and also had powerful foreign allies. The English would likely rally to their crowned king in great numbers, as had happened before in 1075 and 1088. The pros were that by invading England he would be standing up for the rights of fellow Normans (Bellême, Mortain, Flambard and others of their ilk) who faced having their lands in England seized, their titles renounced and their assets frozen.

An invasion date was set for mid-July 1101. Robert tasked his duchess to guard and oversee the running of the duchy in his absence, in much the same manner his mother Matilda had done in 1066 for William. After embarkation, the Norman invasion fleet contrived to circumvent any mid-Channel clash with the English warships known to have been patrolling the Channel. Avoiding the Kent and Sussex coasts, they sailed somewhat further westward than would have been expected, entering the Solent unopposed, casting anchor in Portsmouth Harbour, probably somewhere close beside Portchester Castle. The date was 20 July. Flambard may have known all along that the English plan was to concentrate at Pevensey and may have suggested Portsmouth Harbour as a good alternative.

Robert had a host of supporters awaiting him at the quayside. Robert's biographer Kathleen Thompson says he enjoyed the support of an alliance of 'discontented Norman nobles from the greatest and wealthiest of the families who held lands in both England and Normandy, and who preferred to see Robert as ruler of both realms'. On Henry's side we know only of Robert Fitz Haimon, Richard de Revières, Hugh d'Avranches and the two Beaumont brothers (Henry and Robert) to have provided the king with their unstinting backing. Others like the Clares might have done so; they too were now heavily invested in Henry's regime. Crucially, Anselm continued to support the English king over Robert. Other churchmen also did the same. As in 1088, the sheriffs of England backed the English crown over the Normans. There is almost a Groundhog Day feel to this.

From his new base at Portchester, the duke might have attacked and occupied Winchester and seized the treasury, but when he learned that his goddaughter, the queen, was in residence (confined there at some early stage of her first pregnancy, possibly because of morning sickness or some other complication) he ordered a change of plan and moved his army to Warnford in the Meon Valley, where it encamped. Winchester in a sense gained its reprieve in this chivalrous act which effectively handed the initiative to Henry. The *Anglo-Saxon Chronicle* refers to Robert Curthose, when setting out against England, harbouring hostility toward his brother, but he was nothing if not respectful when putting the queen's needs above his own. Shriven of sin after crusading, he was not of a mind to attract heavenly condemnation by taking up arms against his goddaughter Edith, a woman he had twenty years ago pledged to protect.

From Warnford, Robert marched his army northward. Henry meanwhile hurried west in a series of forced marches to confront the ducal army before it reached Basing. The brothers faced each other near Alton. Most accounts tell of Henry being outnumbered, outmanoeuvred and apprehensive, yet the king must have had a host of knights and an army of militia to back him up, so the truth of this claim is questionable. Archbishop Anselm, for example, put sixty fighting men into the field from his estates in Kent. Other knightly contingents hailed from Abingdon, Ely, Salisbury, Hereford and Glastonbury. Henry had made sure to fill all the vacancies for abbots at abbacies owing him a knightly fee. Even so, the opposing armies may only have numbered in the high hundreds or low thousands. Nobody today knows the size or makeup of the forces deployed at Alton; neither brother can have had an army to match their father's in 1066, where upwards of 6,000 fighting men had made landfall in Sussex – but the opposing lines of fighting men were still a sobering sight for all but the most hardened to war.

William of Malmesbury claims Henry on the day 'preferred diplomacy to battle', saying '[the king] would rather contend by counsel than by the sword'. Perhaps a retrospective embellishment, Malmesbury adds that the king's advisors recommended he soothe his enemies with promises ... since he could drive them into exile later, when better placed to do so. Robert too might have baulked at fighting a set-piece battle, the outcome of which would inevitably mean the shedding of Christian blood. He would also have feared ousting an already consecrated king. Robert had turned down the kingship of Jerusalem because he felt the crown belonged to Christ alone. He was not ambitious to the extent he would risk offending God and suffering damnation.

At the subsequent Treaty of Alton (signed at Winchester, and sometimes referred to as the Treaty of Winchester), a deal was struck whereby Robert renounced any claims to England and in turn Henry renounced claims to all of his landholdings in Normandy except for the region around Domfront, for which he claimed he had in the past made a solemn vow to the inhabitants he would never relinquish control. Robert was not minded to press the issue to the point where his brother would have had to recant on a solemn promise. Henry, by treaty, was also released from an earlier oath of homage, when, as a count, he had been Robert's vassal. Both men swore to support the other if ever threatened by a third party: Kathleen Thompson points out that the agreement was very similar to that reached by Robert and William Rufus ten years earlier at Caen; John Gillingham considers the treaty in 1091 may, for convenience, have been used as a template in 1101. The brothers also agreed to be each other's heir should neither of them sire a son. This was a hollow pledge: both men were now married to young brides, one of whom was already pregnant.

The agreement was sweetened by Henry with the promise of a large pension to be paid to the duke annually. An amount of £3,000 was agreed upon. Robert may still have owed the English crown £10,000 for his crusading expenses. The sum advanced to Robert by Henry in 1087 cannot have been repaid, so, all in all, he was financially well settled. The pension may only have been paid once, however, and maybe then not in full. There is a story of Queen Matilda tricking the duke out of the money at Henry's urging. There may be truth in this. The queen's great fear of her husband meant she would likely have done his bidding even if abhorrent to her.

Robert's supporters in the main had their rights to their lands in England reconfirmed. Ranulf Flambard, for his part, was restored to his see at Durham. Like William St Calais a decade earlier, the bishop's peacemaking was rewarded with a pardon at an early stage of the proceedings. Prudently, he had remained in Normandy until word reached his ears that the brothers were reconciled and had arranged for his rehabilitation. He may have been playing both ends against the middle all along. He was intelligent and corrupt, a man once accused of inveigling the prestigious vacant see at Lisieux for his almost illiterate brother and then seeking to elevate his sons to an equivalent rank although they were still children, a glaring misuse of power that came to the attention of the papal authorities and at the time attracted criticism. Orderic, with Flambard in mind, imagined the 'Lord's flock [now] to be at the mercy of wolves'. Bellême and others who had harboured fear for their cross-Channel landholdings had their concerns addressed and lands reinstated.

After the negotiations were concluded, Robert did not immediately leave for Normandy. He waited for the harvest to be brought in, perhaps so that the first instalment of his pension could be paid. The English chronicler says Robert remained in England until Michaelmas and that his knights proved ill disciplined and 'did great harm' wherever they travelled; they were of course waiting to be paid and therefore restless. Robert is known to have been with the king at Winchester on 3 September. Formalities undertaken there, including the witnessing of a charter, have since been seen as an acknowledgement that the Conqueror's sons might in future share the burden of the once again conjoined Anglo-Norman realm. Robert, in fact, may have genuinely hoped to work with Henry for the common good. The same may not have been true for Henry, who remained by far the more ambitious of the two men.

For a time the alliance held. Henry proved to be a good king. He is described by Hollister as 'unique among medieval monarchs in maintaining [a] strict peace throughout his kingdom of England – an achievement widely and deeply appreciated by his subjects'. Justice, severe punishment for wrongdoing and the judicious use of royal patronage are all cited as examples of his intelligent stewardship. The insurrections of 1075, 1088 and 1095 provided him with a ready template for the introduction of strong preventative measures against any repeat. Yet, as in the past under Rufus, the English are said to have been harshly taxed; the chronicler for the year 1104 wrote of the king's demands never ceasing and remaining undiminished. The king also laundered the revenues of the vacant see of Canterbury, treating the cash as a windfall to fund his campaigning.

He must have come to fear his brother less than he feared a number of his own subjects, some of whom, the usual suspects, may have been actively plotting against him. Henry over time conjured forty-five separate indictments against Robert de Bellême, whose castles in England soon fell to the king one by one during a whirlwind royal campaign in the spring and summer of 1102: Arundel (Sussex), Bridgewater (Somerset), Bridgnorth and Shrewsbury (both in Shropshire) were all targeted. One of the charges against Bellême was that Bridgnorth Castle had been built by the earl without first gaining royal permission. In fact, Bellême proved as big a castle builder and improver in England as he had been in Normandy; many of his castles became noted for their broad moats. Bradbury claims he held thirty-four castles and was a lord over thousands of men. He notes Bellême's harshness – putting out men's eyes, hacking off hands and feet and torturing his victims – but also his innovations – bringing to England warhorses bred in Spain, inventing new methods of siege warfare.

Bellême sought Welsh support from his brother Arnulf in Pembrokeshire, but Arnulf had also by this time been arraigned and would later even be accused by Henry of plotting an Irish invasion. The remaining Montgomery brother at large, Roger the Poitevin, still held extensive lands in Lancashire, Yorkshire and East Anglia, but he too may have been impeached.

Orderic has left us with a vivid account of the king's campaign against the strongly sited castle at Shrewsbury, built on high ground and protected on three sides by the backwaters of the River Severn. Henry, he says, ordered his army to march from Bridgnorth to Shrewsbury via what was known as the 'evil road', a rough track through overarching woodland, so narrow that two mounted men could hardly ride abreast. Orderic tells of ambushes and of a rain of 'hissing bolts and arrows' directed at the royal army. An extensive swathe of the woodland was later cleared using axes to ensure safe passage for Henry and his retinue in the years to come. The once dreaded passage thus became as safe as any other length of the king's highway.

After Shrewsbury's fall, the Montgomery brothers had no option but to sue for peace. As a consequence they faced banishment and the loss of their estates. By the end of the year 1102, they had all left the kingdom. Another nobleman hounded from England at this time was Henry's cousin William of Mortain. Historian J. F. A. Mason says one of the reasons for Mortain's downfall was his support for the Montgomery brothers, who were his maternal uncles. We should not see Mortain as a blameless victim; Henry had sought to woo his cousin, only to be rebuffed. When exiled, Mortain lost all his lands, including the vast county of Cornwall, which Mortain had previously been divested of but apparently reoccupied.

*

Robert was now in some senses better placed than he had been in 1095, prior to his departure for crusade. Upper Normandy at that time had remained firmly under Rufus' control and much of western Normandy in Henry's. Both brothers had established substantial bridgeheads into Normandy by the mid-1090s. Rufus was now dead and Henry had conceded most of his rights to western Normandy. Yet Robert still had enemies at large: Robert de Beaumont, for example, was Henry's man through and through. He had become the English king's main lay counsellor and still controlled landholding in the duchy. He was also an implacable enemy of the Montgomery family, who were now Robert Curthose's allies. Another was Eustace of Boulogne, who had married Henry's sister-in-law Mary (the sister of Edith/ Matilda of Scotland), and had therefore been wrested from the ducal to the English camp.

Even while retaining an aura of crusader glory, the middle-aged, now portly duke was fast becoming a diminished figure on the European stage, and this process would accelerate after the death of the duchess Sibylla in 1103. Sibylla had given birth to a son and ducal heir named William the year before, but there had been medical complications. William of Malmesbury says she had bound her breasts too tightly, bringing on an infection. Within six months of giving birth she was dead. Rumours of her being poisoned by one of Robert's jealous paramours are hard to credit, but some modern historians give credence to the tale of a fatal love triangle. Robert's ally William of Breteuil died in Normandy the same year. Robert may have suffered a recurrence of the depressive illness that had dogged him throughout his life. Losses, age and temperament were against him in his dealings with the younger, more dynamic Henry. Orderic says that 'after the death of Sibylla, war [in Normandy] flared up for various reasons almost everywhere'. Judith A. Green says 'Duke Robert was unable to restore order'.

When at his most vulnerable, Robert came to face threatening demands from Henry to harry Montgomery lands. Henry claimed

Bellême had escaped punishment in England but continued to pose a threat to the English polity. The call at first went unanswered,' and Henry accused his brother of failing to make good on his pledges. There are reverse echoes here of Robert and Rufus' troubled relationship in the 1090s. Robert, paying lip service, ordered his knights to lay siege to Bellême's castle at Vignats, not far from Caen. Some disorder was stirred up in the area, but mainly to the detriment of the duke. Robert Curthose, after suffering a minor reverse, was forced to cut and run, and old enmities between Bellême and the duke were stirred once more. Robert marched an army against Bellême's stronghold at Exmes in the summer of 1103, but he was beaten off. This was the first major defeat Robert had ever suffered that we know about – a harbinger for chroniclers and historians down the years to hark back upon and hang their hats. The levels of violence and mayhem in the duchy caused by the breakdown in relations between the two Roberts forced a number of churchmen to abandon their monasteries and take ship to England and place themselves under the protection of King Henry. This, in turn, only stoked pressure for Henry to intervene in Normandy.

Robert seems to have managed to maintain a degree of control over his subjects until around the year 1104, but Bellême remained unpunished and for this Henry criticised his brother. The instability this engendered proved untenable. Robert had to formally break his accord with Henry and come to an understanding with Bellême for the sake of restoring order. This, in turn, proved to be the last straw for Bellême's many other enemies in Normandy, who now more openly backed Henry over Robert. Henry arrived in Normandy on an impromptu State visit, at the head of a strong knightly retinue. He set out his stall by denouncing his brother for breaking the terms of their treaty and siding with traitors. The price the king demanded by way of compensation was the county of Evreux, which Robert, in a weak moment, ceded to him. Henry also made time to reoccupy his old bolthole at Domfront, renewing his alliances in the region. The next year he came back to Normandy to demand yet more concessions. Caen and Bayeux were stripped from Robert and Falaise Castle came under attack. Robert Fitz Haimon became a casualty at the latter place. Mortally wounded, he lingered on, but with his senses addled. He died later, in March 1107, and was buried in the chapterhouse of Tewkesbury Abbey. In 1241 his body was transferred to the church, and a stone chapel, which still survives, was erected over his tomb.

The Battle of Tinchebrai, 26 September 1106

By the autumn of 1106, Henry was again back in Normandy. He claimed ownership and control over the fortified abbey of Saint-Pierre-sur-Dives, near Falaise, and the right to place William de Mortain's castle at Tinchebrai, just twelve miles from Domfront, under close siege by investing the place and building a *malvoisin* (bad neighbour) nearby. Henry was by this time acting in the manner of an overlord of the Cotentin, able to take vengeance on his enemies in western Normandy without recourse to his elder brother. Stung into action by the complaints of Mortain, Robert marched an army west to raise the siege. With the duke was the ever-reliable Edgar *atheling*, for whom friendship trumped familial ties.

Robert was confronted by a much larger force under Henry's command. A full division of knights had travelled with the king from England and had been bolstered by a strong additional contingent from Maine. Helias had, it seems, abandoned Robert. The duke's earlier soft handling of the count on his return from crusade must have been seen as a sign of weakness. No matter how much Helias may have liked Robert, he had to follow the main chance, so he now looked to Henry for patronage. Another man who abandoned Robert was Count Rotrou of Perche, the duke's crusading companion. Like Eustace of Boulogne, he had married one of Henry's illegitimate daughters, a girl named (yet again) Matilda, whom historians tag with the surname FitzRoy; he too was now the English king's son-in-law. Henry's alliance building coming at the cost of his many natural daughters as lures is a key feature of the way the king spun his sticky webs. There were also contingents in Henry's army hailing from Brittany, headed by Henry's brother-in-law Alan, the widower of the long-dead Constance. There were also knights from the Cotentin, Domfront and Evreux. Foremost in the king's retinue rode Ranulf of Bayeux, Robert de Beaumont (now Earl of Leicester), William II de Warenne, Earl of Surrey (Warenne was a late convert to the king's side), William d'Evreux, Ralph de Tosny (whose loyalty Robert had lost when failing to back him against d'Evreux), Robert de Montfort and Robert de Grandmesnil.

Negotiations entered into between king and duke on the eve of battle broke down. The official battle report states that on 'a named and specified day battle was joined'. Robert Wace's *Roman de Rou* recounts how Duke Robert's vanguard 'attacked well', but that Henry's army held out 'with scarcely any casualties incurred'. The king remained safely back in the second line of the royal army. William of Mortain, whose castle was threatened by Henry, is said to have fought manfully in the front line of the ducal force and to have driven in his immediate opponents, only to be surprised when attacked in the flank by a combination of Manceaux and Breton knights. The men of Maine and Brittany are credited with charging so well that they 'broke the ducal army to pieces'.

The battle was over in the space of less than an hour. Robert de Bellême became the scapegoat. He and his contingent, described as held back in reserve, fled at the first sign the day might be lost: 'Bellême received no blow, nor gave no blow.' However, it was Mortain's castle being threatened so Bellême had little skin in the game. Robert Curthose's apologists nevertheless felt he and Mortain had been badly let down. It seems Robert, possibly making a mounted charge, continued to carry the fight to Henry but was sorely pressed and made little headway. Common soldiers in the ducal army were slain almost to a man. Robert Curthose, Mortain and Edgar were all captured. The duke was taken into custody by Henry's chancellor, a man named Gaudry Waldric – another crusader, therefore likely well known to the duke.

Waldric fought in the front line at Tinchebrai. In a sense, he won the battle for Henry when capturing the duke. Had Robert Curthose escaped, the victory, though still a laurel in Henry's cap, might not have proved decisive. Henry afterwards went on to conquer all of Normandy and is said to have 'set it under his will and control'. Of the Bastard's sons, Henry, the runt, had gained all his father had ever had, save the glory.

*

The final seal on Henry's victory was date-stamped 16 October 1106 at Lisieux. Power over the duchy was formally transferred; Robert's claims to either dukedom or kingship were airbrushed from the record. He was now known as 'the count of Normandy' – no longer a duke. Captured noblemen considered by Henry to be dangerous were brought back to England and 'thrown into dungeons'. Orderic adds a gory addendum, writing that 'some had their eyes torn out, while others were exposed to horrible and long-continued cruelties'. Robert would have been treated better than most, yet even he came to face indefinite imprisonment. Like the Conqueror with respect to Roger de Breteuil and Bishop Odo, Henry proved inflexible when pressed by noblemen and churchmen to release his brother: all 'entreaties, promises and gifts' designed to 'mollify his resentment' against Robert are said to have been spurned. Possibly it was payback time for the king having been imprisoned by his brother in 1088.

A successful petition made by Matilda did, though, see her uncle Edgar freed. A true survivor if there ever was one, Edgar retired to Hertfordshire. He had earlier turned down offers of employment from the Byzantines and also the Germans in order to support Robert and fight at Tinchebrai. Orderic says of Edgar that he had given up his travelling 'to again breathe his native air'.

For Robert, when moved on to the immense building site which would one day become Devizes Castle after a period of imprisonment at Wareham in Dorset, the air the duke breathed was in large part mortar dust. Some years later still, he was moved further to the west; perhaps out of sight and out of mind for Henry, first to Bristol Castle and then to the late Robert Fitz Haimon's castle at Cardiff. He was likely allowed a degree of freedom at all these places: Gloucester Abbey today claims him as a patron. He is held to have learnt Welsh by way of a pastime, and he also wrote poetry. His faculties, it seems, had not noticeably deteriorated. It is plausible to accept he was not overly unhappy with his lot. Even when he was captured at Tinchebrai, aged around fifty-seven, he had been old for a medieval nobleman. He would live much longer yet, remaining under loose guard for twenty-eight years at the various castles where he was held. On occasion he may have shared apartments with William de Mortain.

Mortain fared the worst of all from Henry's close family: not only was he made captive, but he was also charged with treason and blinded. Being close in line to the throne, this was a way for Henry to ensure that no future plot to raise his cousin as a contender against him would ever be mounted. Upon Mortain's eventual release in 1140, after thirty-four long, sightless years of incarceration, he retired to become a Cluniac monk at Bermondsey, one of Rufus' great monastic foundations.

By this time both Robert Curthose and King Henry were dead. Robert likely died either at Cardiff or Gloucester. He is buried in Gloucester Abbey. His death occurred on or around 3 February 1134. Henry had earlier described his brother as now being 'worn out through many hardships, and living the life of a noble pilgrim'. The old duke's tomb displays an impressively coloured wooden effigy of a crusading knight with legs crossed, but is not thought to be a good likeness, since it was not commissioned until the reign of Henry III. The more impressive marble tomb of Richard II lies nearby. Henry, it is alleged, did no more than fund a single candle to burn before the high altar in Robert's memory.

Henry himself died just under two years later, on 1 December 1135, at Lyons-la-Forêt. His death came after suffering an abdominal complaint, the consequence of devouring a 'surfeit of lamprey eels'; an atypical end for a man held to have been abstemious to a fault when it came to food. Hollister says that having journeyed to Lyons-la-Forêt for a hunting trip, Henry fell ill after feasting on 'a delicacy that his physician had forbidden him'. Hollister adds that the legend implying gluttony or extreme hunger has little real basis in fact, explaining, 'It was not that he ate too many lampreys, but that his physician had advised him not to eat any.' After the king's corpse was boiled down to rid it of its flesh (which would otherwise have putrefied during the long journey back to England), the king's bones were shipped back and buried at his unfinished abbey at Reading, which he had founded in 1121. William of Malmesbury wrote that the abbey was built on a gravel spur between the rivers Kennett and Thames, making it highly accessible for travellers. We can imagine the king's remains arriving down the river by royal barge. His entrails remained in Normandy for burial.

The queen had died seventeen years earlier and had been interred at Westminster. Mercifully, she passed two years prior to the infamous *White Ship* disaster, which, on 25 November 1120, carried off her only son, William Adelin, as well as many other young men and women from the royal court. William of Malmesbury wrote, 'No ship that ever sailed brought England such disaster, none was so well known the wide world over.' Henry had been left with no legitimate male heir. Matilda was fondly remembered by her English subjects as Matilda the Good Queen, and Matilda of Blessed Memory, and she is thought perhaps to have been the source for the 'my fair lady' in the nursery rhyme 'London Bridge Is Falling Down'. Robert's only son, William Clito, died in 1128, eight years after the *White Ship*'s foundering and seven years before his father's death. His end came after a series of unsuccessful rebellions he had launched against Henry with his supporters in Normandy. The duke's son had been laying siege to a castle in modern-day Alsace when struck down by gangrene after wounding himself when grasping the business end of a lance.

Edgar *atheling*'s death went unrecorded. Orderic wrote of him in 1125 as growing old 'in privacy and quiet'. If, as suggested by his critics, he was a man of no political relevance after 1071, he was, with respect to Robert Curthose at least, a remarkably loyal one – and, in the author's opinion, remains one of the unsung heroes of the period. Bellême, the antithesis of a hero, managed through power and influence to retain his Continental fiefs after Tinchebrai, but was never again trusted by Henry. In 1112, his luck ran out. The context is hazy, but Bellême seems to have accepted a mission from the French king to negotiate a renewal of ducal authority under Robert Curthose, whose release from prison must have been pressed for. He met Henry at Bonneville, but was at once arrested on a long list of charges, many no doubt trumped up. He spent time in prison at both Cherbourg and Wareham and is known to have still been alive in 1131. The details of Bellême's treatment at the hands of Henry, like much else, went unrecorded. His lands in Normandy were made forfeit and handed over to Henry's illegitimate daughter Maud FitzRoy and her husband Count Rotrou of Perche.

Maud, like William Adelin, would also come to lose her life on the *White Ship*. William of Malmesbury wrote,

The water having washed some of the crew overboard and entering the chinks drowned others, the lifeboat was launched, and the young prince [William Adelin] getting into it might certainly have been saved by reaching the shore, had not his illegitimate sister, the countess of Perche, now struggling with death in the larger vessel, implored her brother's assistance, shrieking out that he should not abandon her so barbarously. Touched with pity, he ordered the boat to return to the ship, that he might rescue his sister; and thus the unhappy youth met his death through excess of affection; for the skiff, overcharged by the multitude who leaped into it, sank, and buried all indiscriminately in the deep. Thus William perished trying to save his sister Maud.

The Conqueror's youngest daughter, the princess Adela, retired to the convent at Marcigny before the disaster, albeit the same year. She wished to be closer to her eldest son, Henry, Abbot of Cluny, who would one day gain the bishopric of Winchester. She only heard about the *White Ship*'s foundering months after the fact. Her own daughter, Lucia, the wife of the late Hugh d'Avranches' son Richard, was among those drowned. Richard drowned too. Adela died in 1137, at Marcigny. By then she had lived long enough to see her second son, Stephen, crowned King of England, and was likely not too old to have fretted when war between Stephen and her niece Matilda broke out – a bruising clash of arms which became known as The Anarchy. Internecine fighting between the Bastard's grandchildren lasted for close on two decades. Even during the reign of Henry II, familial infighting would plague the realm; and in the reign of King John, the Conqueror's great-great-grandson, Normandy (and much else besides) would be lost to the French.

APPENDIX I
Letter from Stephen of Blois to Adela (March 1098)

Source: *Epistolae*, Medieval Women's Latin Letters (epistolae.ctl. columbia.edu/letter/79.html)

Count Stephen to Adele, his sweetest and most amiable wife, to his dear children, and to all his vassals of all ranks, his greeting and blessing.

You may be very sure, dearest, that the messenger whom I sent to give you pleasure, left me before Antioch safe and unharmed, and through God's grace in the greatest prosperity. And already at that time, together with all the chosen army of Christ, endowed with great valour by Him, we had been continuously advancing for twenty-three weeks toward the home of our Lord Jesus. You may know for certain, my beloved, that of gold, silver and many other kind of riches I now have twice as much as your love had assigned to me when I left you. For all our princes, with the common consent of the whole army, against my own wishes, have made me up to the present time the leader, chief and director of their whole expedition.

You have certainly heard that after the capture of the city of Nicaea we fought a great battle with the perfidious Turks and by God's aid conquered them. Next we conquered for the Lord all Romania and afterwards Cappadocia. And we learned that there was a certain Turkish prince Assam, dwelling in Cappadocia; thither we directed our course. All his castles we conquered by force and compelled him to flee to a certain very strong castle situated on a high rock. We also gave the land of that Assam to one of our chiefs and in order that he might conquer the above-mentioned Assam, we left there with him many soldiers of Christ. Thence, continually following the wicked Turks, we drove them through the midst of Armenia, as far as the great river Euphrates. Having left all their baggage and beasts of burden on the bank, they fled across the river into Arabia.

The bolder of the Turkish soldiers, indeed, entering Syria, hastened by forced marches night and day, in order to be able to enter the royal city of Antioch before our approach. The whole army of God learning this gave due praise and thanks to the omnipotent Lord. Hastening with great joy to the aforesaid chief city of Antioch, we besieged it and very often had many conflicts there with the Turks; and seven times with the citizens of Antioch and with the innumerable troops coming to its aid, whom we rushed to meet, we fought with the fiercest courage, under the leadership of Christ. And in all these seven battles by the aid of the Lord God, we conquered and most assuredly killed an innumerable host of them. In those battles, indeed, and in very many attacks made upon the city, many of our brethren and followers were killed and their souls were borne to the joys of paradise.

We found the city of Antioch very extensive, fortified with incredible strength and almost impregnable. In addition, more than [the number is unclear] bold Turkish soldiers had entered the city, not counting the Saracens, Publicans, Arabs, Turks, Syrians, Armenians and other different races of whom an infinite multitude had gathered together there. In fighting against these enemies of God and of our own we have, by God's grace, endured many sufferings and innumerable evils up to the present time. Many also have already exhausted all their resources in this very holy passion. Very many of our Franks, indeed, would have met a temporal death from starvation, if the clemency of God and our money had not succoured them. Before the above-mentioned city of Antioch indeed, throughout the whole winter we suffered for our Lord Christ from excessive cold and enormous torrents of rain. What some say about the impossibility of bearing the heat of the sun throughout Syria is untrue, for the winter there is very similar to our winter in the west.

When truly. the emir of Antioch, that is, prince and lord, perceived that he was hard pressed by us, he sent his son... to the prince who holds Jerusalem, and to [here there are a number of names and titles which are difficult to translate]... These five emirs with 12,000 picked Turkish horsemen suddenly came to aid the inhabitants of Antioch. We, indeed, ignorant of all this, had sent many of our soldiers away to the cities and fortresses. For there are one hundred and sixty-five cities and fortresses throughout Syria which are in our power. But a little before they reached the city, we attacked them at three leagues' distance with 700 soldiers, on a certain plain near the "Iron Bridge." God, however, fought for us, His faithful, against them. For on that day, fighting in the strength that God gives, we conquered them and killed an innumerable multitude, God continually fighting for us, and we also carried back to the army more than two hundred of their heads, in order that the people might rejoice on that account. The emperor of Babylon also sent Saracen messengers to our army with letters, and through these he established peace and concord with us.

I love to tell you, dearest, what happened to us during Lent. Our princes had caused a fortress to be built before a certain gate which was between our camp and the sea. For the Turks daily issuing from this gate, killed some of our men on their way to the sea. The city of Antioch is about five leagues' distance from the sea. For this reason they sent the excellent Bohemond and Raymond, count of St. Gilles, to the sea with only sixty horsemen, in order that they might bring mariners to aid in this work. When, however, they were returning to us with those mariners, the Turks collected an army, fell suddenly upon our two leaders and forced them to a perilous flight. In that unexpected flight we lost more than 500 of our foot-soldiers – to the glory of God. Of our horsemen, however, we lost only two, for certain.

On that same day truly, in order to receive our brethren with joy, and ignorant of their misfortunes, we went out to meet them. When, however, we approached the above-mentioned gate of the city, a mob of horsemen and foot-soldiers from Antioch, elated by the victory which they had won, rushed upon us in the same manner. Seeing these, our leaders sent to the camp of the Christians to order all to be ready to follow us into battle. In the meantime our men gathered together and the scattered leaders, namely, Bohemond and Raymond, with the remainder of their army came up and narrated the great misfortune which they had suffered.

Our men, full of fury at these most evil tidings, prepared to die for Christ and, deeply grieved for their brethren, rushed upon the sacrilegious Turks. They, enemies of God and of us, hastily fled before us and attempted to enter their city. But by God's grace the affair turned out very differently; for, when they wanted to cross a bridge built over the great river... we followed them as closely as possible, killed many before they reached the bridge, forced many into the river, all of whom were killed, and we also slew many upon the bridge and very many at the narrow entrance to the gate. I am telling you the truth, my beloved, and you may be very certain that in this battle we killed thirty emirs, that is princes, and three hundred other Turkish nobles, not counting the remaining Turks and pagans. Indeed, the number of Turks and Saracens killed is reckoned at 1,230, but of ours we did not lose a single man.

While on the following day (Easter) my chaplain Alexander was writing this letter in great haste, a party of our men lying in wait for the Turks, fought a successful battle with them and killed sixty horsemen, whose heads they brought to the army.

These which I write to you, are only a few things, dearest, of the many which we have done, and because I am not able to tell you, dearest, what is in my mind, I charge you to do right, to carefully watch over your land, to do your duty as you ought to your children and your vassals. You will certainly see me just as soon as I can possibly return to you. Farewell.

APPENDIX 2
The Battle of Priestholm (July 1098)

Magnus 'Bareleg' Olafsson, the victor of the Battle of Priestholm, was a Norseman without the frills and frippery of the francophone Norman elite lording it over Anglo-Saxons, Danes and Welsh alike. Men like him were born opportunists. Christianised through a gradual process (often requiring coercion and sustained missionary zeal), men like him maintained a markedly polytheistic outlook, described by historian Huw Pryce as comprising 'an intermediate stage between paganism and full Christianisation'. In the Western Isles and beyond, Thor and Woden still on occasion held sway over the crucified 'White Christ'. Dead saints would have given Magnus room for pause: once, at Iona in the Western Isles, he is said to have given 'peace and safety to all men there' after opening the door of the kirk wherein St Columba's shrine lay; when pressed to enter, he feigned to do so, saying according to the skald Snorri Sturluson that 'no man should be so bold'. King Edgar of Scots later formalised the handover of control of the Hebrides to Magnus rather than engage in a war he knew he was likely to lose. The inhabitants he came to rule over would have been of mixed Norwegian and Irish stock, the grandchildren of past colonisers of lonely stopover islands on the sea-road from Scandinavia to Ireland.

When in battle Magnus is said to have worn an iron helmet and to have clasped a red shield, inlaid with the motif of a gilded lion. He also bore a famous sword called 'leg biter', its hilt inlaid with ivory with a golden thread wound around the handgrip. In his other hand (how many hands did Magnus have!) he wielded a short spear. Across his shoulder and down his back lay a red, silken cloak, which, both before and behind, was embroidered with a lion in yellow silk. Snorri claimed, 'Never before was there such a brisk, stately man as Magnus Olafsson.'

The course of Magnus' summer cruise in 1098 included stopovers at Lewis, Uist, Skye, Tiree and Mull (Dublin also must have been on his itinerary, since it was in Ireland he is alleged to have heard tell of the Norman chevauchee across Gwynedd and Anglesey and the terrorising of his subjects).

> In Lewis isle, with fearful blaze, the house destroying fire plays.
> To hills and rocks the people fly, fearing all shelter but the sky.
> The hungry battle birds were filled in Skye with blood of
>   foemen killed...
> And wolves on Tiree's lonely shore dyed red their hairy jaws
>   in gore.
> The men of Mull were tired of flight.
> The Scottish foemen would not fight.
> And many an island girl's wail was heard as through the isles
>   we sail.
>
> Bjorn Cripplehand

The Norse king is imagined elsewhere in the skaldic literature as coming 'west-over-sea' from Orkney to plunder:

> [From Orkney] King Magnus, with his followers, proceeded to the Sudrevjar, and when he came there began to burn and lay the inhabited places, killing the people and plundering wherever he came. [However] at Holy Island [Iona] he gave

peace and safety to all men there. From thence King Magnus sailed to Islay, where he plundered and burned; and when he had taken that country he proceeded south around Kintyre, marauding on both sides of the Irish Sea.

Snorri Sturluson

It may have been the Welshmen Cadwgan or Gruffydd (both of whom had earlier been driven into exile to Ireland by the earls of Shrewsbury and Chester – the two Hughs) who sponsored Magnus to square accounts for their killing spree. Magnus set out from Dublin for Anglesey with six longships. His voyage has been described by historian Barbara E. Crawford (*From the Vikings to the Normans*) as a reassertion of authority over the centuries-old 'Viking sea-route south and west round north Britain, the Hebrides and Ireland'.

> South of Kintyre the people fled
> Scared by swords in blood died red.
> [From there] our brave champion onward goes,
> To meet in Man the Norseman's foes.
>
> Snorri Sturluson

At the obscure battle known variously as Priestholm or Anglesey Sound, fought on a beachhead near Beaumaris close to modern-day Puffin's Island in the midsummer of 1098, Magnus's warriors gave the surprised Normans a bloody nose. The *Orkneyinga Saga* describes 'a great battle in Anglesey Sound', suggesting a fight somewhere inside the northern approaches to the Menai Strait. The Normans had camped out in a wooded valley between Beaumaris and Penmon (Penmon Priory might plausibly have been a Viking target). According to military historian Richard Brooks (*Battlefields of Britain & Ireland*), Magnus' boats most likely made landfall at the gently shelving bay at Aberlleiniog, where there would have been shelter from the westerly winds off the Irish Sea. Among those who fell in battle was Hugh de

Montgomery, Earl of Shrewsbury, struck dead by an arrow to the eye – the only unprotected point on his body. Hugh is said by Gerald of Wales to have dashed 'wildly on a mettlesome horse into the sea' to attack the Norse. So deep did Hugh's horse wade before he was killed, claimed Gerald, the Normans were afterwards prevented from recovering their heavily armoured leader's body until the tide went out. This has all the hallmarks of a 'tall story'; more plausibly, Hugh fell victim to an indiscriminate shooting off of arrows, the Vikings from their beached longships and the Normans from further up the beach.

Hugh of Shrewsbury should have seen his death coming. A few weeks before, he had irreligiously shut his dogs up in a nearby church dedicated to the holy Saint Tyfrydog; the next morning, upon letting his hounds loose, he discovered they had gone raving mad – this was the saint's work no doubt, as was the forthcoming arrival of the Vikings, or so legend has it.

Orderic remembered Hugh as the only son of Roger de Montgomery and Mabel de Bellême who might be considered an agreeable man, calling him 'mild and lovable'; yet he stands accused in the annals of ordering the mutilation of a priest on Anglesey, whose only crime was to have complained when the earl had kennelled his soon-to-be-maddened dogs inside Llandyfrydog Church. Probably shunning the fateful chapel on the return leg, the earl's corpse was transported and interred at Shrewsbury. How many other Normans died that day is unknown; but the clash of arms and Magnus' 'nonchalant demonstration of sea power' is said to have rattled the surviving Normans to an extent sufficient to curtail Norman penetration of north-east Gwynedd for a century or more. Some fugitive Welsh princes had afterwards been reinstated by the Normans in Gwynedd in an attempt by the Anglo-Normans to place a buffer against Magnus and his kind; though he sailed away after the battle, he later returned and for a time based himself on Anglesey. He is claimed in *The Chronicles of Man* to have built a number of forts there to protect his gains.

One of the men sponsored by the Normans as a custodian in the far west was Cadwgan ap Bleddyn, the victor at Coed Yspwys four years earlier, who it seems regained his lands in Powys and Ceredigion under the Norman overlordship of Robert de Bellême – the late Hugh de Montgomery's elder brother and the successor to Hugh's lands and titles in England. Some accounts hold that Cadwgan, having initially strengthened his position and having entered once again into alliance with Gruffudd ap Cynan, was forced to come to a mutually beneficial arrangement with Magnus, who was awarded by the Welsh with 'gifts and honour'. This would indicate the kingdom of Gwynedd for a time capitulated and fell under Magnus' 'helmet of terror' (to use a phrase better known to describe Eric Bloodaxe's regime at York in the mid-tenth century). A strong Norse presence in north Wales would have been of immediate concern to the Norman kings. An emerging Viking–Welsh coalition might threaten the west Midlands. As we have seen, Magnus' grandfather Harald Hardrada had invaded England in 1066, and the Danish king Swein Estrithsson had supported the English against the Normans in 1070. Cnut IV briefly threatened Norman England fifteen years later in 1085. As pointed out by John Gillingham, 'nobody had told the Vikings (or the Normans for that matter) that the Viking Age was over'.

APPENDIX 3
Tinchebrai Battle Reports

1. The following summary of the battle is contained in an extract from a letter sent by a priest at Fécamp to a colleague at Sees.

To his lordship the priest of Sees, the priest of Fecamp, greetings and prayers. I bring good news, my lord, because I knew you desirous of these tidings. Our lord the king fought with his brother at Tinchebray on the third Kalends of October [26 September] at the third hour [about 9 a.m.] and the battle was disposed as follows. In the first line [of Henry's army] were the men of Bayeux, all on foot. In the second, the king, with innumerable barons, all similarly on foot. Seven hundred mounted knights were deployed with each of these divisions; besides [Helias] the Count of Maine and Count Alan of Brittany surrounding the army, with up to a thousand knights, the grooms and servants having been sent away. For the whole army of the king was estimated at not far off 40,000 foot [this would yield an incredible total of 42,400 foot and knights; we should likely divide by at least ten]. The Count [Duke of Normandy] had up to 6,000 [of whom] 700 knights, and the battle hardly lasted an hour, Robert of Bellême turning his back immediately, by whose flight everyone was scattered in flight. The duke was captured and the Count of Mortain, with his barons, and Robert of Estouteville, my friend; the rest scattered fugitives. Thus the land is delivered to the king, and I shall not omit the most remarkable thing, that the king hardly lost two [noble] men in the battle. Only one is wounded...

2. King Henry wrote to Archbishop Anselm what is claimed as the first ever battle report penned by an English monarch when fighting overseas.

Holy Father, we report Robert of Normandy to have fought fiercely with all the forces he could bring by prayers or payment upon a named and specified day, before Tinchebrai, and at length by God's mercy we were victorious. What more? Divine mercy delivered into my hands the Count of Normandy, Count of Mortain, William Crispin, William Ferrars, and Robert Estouteville the older, and up to 400 other knights, and 10,000 foot, and Normandy. There is no count of those on their side who perished by the sword...

NOTES

1. Robert while at L'Aigle is claimed by Orderic Vitalis to have reacted badly to being disrespected by his younger brothers, who are alleged by the chronicler to have urinated on the prince and his knights from an upper tier of the building in which they were housed. In a metaphorical sense, they are depicted by the churchman as able to openly abuse their elder brother without censure, having by this time risen high above Robert in their father's affection. Orderic portrays the younger siblings as aware that their father and elder brother are at odds, and also mindful that their mother dotes on him. It is as if William's antagonism for Robert gave them licence and Matilda's undisguised affection for him gave them cause. Robert, though, would not have been driven to rebel by such antics: Henry was just ten years old and Rufus but a teenager. Even the idea Henry, when a child, was present with his father's army in a war-zone, on the eve of a major campaign, is not, in the author's opinion, credible.

2. William of Malmesbury imagined Edgar, with echoes of the way Robert Curthose is sometimes portrayed, 'at [the Norman] court, silently sunk into contempt through his indolence, or ... his simplicity'. It might be the case that the historian wilfully marshalled the alleged attributes of one to unfairly condemn the other.

3. A traditional tale tells of Queen Matilda being present at Edith's christening during the ceremony the baby reached out and grasped

her hand as if to announce a bond between them. The proffered baby's hand became symbolic of the close ties between the families from then on. It is, though, just a story. The English queen's journeying through a recent warzone so late in the year is now thought unlikely. It would also have been something of a rush, since she is known to have been in Normandy, acting on her husband's behalf in a land plea. Perhaps the queen became a godmother to Edith in absentia; either that or Margaret and the baby Edith later travelled south for a repeat ceremony held in England.

4. Bishop Odo is said by Orderic to have encouraged Robert to act harshly against the St Ceneri garrison. In words imagined by the chronicler, he told the duke to 'extirpate the clan and rid the land of their evil seed'. This is made up to discredit both men, casting Odo as rapacious and Robert as easily led.

5. Standing today above the village of the same name, the great donjon of Brionne we see likely post-dates 1090. The place had been besieged before by William after the famous victory at Val-ès-Dunes, albeit on that occasion it had taken several years to gain its capitulation; this despite the erection of two counter-castles on either side of the River Risle to blockade access to supplies for the garrison. This first siege of Brionne may have been such a protracted affair because William was active as well elsewhere in 1048, remaining on campaign outside Normandy as late as the winter of 1049/50. Although less urgency may have been assigned to the reduction of the castle than in 1088, some historians now doubt the single source's – Orderic's – veracity, and suggest a much shorter duration.

6. Philip was a man well past his prime and perhaps an overweight and physically unreliable ally for the duke. He is said by the ever-critical Orderic to have hiccupped and belched incessantly; either this was a nervous trait or the result of overeating.

7. Despite his noted generosity and friendly and welcoming nature, Orderic would have us believe Avranches was an unpleasant man both physically and morally, claiming a lust for young maidens to have come second only to a great appetite for food on the earl's 'things to do' list. A pot belly, it seems, did not prevent Avranches from fathering many bastards. We should not make too much

of any of this, however; Orderic clearly had an agenda when besmirching Avranches.

8. Orderic thought mid-Lent, which places the start of the siege proper sometime in March 1091. John of Worcester says it was the beginning of Lent, around 26 February, with the siege lasting throughout the period of religious observance. Since Rufus had only arrived in the duchy at the beginning of February, this would have left little time for him to establish himself, hold talks with Robert, agree an outcome, then set out with the duke to confront their brother. The later timeframe, posited by Orderic, would therefore seem the more likely.

9. This series of disputes and their ramifications may, arguably, have been given greater emphasis than is warranted by Orderic, who devotes a complete chapter of his *Historia Ecclesiastica* to them, titled 'The distracted state of Normandy, principally caused by the ambition of Robert de Bellême: His feuds with the neighbouring lords, cruelties and exactions'. Orderic was an astute but rarely impartial reporter, very sensitive to the dangers posed to his monastery during any hiatus in ducal authority. Based on what he may have learned from an older generation of monks, no less partial, he wrote, 'Ecclesiastical order and monastic discipline were often disturbed by disorders resulting from the neglect of secular rulers.'

10. Two stone coffins lying near the west door of Dunfermline Abbey were discovered in 1849. The larger one contained a leather shroud which had been wrapped round the body and stitched with a thong from head to heel and along the sides of the feet. Within were found fragments of bone and a little dark-coloured hair. The remains are said to have been those of Prince Edward, interred near his mother. The leather shroud is preserved in the National Museum of Antiquities, Queen Street, Edinburgh, and there is a photograph of it at the entrance to the Abbey Church.

11. It should in passing be noted that, at odds with Rufus' reputation for irreligiousness, monastic orders like the one at Bermondsey flourished during his reign. In all, Rufus founded twenty-six Benedictine and six Cluniac houses.

BIBLIOGRAPHY

Primary Sources

Burgess, G. S. (trans.), *The History of the Norman People, Wace's Roman de Rou* (The Boydell Press, 2004)

Dawes, E. A. S. (trans.), *The Alexiad of Anna Comnena* (Stonewell, 2015)

Forester, T. (trans.), *Ordericus Vitalis, The Ecclesiastical History of England and Normandy* (archive.org/details/ecclesiasticalhio3orde/)

Giles, J. A. (ed. & trans.), *William of Malmesbury, Chronicle of the Kings of England*

Greenway, D., (trans.), *Henry of Huntingdon, The History of the English People* (Oxford, 2002)

Morillo, S. (ed.), *The Battle of Hastings, Sources and interpretations* (The Boydell Press, 1999)

Peters, E. (ed.), *The First Crusade* (University of Pennsylvania, 1998)

Guibert of Nogent, *The Deeds of God through the Franks* (http://www.gutenberg.org/ebooks/4370)

Stevenson, J. (trans.), *Florence of Worcester: A History of the Kings of England*

Stevenson, J. (trans.), *Simeon of Durham, Historical Works*

Swanton, M. (ed. & trans.), *The Anglo-Saxon Chronicles, New Edition* (Phoenix, 2000)

Thorpe, L. (trans.), *Gerald of Wales, The Journey through Wales* (Penguin, 1978)

Tyerman, C. (ed.), *Chronicles of the First Crusade* (Penguin, 2012)

Secondary Sources

Aird, W. M., *Robert Curthose* (The Boydell Press, 2011)

Allen Brown, R., *The Norman Conquest of England* (The Boydell Press, 2002)

Anderson, B. S & J. P. Zinsser, *A History of Their Own: Women in Europe from Prehistory to the Present, Volume 1* (Penguin, 1988)

Barlow, F., *The Feudal Kingdom of England 1042–1216* (Longman, 1088)

Barlow, F., *William Rufus* (Yale, 2000)

Bartlett, R., *England under the Norman and Angevin Kings* (Oxford, 2000)

Bates, D., *William the Conqueror* (The History Press, 2004)

Bennett, M. (ed.), *Fighting Techniques of the Medieval World* (Thomas Dunne, 2005)

Blair, J., *The Anglo-Saxon Age, A Very Short Introduction* (Oxford, 1984)

Borman, T., *Matilda, Wife of the Conqueror* (Vintage, 2012)

Bradbury, J., *The Routledge Companion to Medieval Warfare* (Routledge, 2004)

Brooks, R., *Cassell's Battlefields of Britain & Ireland* (Weidenfeld & Nicolson, 2005)

Brown, R., *Robert Guiscard, Portrait of a Warlord* (Authoring History, 2016)

Carpenter, D., *The Struggle for Mastery* (Allen Lane, 2003)

Chibnall, M., *The World of Orderic Vitalis* (The Boydell Press, 1984)

Cole, T., *The Norman Conquest* (Amberley, 2016)

Cole, T., *After the Conquest, The Divided Realm 1066–1035* (Amberley, 2018)

Crouch, D., *The Normans, A History of a Dynasty* (Hambledon, 2006)

Davies, R. H. C., *The Normans and their Myth* (Thames and Hudson, 1976)

Davies, W. (ed.), *From the Vikings to the Normans* (Oxford, 2003)

Delbruck, H., *Medieval Warfare* (University of Nebraska, 1990)

DeVries, K., *The Norwegian Invasion of England in 1066* (The Boydell Press, 1999)

Dodds, J. F., *Bastions and Belligerents, Medieval Strongholds in Northumberland* (Keepdate Publishing, 1999)

Douglas, D. C., *William the Conqueror* (University of California, 1964)

Duby, G., *France in the Middle Ages, 987-1460* (Blackwell, 1991)

France, J., *Victory in the East, a History of the First Crusade* (Cambridge, 1996)

Frankopan, P., *The First Crusade: The Call from the East* (The Bodley Head, 2012)

Fuller, General J. F. C., *The Decisive Battles of the Western World, Volume 1* (Cassell & Co., 2001 edition)

Gillingham, J., *William II, The Red King* (Allen Lane, 2015)

Green, J. A., *Henry I, King of England and Duke of Normandy* (Cambridge, 2009)

Grinnell-Milne, D., *The Killing of William Rufus* (David & Charles, 1968)

Harvey Wood, H., *The Battle of Hastings* (Atlantic, 2008)

Hay, D., *The Medieval Centuries* (Methuen, 1064)

Hilton, L., *Queens Consort, England's Medieval Queens* (Phoenix, 2009)

Hollister, C. W., *Henry I* (Yale, 2003)

Hume, D., *A History of England* (ebooks.adelaide.edu.au/h/)

King, E., *Henry I: The Father of His People* (Penguin, 2018)

Lack, K., *Conqueror's Son, Duke Robert Curthose, Thwarted King* (Sutton, 2007)

Lambert, M., *Crusade and Jihad* (Profile Books, 2016)

Lavelle, R., 'The Dark Side of the Anglo-Saxons', *BBC History Magazine*, vol. 13 no. 13 (2012)

Le Patourel, J., *Normandy and England 1066-1144* (University of Reading, 1971)

Leyser, H., *Medieval Women* (Phoenix, 1996)

Marsden, J., *The Fury of the Northmen* (Kyle Cathie, 1996)

Mason, E., *William II, Rufus, the Red King* (Tempus, 2005)

Mason, J. F. A., 'Roger de Montgomery and His Sons (1067-1102)', *Transactions of the Royal Historical Society*, 5th series vol. 13 (1963)

Mitchison, R., *A History of Scotland* (Routledge, 2002)

Morris, M., *Castle* (MacMillan, 2003)

Morris, M., *The Norman Conquest* (Windmill Books, 2013)

Nelson, L. H., *The Normans in South Wales 1070-1171* (University of Texas, 1966)

Norton, Elizabeth, *England's Queens* (Amberley, 2011)

Oxford Dictionary of National Biography

Poole, A. L., *Domesday Book to Magna Carta, 1087-1216* (Oxford, 1955)

Prestwich, J., 'The Military Household of the Norman Kings', *English Historical Review*, vol. 96 no. 378 (January 1981)

Rex, P., *William the Conqueror, the Bastard of Normandy* (Amberley, 2016)

Riley-Smith, J., *The First Crusaders, 1095-1131* (Cambridge, 1998)

Rud, M., *The Bayeux Tapestry and the Battle of Hastings* (Copenhagen, 1996)

Rowley, T., *The Man behind the Bayeux Tapestry* (The History Press, 2013)

Southern, R. W., *Western Society and the Church in The Middle Ages* (Pelican, 1970)

Spencer, Dan., *The Castle at War* (Amberley, 2018)

Stafford, P., *Unification and Conquest* (Edward Arnold, 1989)

Stenton, F., *Anglo-Saxon England* (Oxford, 1971)

Strickland, M. (ed.), *Anglo-Norman Warfare* (The Boydell Press, 1992)

Walker, I., *Lords of Alba* (The History Press, 2006)

Weir, A., *Queens of the Conquest* (Jonathan Cape, 2017)

INDEX